ETHNIC GROUPS IN MOTION
Economic Competition and Migration in Multiethnic States

CASS SERIES: NATIONALISM AND ETHNICITY
ISSN 1462-9755
General Editor: William Safran

This new series draws attention to some of the most exciting issues in current world political debate: nation-building, autonomy and self-determination; ethnic identity, conflict and accommodation; pluralism, multiculturalism and the politics of language; ethnonationalism, irredentism and separatism; and immigration, naturalization and citizenship. The series will include monographs as well as edited volumes, and through the use of case studies and comparative analyses will bring together some of the best work to be found in the field.

Ethnicity and Citizenship: The Canadian Case (NEP 1/3 Aut 1995)
Edited by Jean Laponce and William Safran

Nationalism and Ethnoregional Identities in China (NEP 4 1&2, Spring/Summer 1998)
Edited by William Safran

Identity and Territorial Autonomy in Plural Societies (NEP 5 3/4/Aut/Win 1999)
Edited by William Safran and Ramon Maíz

Ideology, Legitimacy and the New State: Yugoslavia, Serbia and Croatia
Siniša Malešević

Diasporas and Ethnic Migrants: Germany, Israel and Russia in Comparative Perspective
by Rainer Munz and Rainer Ohliger

Ethnic Groups in Motion: Economic Competition and Migration in Multiethnic States
by Milica Z. Bookman

ETHNIC GROUPS IN MOTION

Economic Competition and Migration in Multiethnic States

Milica Z. Bookman
St Joseph's University, Philadelphia

FRANK CASS
LONDON • PORTLAND, OR

First published in 2002 in Great Britain by
FRANK CASS PUBLISHERS
Crown House, 47 Chase Side
London N14 5BP

and in the United States of America by
FRANK CASS PUBLISHERS
c/o ISBS, 5824 N.E. Hassalo Street
Portland, Oregon, 97213-3644

Website: www.frankcass.com

British Library Cataloguing in Publication Data

Bookman, Milica Zarkovic
  Ethnic groups in motion: economic competition and
  migration in multiethnic states. – (Nationalism and
  ethnicity)
  1. Ethnic groups 2. Emigration and immigration 3. Migration,
  Internal
  I. Title
  304.8

ISBN 0-7146-5231-8 (cloth)
ISBN 0-7146-8211-X (pbk)

Library of Congress Cataloging-in-Publication Data

Bookman, Milica Zarkovic.
  Ethnic groups in motion: economic competition and migration in multiethnic
states /
  Milica Z. Bookman.
    p. cm. – (Nationalism and ethnicity, ISSN 1462-9755)
  Includes bibliographical references and index.
  ISBN 0-7146-5231-8 (cloth) – ISBN 0-7146-8211-X (pbk.)
    1. Emigration and immigration – Economic aspects. 2. Migration, Internal–
Economic aspects. 3. Competition. 4. Ethnic conflict. I. Title II. Cass series –
nationalism and ethnicity.

JV6098.B66 2002
304.8–dc21

2002071600

Typeset in 10.5/12pt Baskerville by Vitaset, Paddock Wood, Kent
Printed in Great Britain by
MPG Books Ltd, Victoria Square, Bodmin, Cornwall

Contents

For Richard,
Let's go for seven out of seven!

Foreword

The Frank Cass series on Nationalism and Ethnicity aims at presenting both in-depth monographic and comparative-theoretical approaches to nationalism, nation-building, and ethnicity. The present study by Milica Bookman fulfills that aim. Ambitious in its scope, thoroughly researched and impressively documented, it deals exhaustively with the relationship between economics, migration, ethnic consciousness and mobilization, interethnic competition or cooperation for obtaining a share of scarce resources, and economic growth and decline.

The author is not an economic determinist or instrumentalist in a dogmatic sense; while discussing the economic motivation for the migration patterns of ethnic groups, she focuses equally on the impact of immigration on the labor market and on economic performance as well as on cultural patterns and political values. Her universe of research is wide ranging; in making her case, the author uses historical as well as statistical evidence from multiethnic countries around the globe.

A major theme of Professor Bookman's work is the relationship between host countries and immigrants. That relationship is determined by the economic system of the receiving country, its general macroeconomic policies, and measures aimed specifically at immigrants who constitute an ethnic minority. The author analyzes a variety of policy choices, both inclusionary and exclusionary. The former include affirmative action, tax concessions, subsidies, and easy access to education, jobs, and welfare state benefits. Among the latter are entry quotas, ethnic restrictions on employment; the resort to scab and 'slave' labor, ethnic cleansing, deportation, and other forms of involuntary migration. The examination of other measures directed at immigrants that have economic consequences includes language policies and the application of the criterion of language use for discrimination in hiring and access to citizenship. In this connection, attention is also devoted to the negative economic impact of ethnic repression on a nation's economy. Finally, there is a discussion of the economic effects of out-migration on the sending country.

Professor Bookman takes up a number of important issues: the role of the market in moderating or sharpening ethnic consciousness; the question of whether capitalism fosters the integration of ethnic minorities or discrimination against them; and the fate of ethnic minority labor in the event of economic stagnation or decline. Questions are also raised concerning the positive or negative impact of immigrants on the host country, especially in terms of economic and political behavior: do they contribute to, or detract from, the ethos of productivity or democratic ideology? Does their presence serve to make the culture of the receiving society more interesting or, on the contrary, contribute to cultural 'dilution' and insecurities with respect to national identity? These questions are, inter alia, applied also to diasporas, whose number and impact have become increasingly important.

William Safran

Acknowledgments

In writing this book, I have depended on many people to help, cajole, enable, introduce, fund, advise, and encourage. I was cognizant of their contribution on a daily basis, whether it resulted in a page well written or a draft quickly shredded. Therefore, I take this opportunity to express my deepest appreciation to them.

I owe a debt of gratitude to those who put me in contact with valuable sources and helped set up interviews: Charlie Schreiner, Wayne Selcher, and Alfonso Obughezi. I am grateful to Gustavo Gonzaga, Adalberto Cardoso, and Miladin Kovacevic for answering my questions and raising new ones.

Selected contents of this book were presented to academic audiences during lectures and at conferences. I want to thank Al Rubinstein, Ljubisa Adamovic, and Stephen Lubermann for their useful comments.

I would like to thank Lisa Baglione, Tony Joes, and Alice Ackermann for their guidance with literature and data. Thanks also to Richard Trench for technical assistance. Chris Dixon and Samantha Quan were extremely helpful in procuring some US data on labor and commuting, for which I am grateful. Moreover, I would like to thank all the participants in the Commuting Survey as well as those who helped recruit participants (especially Linda Wagner and Joe Arcadia).

The anonymous reader for Frank Cass Publishers has contributed suggestions that have improved the manuscript. I am also grateful to those I have worked with at Frank Cass, especially Sarah Clarke, Sally Green and Lisa Hyde.

Dori Pappas has been much more than my secretary for the past 13 years. Her help and friendship in the course of this manuscript preparation have been indispensable. Also, George Prendergast has been more helpful than he can imagine. From 1983 onwards, he gave me peace of mind by protecting my interests while I concentrated on research and writing.

I have received funding from St Joseph's University for the Labor Commuting Survey. Moreover, I have received travel grants for research in Brazil, Singapore, Hong Kong, and Russia. For this funding, I am very grateful to Judi Chapman, Dan Curran, and George Prendergast.

In addition to professional colleagues, I am also grateful to friends and relatives for their friendship, cooperation and practical assistance. Most of all, I owe a tremendous debt to the cooperative and tolerant members of my family, Richard, Aleksandra, and Karla. Each one of them, in their own way, has inspired me to attain my goals. Together, they have provided the peace and harmony that is a necessary component of concentrated research and writing.

Moreover, I would not have had the motivation and discipline to spend hours and hours at the computer if I had not had a deep love of the writing process and the written product. For that, I am indebted to several people. I would like to thank Andy Hine, who kept my nightstand piled high with novels. To Elissa Vanaver, thanks for the shared dreams of future full-time writing. Marco Martinelli showed me what quality prose is all about. *Grazie!* To Desmond O'Grady, thanks for teaching me, years ago, that the most important ingredient for successful writing is passion.

List of tables

Preface

During a single month in the year 2000, the following seemingly unrelated events occurred across the world. In Kosovo, Serbs and Albanians continued to evict each other from their respective homes. In China, the regulation of internal migration by the central authorities was reconsidered as Uygur Muslims protested the reigns on their mobility. In Austria, Jörg Haider of the Freedom Party came to power advocating the repatriation of immigrants from Eastern Europe. In the United States, Alan Greenspan, chairman of the Federal Reserve, testified before Congress that it may be necessary to loosen immigration regulations on foreign labor in order to satisfy the demands of the growing US economy.

These events share a common denominator, namely the movement of populations. Whether voluntary or involuntary, induced or restricted, domestic or international, large-scale population movements are a feature of the world at the turn of the new millennium. While migrations have been ongoing since time immemorial, recently the nature of the migrant, the process of migration, and the policies of host and home countries have changed.

This book focuses on one aspect of migration, namely its ethnic composition. Rather than observe population movements in general, this study is limited to the movements of specific ethnic groups and explores the role played by ethnicity in determining which groups move and which groups stay. It is based on the premise that not every ethnic group has the same restrictions with respect to migration. Indeed, there is ethnic variation in the propensity to migrate and there is ethnic variation in the reception that awaits migrants at their destination.

In this book, I argue that ethnic variations in migration follow from interethnic competition. In other words, the nature (and the ethnic composition) of migration in multiethnic societies is often the outcome of economic competition among ethnic groups. Groups compete for preferences, power, advantages, and opportunities. They also compete for jobs, housing, natural resources, capital, education, and so forth. Such competition determines not only 'who gets what' but also affects who migrates and the conditions under which they migrate.

The relationship between economic competition and migration is not static and does not exist in a vacuum. In order to encompass this dynamism and breadth into the book, I have introduced three variables that affect both competition and migration: economic change, freedom of choice, and discriminatory policy. Each contributes an additional dimension to migration; each underscores the complexity of migration.

Economic change alters interethnic competition. During periods of decline, interethnic competition sharpens as groups compete for a share of the dwindling economic pie. During periods of growth, competition subsides as all ethnic groups participate, in varying degrees, in the economic expansion. Moreover, economic change alters the manpower requirements of the economy, inducing migration into high-growth regions and out of regions with declining economic opportunity.

With respect to freedom of choice, interethnic economic competition affects both voluntary and involuntary migration. This book emphasizes the differences among ethnic groups with respect to their capacities and incentives to voluntarily migrate. It also explores ways in which competition may result in involuntary migrations, such as when targeted ethnic groups are forced to move (as in Bosnia) or to stay (as in Romania).

With respect to discriminatory policy, this book shows that during interethnic competition dominant groups often institutionalize discriminatory policies that influence migration in a variety of ways. The range of such policies is broad: it includes the denial of income-generating property rights to target ethnic groups in order to induce emigration (as experienced by Russians in Estonia and Indians in Fiji) and the denial of working permits to undesirable ethnic groups in order to restrict immigration (as experienced by Chinese in the Czech Republic and Palestinians in Israel). Discriminatory policies that affect people's capacity to move or to stay do more than favor one group over another. They prevent the functioning of *laissez-faire* migration by tampering with the market forces that might otherwise determine which ethnic group goes and which one stays.

The combination of interethnic competition, economic change, and discriminatory policies pertaining to people's right to voluntarily stay or go is potentially explosive, as it can easily destabilize what is all too often a precarious balance between ethnic groups. Indeed, in the current climate of competing nationalisms (in which in the period 1989–92, 79 of the world's 82 conflicts took place within national borders and among different ethnic or religious groups), any change in any of the above variables may trigger an interethnic crisis. Given such a reality, a foremost goal of social scientists must be exploration of effective means of diffusing actual and potential conflict. In that spirit, this study contributes to the dialogue on the resolution of inter-ethnic conflict by exploring several chains in the link between harmony and disharmony.

This study also strives to push the boundaries of the academic discourse on the relationship between economics and ethnicity that has, until recently, been outside the scope of mainstream economics. It is only in the recent decade, with evidence of explosive nationalist sentiment, interethnic warfare, secessionist movements, and the emer-gence of independent states, that scholarly attention has of necessity confronted these issues in a rigorous and thorough manner. Moreover, conventional wisdom until the 1980s upheld the idea that moderni-zation eliminates interethnic conflict, only to be disproved by clear evidence of highly developed countries succumbing to ethnic mobili-zation and even interethnic strife. Yet, there has been no compre-hensive replacement of this classical view. Finally, the literature on economic competition among ethnic groups has not kept pace with events while the literature on migration by ethnicity has grown precipitously. This imbalance is coupled with a void in the literature pertaining to the link between these two variables. Here I strive to redress the imbalance and fill the void.

The book is arranged as follows. Chapter 1 contains an introduction to the concepts as well as the countries that are discussed throughout the book. Also, the theoretical framework that underlies this study is presented along with propositions pertaining to the effect of inter-ethnic economic competition on migration. In chapter 2, the manifes-tation of economic competition and migration under conditions of economic decline is discussed, while chapter 3 follows the same format for economic growth. In both chapters, the sources of economic change are studied, as well as the way in which they may cause ethnic bifurcation within society. Voluntary migration is assessed in chapter 4, with emphasis on differences by ethnicity in capacities and incentives to migrate. Involuntary migrations are discussed in chapter 5, including ethnic cleansing, ethnic consolidation and ethnic dilution. Chapter 6 is devoted to the study of domestic discriminatory policy that induces or impedes migration of targeted ethnic groups. Chapter 7 focuses on discriminatory policy that regulates international migra-tion of ethnic groups. Finally, chapter 8 links competition, migration, economic change, and discrimination to interethnic conflict. It shows how easily conflict can erupt and offers suggestions for its prevention and/or resolution.

1

Introduction: Interethnic Competition, Economic Change, and Labor Migration

Over the last decade three trends pertaining to interethnic competition, economic change, and population movements have become visible across the world. First, there has been a marked increase in interethnic competition resulting in open and violent conflict. Indeed, the number, intensity, and violence of interethnic struggles within states have increased. As noted in the preface, most of the world's recent conflicts have taken place within borders and among different ethnic or religious groups.[1] The global extent of interethnic turmoil has been pointed out by Helman and Ratner, who claim that

> from Haiti in the western hemisphere to the remnants of Yugoslavia, from Somalia, Sudan and Liberia in Africa to Cambodia in southeast Asia, a disturbing new phenomenon is emerging: the failed nation-state, utterly incapable of maintaining itself as a member of the international community ... those states descend into violence and anarchy, imperiling their own citizens and threatening their neighbors through refugee flows, political instability and random warfare.[2]

Many ethnic groups in multiethnic states are taking their frustrations one step further, demanding secession from their unions at unprecedented rates. Indeed, the 1990s came to resemble two other periods in their century of active secessionist activity, namely the aftermath of the First World War and the independence movements of Africa and Asia that gained momentum in the aftermath of the Second World War. In the 1990s, no longer restrained by a Cold War polarization and encouraged by the winds of rapid overall change, subnational groups are seeking to free themselves from central authorities and have created dramatic changes in national boundaries.

Second, there has been an increase in the variety and pervasiveness of economic changes that countries have experienced. In some places, very rapid rates of economic growth and sustained periods of prosperity were experienced while in others there were precipitous declines in national income. Some countries experienced a transformation of their economic systems from communism to capital-ism while others replaced economy-wide public sector involvement with deregulation, privatization, and price liberalization. In some countries, peace brought about an economic rebirth while in others wars devastated the economic infrastructure. International sanctions and boundary changes affected rates of growth as well as the nature of growth. Moreover, all these economic changes occurred against a background of (a) the changing division of labor within the global economy, (b) the structural transformation of domestic economies during modern economic growth, and (c) a widespread tendency away from authoritarian rule and an embracing of democracy of the kind that Huntington described as the 'third wave'.[3]

Third, the increase in population movements across the globe has been dramatic and overwhelming, leading scholars to refer to the 1990s as the 'age of migration'.[4] Widespread famines and environ-mental disasters are causing unprecedented numbers of refugees to relocate; wars and secessions are inducing voluntary and involuntary migrations as people of varying ethnic groups adjust to new leaders and new borders; differences in human capital needs are causing workers to relocate voluntarily in order to maximize their employment options; wage differentials are attracting workers from low income to high income regions; and movements of enterprises in search of profit maximization induce workers to follow.

Interethnic competitions, economic change, and migration are three ongoing processes that, although they are discussed separately in this chapter, interact in very important ways. The theoretical under-pinnings of their interrelationships are presented below.

DEFINITIONS AND CONCEPTS

Some terms used in this book need clarification since there is little agreement about them in the literature. The introduction of these terms serves merely to describe how they are used in the text, rather than to offer a definitive explanation or resolve some outstanding contradictions in the literature.

Ethnicity, Nations, and Nationalism

Ever since Vilfredo Pareto said that the term *ethnic* is one of the vaguest known to sociology,[5] research has attempted to clarify it. According to Anthony Smith, an ethnic group is composed of a people that share a cultural bond and that perceive themselves to share a common origin.[6] While Brock's definition of an ethnic group is perhaps the most apropos this time (he defines an ethnic group as a people united by a common dislike of their neighbors and a common myth of their origin[7]), it is Smith's definition that will be used in this study.[8] Moreover, ethnic affiliation is viewed as flexible and in some instances transitory, underscoring that ethnicity is neither primordial nor immutable. This dynamic view is based on evidence of changing ethnic affiliations from across the globe.[9]

A nation differs from an ethnic group insofar as it refers to a group of people who share culture, history and usually language, in a specific territory, and who give political expression to this common identity. (It is noted that confusion shrouds this term because *nation* and *state* are sometimes used synonymously. For the purposes of this study, state and nation are not interchangeable. A state is a political term that connotes a country.) According to Smith, a nation is 'a body of citizens bound by shared memories and a common culture, occupying a compact territory with a unified economy and identical rights and duties'.[10] A nation is therefore a wider concept than an ethnic group.[11] Moreover, it *de facto* carries with it an association with rank and status: the status of a nation is perceived to be the highest order in the ranking of peoples.[12]

The term nation underlies the concept of nationalism, a phenomenon that has received much attention in the literature. While its dictionary definition is simply 'the devotion to one's nation; patriotism or chauvinism',[13] it does in fact connote more, embodying culture, ethnicity, and language. According to Smith, nationalism is 'a doctrine of autonomy, unity and identity, whose members conceive it to be an actual or potential nation'.[14] Just as the term nation is submerged in contradictory terminology, so too is the term nationalism. Connor has attempted to rectify the semantic sources of misunderstanding by clarifying words: a sloppy use of the term nationalism connotes loyalty to the state. It is, in fact, loyalty to the nation.[15] Kellas's definition takes nationalism one step further by claiming that it is 'both an ideology and a form of behavior'.[16] That extension underscores its political character, which is clearly identified by Brass, who claimed that 'nationalism is a political movement by definition'.[17]

The term nation also underlies the term nation-state, in which national and political borders coincide. According to Ra'anan, the term refers to 'a polity whose territorial and juridical frontiers coincide with the ethnic boundaries of the national entity with which that state is identified, frequently by its very name'.[18] Most countries of the world are not nation-states.[19] Indeed, a study by Connor found that of a total of 132 contemporary states, only 12 are ethnically homogeneous.[20]

The debate pertaining to the relationship between race and ethnicity is extensive and largely irrelevant for the purposes of this book.

Race is the distinguishing feature among peoples in some population classifications. Suffice it to say that while race emphasizes physical properties and biological heredity, ethnicity emphasizes social organization and cultural characteristics. Racism is the ideology associated with race as nationalism is the ideology associated with nations.

The question of how to classify and define peoples remains unresolved and continues to dominate debates on ethnicity and nationalism. Possible categories abound, such as ethnicity, race, language and so forth, and despite their overlap and imprecision, they serve to group populations across the globe. For the sake of simplicity and convenience, in this study *ethnicity* is referred to as the distinguishing characteristic even though it is not universally applicable. Indeed, sometimes race is the crucial distinguishing characteristic (as in South Africa) or it is language (as in Canada) or religion (as in Bosnia). Ethnicity is, therefore, used in the text as an umbrella term that includes race, religion, language, nation, as the case may be. In that sense, this study heeds the 1997 proposal of the American Association of Anthropologists, suggesting the US government use ethnic categories in federal data to reflect the diversity of the population and to phase out the use of race which is a concept that has no scientific justification in human biology.[21] Olzak, in her study of competition and ethnic conflict, says that 'since ethnicity is an outcome of boundary creation and maintenance, there is no obstacle to treating race as a special case of an ethnic boundary, one that is believed to be correlated with inherited biotic characteristics. Hereafter, the term ethnicity refers to both racial and ethnic boundaries, unless otherwise qualified'.[22] Finally, Van den Berghe also made a convincing argument for using ethnicity as an umbrella term: 'While I still think that the greater rigidity and invidiousness of racial, as distinct from cultural distinctions makes for qualitatively different situation, both race and ethnicity share the basic common element of being defined by descent, real or putative. Therefore, I now tend to see race as a special case of ethnicity.'[23]

Labor and Migration

Labor migration has been studied by a variety of social scientists. Demographers have the longest record, with their studies of population movements and the resulting transformation of the demographic structure of societies. Economists joined in because of their concern with the movement of labor and its relationship to economic growth and development. Sociologists, psychologists, industrial analysts, and marriage specialists all looked at family issues relating to work and geographical mobility. Regional scientists studied population movements as they related to location of industry and economic activity. Migration is a field of study within anthropology, geography, political science, history, and international law. The research in all these disciplines, bountiful albeit often unrelated across disciplines, has yielded some clarity in definitions and concepts pertaining to the geographical mobility of labor.[24] Those relevant for this study are described below.

In Western culture there was a time when all work was for survival of the household unit and took place in the home and its immediate vicinity. Before specialization and the complex division of labor became widespread, simple economic systems focused on subsistence and on the short term, relying on the ideology of self-sufficiency and the practice of minimal barter arrangements. Similarly, in traditional societies today, the lack of complexity in economic relations underlies the lack of separation between work and home. Over time, with increasing complexity and an enlarged perimeter of economic activity, work inched away from the home, especially for men. The divergence between the geographical location of home and work culminated in industrial and post-industrial societies in which the demands of a growing economy, the individual pressure for economic adaptability and survival, an increasing cultural acceptance of geographical mobility as an economic fact of life, and an accommodating transportation system, enabled large scale labor movements and/or commuting to distant workplaces (we are now witnessing gradual return to work in the home, albeit of a qualitatively different kind (spearheading this trend is the US, where in 1993, 33% of the adult labor force worked at home at least some of the time[25])).

The labor market is assumed to have players who voluntarily take jobs, who take jobs for pay, and who can leave those jobs. They are assumed to make choices, conduct personal cost/benefit analyses, and pursue their own self-interest. This definition of the labor market excludes systems in which slavery is the dominant form of labor, according to which workers are not free to sell their labor to an employer of their choice (as was the case, historically, on US plantations and, presently, in parts of Africa[26]). It also excludes present-day feudalism, in which workers are bound to employers as a result of a series of constraints and thus cannot respond to labor market incentives (as in regions of rural India where indebted farmers and their future offspring are bound to a landlord). Wherever people have no effective choice to respond to labor market conditions, where they have no choice to travel and take new jobs, where they cannot freely sell their labor, there is no functioning labor market. Therefore, assuming the absence of structural constraints to selling one's labor, a functioning labor market consists of employers who respond to changing economic circumstances by hiring, transferring, or discharging workers; closing or opening facilities, or moving their operations to new locations. Workers respond to changing economic or personal conditions by changing employers, occupations, or geographical locations. Clearly, the supply and demand of labor are crucial concepts in understanding where people try to find work and where the jobs are located.

Labor mobility in its broadest form includes the following. When product demand, labor productivity, level of investment in human capital, family circumstances, or general economic conditions change, some workers find it advantageous to change employers, occupations, geographic locations, or some combination of these three. Alternatively, it is the employers who might initiate changes in the labor market. Indeed, they might respond to changing economic circumstances in the ways described above, namely by hiring, transferring, or laying off workers; closing or expanding facilities; or moving operations to new locations. Together, the actions by workers and firms generate movement of labor from job to job and place to place.

Numerous scholars have defined labor mobility in a variety of similar ways. According to Reynolds, labor mobility entails movement into and out of the labor force, between employment and unemployment, between employers, industries, and occupational levels, and between geographical areas.[27] A single job change may involve several types of movements simultaneously. According to McConnell and Brue, the following possibilities for labor mobility exist: (a) job change with no change in occupation or residence; (b) occupational change with no change in residence; (c) geographic change with no change in occupation; and (d) geographic change and change in occupation.[28] It is clear from both of these definitions that labor mobility entails a lot more than simply changing the geographical location of one's work. In the Reynolds classification, only one out of six movements of labor is geographical, while according to McConnell and Brue, two out of four connote geographic mobility. Labor mobility then includes a broad range of changes, of which only some entail a spatial dimension. Geographical mobility of labor is a subset of labor mobility, and is significantly narrower in scope and characteristics.

Migration is the broadest term pertaining to population movements, since it embodies movements of workers and nonworkers alike. Geographical mobility of labor is a subset of migration as well as of labor mobility. Labor migration is a subset of migration, entailing only workers in the labor force. In this study, sometimes labor migration and total migration are used interchangeably. Not only are comparable labor migration statistics sometimes not available for the countries under study, but also some concepts do not necessitate disaggregation. Most voluntary migration occurs in response to economic incentives, which have to do with employment. Most involuntary migration is aimed at the working-age population and is usually male. (As discussed in chapter 5 below, ethnic cleansing tends to be aimed at those who work (and are fertile and of military age), while children and the elderly are viewed as irrelevant. Recent experience in Kosovo indicates that the efforts at ethnic cleansing by both the Serbs and the Albanians were focused on skilled workers: 'much as the Serbian authorities singled out educated Albanians before, now Albanians are singling out the dwindling number of educated Serbs in an effort to expel all Serbs from the province'.[29])

INTERETHNIC COMPETITION

Irrespective of their ethnic, racial, and religious orientations, all people compete and cooperate. Competition is a fundamental component of the incentive/motivational structure that most societies share and that forms the basis for personal gain at the micro level. Cooperation enhances overall efficiency and enables complexity in production. At the same time, it is the glue that ties together groups of competitors and that smoothes economic interaction at the macro level. Both competition and cooperation are necessary (but not sufficient) conditions for sustained, long term economic growth. In this chapter, attention turns to competition between groups of people (while cooperation is revisited in chapter 8).[30]

Scholars as diverse as Marx and Kuznets have described the growth-promoting characteristics of competition.[31] However, their discussion of competition focused on the process that transpires between individuals or firms, rather than between ethnic groups. More recently, Hawley said that competition exists between two populations when the presence of one reduces the opportunities of the other.[32] Blalock defined it as 'involving the idea that two or more individuals are striving for the same scarce objectives, so that the success of one implies a reduced probability that others will also attain their goal'.[33] Interethnic competition occurs because ethnic groups are motivated to increase their economic and political power relative to other groups. It arises because economics and politics are viewed as a zero-sum game in which the loss to one ethnic group is perceived as a gain to another.

Interethnic Competition for Economic and Political Power

Ethnic groups compete for economic power and rewards in the following ways. First, they compete for access to scarce resources. The distribution of scarce resources is often the primary source of conflict among ethnic groups. If there is no scarcity, there is no economic source of conflict.[34] According to Van den Berghe, 'Ethnic conflicts, like class conflicts, result from the unequal distribution of and competition for scarce resources.'[35] According to Hoetnik, 'Group competition is commonly used if two or more groups try to limit each others access to scarce resources.'[36] It is exactly this relationship between ethnic competition and scarce resources that has been the underlying source of conflict in the Yugoslav wars of secession, since the size of the economic pie shrunk in the 1980s, and competition for resources took place along ethnic lines (just as Skinner claimed it did in the African context as the countries prepared for independence and African nationalism developed[37]).

Second, ethnic populations compete for input into policy-making. As a result of their right to voice concerns and make demands, ethnic groups also obtain economic rewards.[38] As a result of the political power associated with the governing group, an ethnic population is capable of influencing policy in order to accumulate benefits. Evidence of this was provided by Horowitz, who pointed out that ethnicity is an important factor in the following economic aspects of governmental functioning: development plans, educational controversies, trade union affairs, land policy, business policy, and tax policy.[39] Clearly, if one ethnic group benefits disproportionately from tax laws, business policies, or development projects, then repercussions will permeate throughout the economic, political, and social systems with broad ramifications and will further perpetuate the initial advantages of the group in question. This was clear with the ethnically biased educational policies of Malaysia and Tanzania, as well as the land policies of Guyana, Ethiopia, and Thailand.

Third, ethnic populations compete for control over productive inputs. This is especially true if ethnic groups dominate in specific territories and there is some measure of decentralization of power. Under those circumstances, the dominant group exercises control over raw materials, industrial sites, urban development, and other infrastructure.

Fourth, ethnic populations compete for the allocation of economic favors. Favors doled out by ethnic groups include jobs, slots in educational facilities, industrial location, and so on. While this was a major issue in the former colonies (in which departing powers allocated economic rights and favors after independence to select ethnic groups), there is mounting evidence of such allocation of favors even in the 1990s (which, however, does not necessarily involve an ethnic group: it may be religion (such as in Iraqi politics); race (such as in the Malay educational system), or horde (such as in the Kazakhstani bureaucracy)).

Ethnic groups also compete for political rewards in the following ways. First, they seek enhanced representation in political bodies, which translates into decision-making that tends to reflect the interests of that group. Second, ethnic groups seek political legitimacy to partake in the political arena and to express ethnic demands in an organized fashion. Even if they are small minorities, they seek to have a channel through which to make themselves heard and avoid being ignored as a group. Third, ethnic groups seek participation in the political system, insofar as it gives the group in question equal or preferential access to legal protection and the legal system, access to civil service positions and access to the military and police service. And, fourth, ethnic groups pursue the right to make demands on the political system (as some groups are of insufficient importance to even be recognized in the political spectrum as groups). The assertion of these rights in the spheres of economics, politics, and ethnocultural issues is classified into three types of demands.[40] The mildest demand of a peoples entails policy changes whose effects will favor the group in question (usually of a cultural nature). Another type of demand is for full integration into the decision-making process. (This usually entails minority groups that strive for rights equal to those enjoyed by the titular majority, including the right to own property and to defend property rights in courts, the right to vote or partake in political life, and the right to enjoy the social welfare of the country.) In the United States, affirmative action legislation, such as the Equal Employment Act of 1972, is an example of legislation to make into law such civil rights. The strongest demand is for autonomy. While this demand may be satisfied by the extension of increased political rights to the region where the group resides, the demand may also include the right to secession based on self-determination. The latter was of increasing importance in the secessionist climate of the 1990s (the Chechens, the Tibetans, the Punjabis, the Kashmiris, and the Albanians of Kosovo are just some of the examples of peoples that have voiced the demand to leave their union).

The Nature of Ethnic Dominance

Two points need to be made with respect to the nature of ethnic dominance. First, while there are numerous exceptions, the relative size of an ethnic population is important in determining its economic and political power. Second, despite some exceptions, economic and political powers usually coincide in order to define ethnic dominance within a state.

The relationship between the size of an ethnic group and its economic and political power is usually positive. Pioneering research has been undertaken in the areas of comparative ethnic demography and its political significance by scholars such as Wright, Guyot, Wriggins, Alonso and Starr, among others.[41] Issues pertaining to the size of an ethnic group and its effect on intergroup power relationships have been analyzed in the literature. According to Allen, the largest group in society engages in distinct behavior because it is both large and the largest: he observed that 'members of the largest group are most "conservative" because they have the most control, status, and privilege to conserve.'[42] Mayhew and Levinger, and later Blau, described how the large group interacts with other groups, while Fisher has claimed that size produces a 'critical mass' in political and social systems.[43] Schermerhorn introduced the term *mass subjects* in describing the strength and legitimacy derived from majority rule. Studies by Tilly and Portes, and more recently Olzak and Olzak and Nagel, have explicitly described the political and economic benefits of size. While they made the case for a strong positive link between ethnic dominance and economic benefits in the United States, many of their arguments are applicable in a wide variety of countries.

In an earlier study of interethnic competition, I provide empirical evidence to support the contention that size affects positively the economic and political issues over which competition takes place, as described above.[44] Indeed, it is claimed that, first, the more (numerically) dominant an ethnic group, the greater its power to appropriate resources through various forms of political manipulation. Second, ethnic dominance is usually positively related to group input in policy making. Third, ethnic dominance is usually positively related to control over productive inputs on a given territory. Fourth, ethnic dominance is usually positively related to the allocation of economic favors.

With respect to political power, I again found population size to be crucial in determining the outcome of interethnic competition. With respect to enhanced representation in political bodies, demographic statistics show that ethnic size serves to distribute representation within the political system (examples include Nigeria, Romania, and Switzerland). Moreover, it is on the basis of size that numerous population groups claim political legitimacy: for example, the Karanga in Zimbabwe or the Serbs in former Yugoslavia. Finally, the granting of rights tends to be associated with ethnic size, as some are more often granted to larger (but not smaller) ethnic groups (for example, the right to education in a nontitular language was granted by the Yugoslav constitution of 1974 to minorities such as the Hungarians and the Albanians, but not the less populous Romanians or Vlahs).

In representative democracies, each person has one vote and power is distributed through balloting. Under those conditions, and when ethnicity is the basis for political choice, the dominant ethnic groups in society retain their power only if they retain the numerical balance in their favor. Universal suffrage is expressed through a multiparty system. In industrial societies, multiparty systems tend to be divided along class lines, but since class barriers are fluid, so is membership in parties. In pre-industrial societies, as well as some industrial ones, there are multiple parties that reflect the countries' vertical split of the population along rigid tribal or ethnic lines that are significantly less fluid.[45] Party systems, according to Horowitz, may be ethnic (such as in the Sudan, Sri Lanka, Kenya, and Nigeria, at various points in their modern history), multiethnic (such as in the United States, Italy, the Philippines etc.), or nonethnic (the vast majority of countries fall in the in-between range).[46] In a system of ethnic parties, ethnic voting takes place, according to which members of ethnic groups vote for their ethnic leaders, thus ethnic considerations take precedence over economic, regional, and social considerations. When ethnic parties exist, the size of an ethnic group is crucial in the determination of who rules. This view of the importance of size is also voiced by Olugbemi, who claims that ethnic groups believe 'might is right'.[47]

Therefore, population size, economic power, and political power combine to create a ranking within societies pertaining to dominance. Often, ethnic groups are simply divided into majorities and minorities. The defining characteristic of a minority ethnic group is usually size: the minority group is simply the numerically smaller ethnic group. According to that definition, clearly the Maghrebis are a minority in France, the Basques in Spain, the Jews in Italy etc. However, depending on one's point of reference, the size distinction between a minority and majority may become blurred. Indeed, are Tamils the minority in Sri Lanka, or are the Sinhalese in fact the minority in the entire South Asia?[48] Similarly, are the Serbs the minority in Kosovo, or are the Albanians the minority in Serbia? Wars have been fought to answer these questions.

A few words are warranted about exceptions to the link between relative population size and ethnic dominance. Evidence shows that in some societies, ethnic (religious/racial) groups simply do not have the power that their size might warrant. History is replete with situations in which numbers did not have concomitant relevance, such as those in which power was concentrated in the hands of a few by divine right or inheritance. These ruling elites usually had at their disposal power-enforcing abilities (weapons, education, economic skills etc.). Lower level power concentrations were sometimes tolerated: across the Ottoman Empire, the millet system allowed religious communities some power, as did the 'estates' system of medieval Europe.

While exceptions to the positive link between ethnic size and power cover a wide range of conditions, geographical areas, and political traditions, the following instances are most common. The link between population size and power does not exist when: there is no universal suffrage, so that size cannot be expressed into power through the political process; the political structure is so defined that the majority population is prevented from exerting power proportional to its size; colonial powers favored one ethnic group, groomed it for powerful positions, and following independence, those colonial power structures remained in place; the majority–minority distinction at the state level does not coincide at the regional level; and a group of people has no state in which they are the titular or dominant nationality and are in diaspora wherever they reside. The existence of the above conditions does not invalidate the importance between relative size and power for two reasons. First, the conditions that are listed do not prevail in most regions of the world and as such do not affect the majority of global ethnic groups. Therefore, the link remains important by sheer magnitude of the ethnic groups and territories that do not exhibit the above conditions. Second, irrespective of evidence of exceptions to the positive link, it is the perception among peoples that size is important that guides human behavior. As long as members of ethnic groups believe that size is relevant, they will attempt to augment that size.

Political and economic powers usually coincide, in other words, an ethnic group that has one also tends to have the other. However, there are times when the two forms of power do not coincide, resulting in a paradox that is the source of much interethnic conflict. A recent study by Gurr indicated that some groups enjoy political power, others enjoy economic power, and while the two often go hand in hand, they do not always coincide. He found that, out of 214 peoples studied, 17 have economic power with little political power (such as the Kikuyu, the Ashanti, the Turks in Germany, Palestinians in Jordan etc.), while very few have more political power than economic power (including native peoples in Canada and the North Irish Catholics in the United Kingdom).[49]

The former, more common divergence of power (i.e., when a minority ethnic group has economic power but lacks political power), usually occurs in societies where minorities are associated with a particular profession. For example, they might be the moneylenders (such as the Jews and Lombards in medieval Europe; the Armenians in the Middle East; the Chinese throughout southeast Asia), the merchants (various communities in south India), or the government bureaucrats (such as Serbs in Croatia in the former Yugoslavia). This phenomenon, described by Zenner as the 'paradox of the middleman-minority position' occurs when 'economic success is combined with political impotency'.[50] When ethnoprofessionalism is present (according to which certain ethnic groups are associated with certain professions), then the economic power of ethnic groups is determined by the status and income accrued to that profession. For example, in Malaysia, Malays are found in farming or civil service, the Chinese in business and the Indians in rubber-tapping and liberal professions.[51] Similarly, in the former Yugoslavia, the Serbs were predominant in the armed forces;[52] in Israel, the Sefardim account for the vast majority of unskilled labor;[53] and in Kenya, the Kikuyu dominate in the government bureaucracy.[54] The evidence of such widespread ethnoprofessionalism led Horowitz to claim that capital and labor in some multiethnic societies are organized along ethnic lines,[55] and Furnivall to say, that 'even in the economic sphere, there is a division of labour along racial lines'.[56] Bonacich focused on the consequences of economic differentiation by ethnic group: she claims that these ethnoprofessional 'trading minorities' can become so powerful, economically and organizationally, that the host country is pushed to ever more extreme reactions in order to break their monopoly on some economic activity.[57]

ECONOMIC CHANGE

Economic changes, differing in scope, timing, and intensity, have altered the pre-existing pace of economic development across the world. Some have affected a small number of people and regions while others have been virtually universal. Some occurred rapidly while others lingered gradually over the course of generations. Some are mere flutters while others transform entire economies and societies. While the possible sources of economic change are numerous, several dominated in the 1990s. The transition from communism to capitalism occurred in the former Soviet Union and Eastern Europe; the overall liberalization of the pre-existing capitalist system is ongoing in South America, Asia, and Europe. The imposition of international sanctions shocked the economies of Yugoslavia, Iraq, Libya, Cuba, and to a lesser extent Israel, South Africa, and India. Actual wars (as in Yugoslavia and Russia) and potential wars (as in Israel and South Asia) highjack economies and prevent the functioning of markets. Successful secessionist movements (as in Singapore, and in the 1990s, Russia, Estonia, the Czech Republic, Yugoslavia) and unsuccessful secessionist attempts (Canada and India) also affected their respective economies. The effect of each of these is amplified because, in many settings, multiple disruptions converge (for example, in Yugoslavia war and sanctions coincided). Moreover, they do not occur in a vacuum but rather have linkage effects throughout the economy. Then, when added to technological innovation, capital accumulation, and foreign investment, disruptions ripple through the economy, over time, producing changes in economic growth, pace, and pattern.

Each of these sources of economic change manifest themselves in a decrease or increase in national income per capita. When such changes are of sufficient duration and breadth, they affect the labor force. What is the mechanism by which this occurs? A little background is necessary in order to answer that question.

When a society experiences economic development (also known as modern economic growth), fundamental alterations occur in the structure of its economy.[58] There is a change in what is produced, how it is produced, where it is produced, and who produces it. During economic development, an increase in income per capita is achieved by the widespread application of innovative technology to the pro-duction process (that serves to make inputs more productive and/or change the way in which they are used in the production function). The definition of economic development also includes an aftermath: namely, it results in a structural transformation of the economy accord-ing to which the sectoral distribution of national income changes, as does the industrial classification of the labor force.[59] With respect to the former, the contribution of the agricultural sector to national income declines while the contribution of manufacturing grows considerably, then stabilizes and even contracts. The importance of the service sector continues to rise in the course of economic development (today, in the United States, it accounts for nearly 70% of the national output).[60]

The structural transformation of the economy manifests itself in the labor force in two ways. First, as the sectoral contribution to national income changes in the course of economic growth, so too does the nature of the work that workers perform. The importance of agri-culture as the principal employer of labor diminishes, while that of the manufacturing sector first increases and then falls off. Services continue to absorb labor. Second, during economic development, the occupational structure of the labor force changes: the proportion of blue-collar workers decreases while the proportion of white-collar workers increases. An analysis of the US industrial classification of the labor force indicates that over the past 100 years, the proportion of agricultural workers dropped significantly, while industrial workers and workers employed in services rose. Moreover, in 1950 blue-collar workers accounted for almost two-thirds of the labor force while by 1990 they decreased to less than half (62.5% to 43%). At the same time, the while-collar work-force grew from 37.5 percent to 57.1 percent over the same time period.[61]

While each country has its own set of particular conditions that mold the nature, pace, and depth of these labor-force changes,[62] a general theory, applicable to all contexts, was provided by Kuznets.[63] It states that as an economy grows and becomes more industry and service oriented, its manpower requirements undergo a transformation. The demand for agricultural workers, being a derived demand, keeps pace with the demand for the product that they produce. As the demand for agricultural goods fails to keep up with overall increases in consumption, so too the demand for agricultural workers tends to fall off. The demand for industrial and service sector workers increases along with consumer demand for products from those sectors. In addition, labor-saving technological change takes place in agriculture and manufacturing, while service sector production tends to be labor intensive, thus absorbing large quantities of white-collar labor.

LABOR MIGRATION AS AN ADJUSTMENT TO ECONOMIC CHANGE

At the end of the twentieth century the global economy witnessed movements across geographical regions that were remarkable in breadth and speed: goods and services were traded across borders, capital was invested in far-away places, labor traveled to jobs in distant locations, jobs traveled to workers in places near and far, ideas flew easily across the globe, and cultures seemed to converge. Efficient advances in transportation and communication systems, coupled with the universal penetration (permeation) of computers and the Internet revolutionized movements of labor, capital, goods, and ideas.

Why do resources migrate from one place to another? With special reference to labor, what determines the migratory flows of workers and how are they related to economic conditions? These questions were answered by scholars from numerous schools of thought. According to world systems theory, the division of labor across the globe sets the stage for movements from the periphery to the core. Following Wallerstein's pioneering work,[64] Cheng and Bonacich claimed that migration occurs in the course of capitalist development as the core requires more workers for its development and the periphery cannot sustain its workers due to underdevelopment.[65] Theories that draw on the concept of the dual labor market stress that immigrant labor tends to be concentrated in the secondary market, where income is low, job security is nonexistent, workers are unproductive, and so forth. Rational choice theories state that as people attempt to maximize their benefits relative to their costs, so they will migrate if that is called for by their personal cost–benefit analysis. Harris and Todaro expanded this idea by combining push and pull factors to indicate that migration will continue from a sending to a target area as long as expected earnings in the latter exceed expected earnings in the former. Earnings tend to be high in a growing region, where there is economic activity that raises the demand for labor and keeps the wages relatively high.

Migration as an economic phenomenon has been studied most comprehensively by Simon Kuznets. Ever since he published his pioneering study of how the manpower demands of a growing economy are met through geographical mobility, scholars have focused on both the volume of labor movements as well as the characteristics of the migrant worker.[66] In the Kuznets tradition, Lansing and Mueller presented their detailed assessment of the nature of mobility in the US economy, thereby setting the stage for the theoretical discussion that ensued over the next few decades.[67] These early studies of the link between economic development and manpower requirements formed the underpinnings of a wide range of academic disciplines. Now, it has become the basis for demographic theories concerned with population movements, sociological theories pertaining to migration, economic theories explaining economic growth and development, and regional studies theories focusing on location of industrial clusters and transportation networks.

The fundamentals of Kuznets's theory can be summarized as follows. Economic change, coupled with new developments in technology and transportation, alters the demand and supply of labor such that the location of productive activity changes (automobile production does not take place on a farm; shipping does not take place inland). As a result, the manpower demands of the economy are no longer necessarily met by the *pre-existing* labor force working in *pre-existing* locations. It is often necessary for labor to relocate, commute, or otherwise geographically respond to market stimuli in new geographical locations. Such migration occurs between rural and urban areas, across regional boundaries and over international borders. Empirical evidence supports this view of migration as an adjustment to economic change. In the period following the Second World War, Germany's economy needed labor for its reconstruction efforts, hence the labor recruitment efforts in Italy to fill labor shortages.[68] Similarly, since the mid-1970s, south Asian migrants have gone to the oil exporting countries of western Asia that are receptive to foreign labor for their growing industries.[69]

When there are impediments to such population movements, then economic expansion fails to reach its potential. Thus, according to Lansing and Mueller,

> The geographical mobility of labor is one of the basic processes of adjustment in the economy ... As new developments occur in

technology, demand and transportation, changes take place in the location of productive activity. Failure of human resources to adjust to these changes leads to inefficiency, poverty and dependency.[70]

INTERETHNIC COMPETITION, ECONOMIC CHANGE, AND LABOR MIGRATION

This chapter has considered the three processes of competition, economic change, and labor migration separately. The remainder of the book will consider the ways in which they interact. These interactions are so complex and dynamic that additional variables must be considered in order to help understand the causality relationships. While the complexity of the interactions precludes a monocausal explanation, nevertheless an effort is made to identify the conditions under which economic processes play themselves out in the ethnic arena, ethnic groups articulate their fluctuating positions, and different migrations follow different logics. The variables included in this study are freedom of choice in migration and discriminatory policies which, in turn, spill over into three others: levels of development, political systems, and interethnic conflict. All these variables are interwoven in the formulation and subsequent elaboration of several propositions that serve to address the gaps in our understanding of the role of competition in migration. An attempt is made to identify a spatial and temporal patterning of interethnic competition and migration, and every effort is made to approach these interlocked phenomena from an interdisciplinary standpoint.

Interaction 1: Competition and Economic Change (Chapters 2–3)

Interethnic competition is altered by economic change. Indeed, the established ways in which ethnic groups compete for scarce resources is discombobulated when rapid or abrupt growth or decline occurs. During such economic change, some ethnic groups become empowered while others become marginalized, and this bifurcation is manifest in the economic, political, and social spheres. But more than mere economic change is relevant. Both the direction and the source of change shed light on the complexity of interethnic competition. It is proposed that the *direction* of change (namely growth or decline) is important in determining the composition of the marginalized groups and the focus of the interethnic animosities on the part of the dominant groups. In other words, during economic decline, when the overall economy is shrinking, interethnic competition among local communities is accentuated while during economic growth, when the economy is expanding, animosities turn to the outside and become focused on the lowest in the pecking order, namely recent and potential immigrants. Moreover, it is proposed that the sources of economic growth and decline are also relevant because they determine just how deep and how entrenched the bifurcation between ethnic groups is. For example, when the source of decline has only a short term effect on the economy, or when discriminatory policies are not introduced to reinforce interethnic imbalances, or when the international community actively monitors changes in minority rights, then bifurcation is less likely to become entrenched.

Interaction 2: Competition and Migration (Chapters 4–5)

Writing in 1889, E. G. Ravenstein proposed that people migrate in order to better themselves, implying that they seek out better employment conditions.[71] In their effort to better themselves by migrating, people compete against other potential and actual migrants. They compete for resources and advantages before the migratory voyage is embarked upon, during the migration, as well as once it is completed. In other words, the entire process of migration entails competition.

Throughout the competition process, numerous impediments arise to restrict the movement of jobs across geographical zones and thus limit the diversification of the demand for labor. At the same time, many constraints limit the way in which workers can migrate from job to job across regions to respond to changes in the demand for their labor. The impediments with respect to both demand and supply of labor fall into the categories of policy, institutions, infrastructure, and personal constraints. Each of these categories includes push and pull forces that act on the employer and the worker in their respective attempts to maximize their profits or utility, as the case may be.

In multiethnic states, competition often takes place along ethnic lines. That ethnic division is also evident in the migration process insofar as members of ethnic groups share advantages and impediments in the migration process. Not every group in a multiethnic state has the same capacities and the same incentives to better themselves through migration. In the case of voluntary migration, ethnic differences manifest themselves in differences in the capacity and incentive of populations to move and thereby affect the relative costs and benefits in their personal cost–benefit analysis of migration. In the case of involuntary migration, ethnicity is crucial in determining who stays and who goes, when going refers to forced population movements such as ethnic cleansing. Competition theories have often said that migration affects competition. While that is true, it is proposed that in addition, interethnic competition also affects ethnic migration. In fact, there is a system of circular and cumulative causation in which competition and migration reinforce each other.

Interaction 3: Competition and Discriminatory Policies (Chapters 6–7)

Interethnic competition is affected by government intervention that serves to advantage one group at the disadvantage of another. Such intervention, embodied in discriminatory policies, is the result of the perceived (or actual) need, by the dominant group, for assistance in retaining its dominance. With respect to migration, discriminatory policies serve to disrupt the functioning of the free market, thereby to interfere with *laissez-faire* migration. Discrimination is reflected in immigration and emigration policies. It is proposed that as a result of discriminatory policies, selective migration ensues, in which ethnic groups are differentiated with respect to 'who goes' and 'who stays'.

Interaction 4: Competition, Migration and the Level of Development and the Political System (Chapter 8)

Multiethnic states differ in their levels of development: some are mostly agricultural and have low income per capita while others are industrial and post-industrial, with strong service sectors and high incomes per capita. Multiethnic states also vary with respect to their political systems. They may be authoritarian, ruled by fiat in a one-party system, or they may be liberal democracies in which individual rights are guaranteed by a system of internationally accepted laws. The process, manifestation, and success of interethnic competition and selective migration are different under different levels of development and different political realities. It is proposed that the most favorable conditions for a minority migrant exist in a highly developed liberal democracy. Indeed, a migrant from Pakistan has more economic opportunities and political rights in Canada than in Turkey.

Interaction 5: Competition, Migration and Ethnic Conflict (Chapter 8)

Interethnic competition can easily result in interethnic conflict. Numerous studies have claimed that when competition for scarce resources becomes accentuated, it can ignite ethnic collective action and result in open conflict.[72] With respect to migration, Park and Burgess have claimed that immigrants increase the competition for resources.[73] Therefore, a receptive immigration policy may be viewed as the spark that ignites conflict. It is proposed that ethnic conflict is not an inevitable consequence of either interethnic conflict or of receptive immigration. Both domestic and international factors can be brought to bear to prevent the development of a crisis situation.

At the same time, discriminatory policies that bias interethnic competition and result in selective migration often push a society over the tipping point and are conducive to embroiling it in interethnic conflict. It is proposed that when selective migration is due to discriminatory policies, it can have the perverse effect of diminishing interethnic conflict. This occurs because the fundamental cause of that conflict, namely interethnic intolerance abetted by forced coexistence, no longer exists.

This book strives to provide theoretical and empirical evidence in support of the above proposals. An effort is made to operationalize the proposals: variables are chosen, their indicators are identified, and the nature of the hypothesized relationships is observed. However, in order to be convincing, evidence must be provided to show that ethnic groups really did compete for jobs, resources, and power; that they did so in response to economic changes; that migration was indeed selective by ethnicity; and that discriminatory policies did in fact induce migration. Empirical evidence must clearly show causality. Alas, this was not possible due to the lack of comprehensive and comparable migration data disaggregated by ethnicity. As a result, there is no survey evidence to report. While an effort is made to address interethnic issues in a systematic way, sometimes only anecdotal evidence is available. While an effort is made to challenge existing views and to offer alternative explanations, at times there is a gap between the theoretical and empirical parts of the book. Nonetheless, every effort is made to offset the data limitations by raising relevant questions that frame a general discussion, by offering commentary of historical processes, and by providing overall depth of detail. The broad nature of the material under study sometimes necessitates a reliance on the possible, rather than the actual, effects and causes.

INTRODUCTION TO THE COUNTRIES UNDER STUDY

The theoretical discourse in this book is illustrated with examples from across the globe. While numerous countries are mentioned and their ethnic policies, growth patterns, and migration characteristics are explored, only 13 multiethnic states have been studied in depth, both with respect to the general patterns as well as their own particularities. They are Russia, Yugoslavia, South Africa, Israel, Brazil, India, Estonia, the Czech Republic, Singapore, Hong Kong, Canada, Australia, and the United States. Why study these countries and not others? While it may have been preferable to draw a random sample of all multinational countries that have experienced economic disruptions and population movements, this was not done for practical reasons. Instead, the 13 countries were chosen on the basis of considerations such as availability of data as well as the author's prior research and experience.

The obvious diversity of these countries raises concerns about the justification of a cross-country comparison. Indeed, the 13 countries differ in their levels of development, systems of governance and legitimization, the degree of integration in the world economy, the nature and role of their markets, and the degree of ethnic homogeneity. However, despite these differences there are some similarities that justify comparison. With respect to the level of development, all countries under study (with the exception of India[74]) are ranked by the World Bank in the middle- or upper-income categories, implying that they are predominantly industrial or service-sector economies. The absence of agricultural economies is deliberate as labor mobility within and from that sector has its own particular set of problems and considerations that are beyond the scope of this study. The GNP per capita in the countries under study ranges from a high in Singapore ($32,940) to a low in India ($390).[75] No other country under study is as poor as India, although Yugoslavia in the late 1990s is relatively close (estimates range from $300 to $1,510), having experienced a massive drop during the decade of war and international sanctions.[76]

With respect to systems of governance and legitimization, all countries under study, with the exception of Hong Kong, have multiparty systems with popular participatory practices. Some are federations (Russia, Yugoslavia, Brazil, India, Canada, and the USA) while others are unitary states (the Czech Republic, Estonia, and Singapore). All are republics with the exception of Canada (which is a parliamentary democracy), Hong Kong (which is a special administrative region of China with its own legislative house), and Australia (which in 1999 voted in a referendum to retain its link to the British monarchy).

With respect to integration in the world economy, while countries differ in the degree to which their economies are dependent on the flow of goods and capital across their borders, they all participate in such flows and their economies are firmly entrenched in the global economy.

With respect to the role of the market, all countries under study are currently market economies. While there is diversity as to what they were in the past, and while there are variations in the precise nature of their capitalist systems, they all reflect some basic characteristics that form the framework of their economies – namely, the predominance of a market economy in which prices are largely determined by the market, the existence of private property rights, the absence of pervasive central planning, the material motivational system (maximization of profits and utility), and so on.

All countries under study have a diverse population. In some, race is the principal distinguishing factor (i.e. South Africa) while in others religion plays that role (i.e. India). It is clear from table 1.1 that in some countries, the titular ethnic group is numerically dominant (such as in Russia, Israel, India, and the Czech Republic, all of which contain more than 80% of one group).[77] Only a few are ethnically bipolar, indicating a demographic parity (or close) between two ethnic groups (Brazil, Estonia, and Canada). Hong Kong, where the Chinese make up 96.8 percent of the population, is an exception. Despite this, it was included in this study of economic competition and migration because of the distinction between the Chinese of the mainland and those of the island, a distinction that is not reflected in ethnicity. In many respects, this difference in history, culture, experience, economic levels, and opportunities is as significant in drawing cleavages among the Chinese as it might be with an altogether other ethnic or racial group (in this sense, the distinction is similar to that between the Albanian population of Albania and Kosovo[78]).

Table 1.1
Population and Ethnic, Racial or Religious Composition, 1997

Country	Population (millions)	Largest ethnic, racial, and religious groups and percentage
Russia	147.231	Russian 81.5, Tartar 3.8
Yugoslavia	10.632	Serbian 62.6, Albanian 16.5, Montenegrian 5.0
South Africa	42.446	Black** 76.3, White 12.7, Colored 8.5
Israel	5.652	Jewish 80.5, Arab and other 19.5
Brazil	159.691	White 54.4, Mulato & Mestizo 40.1, Black 4.9
India	967.613	Hindu 80.3, Muslim 11.0, Christian 3.0
Estonia	1.463	Estonian 64, Russian 30
Czech Republic	10.307	Czech 81.2, Moravian 13.2, Slovak 3.1
Singapore	3.104	Chinese 77.3, Malay 14.1, Indian 7.3
Hong Kong	6.491	Chinese 96.8, English 2.2
Australia	18.508	White 95.2, Aborigine 2.0
Canada	30.287	*French 22.8, British 20.8, Amerindian and Inuktitut 1.7
USA	267.839	Non-Hispanic W 71.3, Non-Hispanic B 12.0, Hispanic 10.7, Asian 3.5, Native 0.7

Notes:
 *Refers to ethnic origin.
**Of which Zulus make up 22% and Xhosa 18%.
Source: various tables in Encyclopedia Britannica, *Britannica Book of the Year 1998*, Chicago: Encyclopedia Britannica, 1999.

Finally, the similarity-within-diversity argument can be further extended to include another point, crucial to this book, namely government policy. All 13 countries have been faced with economic change of some sort or other, and in all countries the governments have had to address this change and its linkage effects throughout the society. While political leaders often prefer to postpone unpopular measures and to allow deterioration, inflation, or stagnation, some-times economic disruptions were so far-reaching that they did not afford them the luxury of waiting out on the sidelines. Moreover, all countries had policies pertaining to population movements (emigra-tion and/or immigration), ethnic rights, and labor-force participation. Thus, while all 13 governments were in some way involved in economic change, interethnic competition and labor migrations (either by causing them or by responding to them), their motivations, actions, and ultimate successes in dealing with social, economic, and political ramifications varied greatly.

NOTES

1 The study was conducted by the United Nations Development Program; armed conflicts are defined as those in which over 1,000 people have been killed. *Economist*, 4 June 1994, p. 43.

2 Gerald B. Helman and Steven R. Ratner, 'Saving Failed States', *Foreign Policy* 89 (winter 1992), p. 3.

3 Samuel P. Huntington, *The Third Wave: Democratization in the Late Twentieth Century* (Norman: University of Oklahoma Press, 1991). The movement towards democracy is first seen among the states of southern Europe, then in the 1970s in Latin America, followed in the 1980s by some Asian countries (such as Korea, Taiwan, Turkey, and Thailand), and culminating with the communist countries of Eastern Europe and the Soviet Union. For a discussion of this trend, see Stephan Haggard and Robert R. Kaufman, *The Political Economy of Democratic Transitions* (Princeton: Princeton University Press, 1995), p. 3.

4 Stephen Castles and Mark J. Miller, *The Age of Migration* (New York: Guildford Press, 1993); Timothy J. Hatton and Jeffrey G. Williamson, *The Age of Mass Migration* (Oxford: Oxford University Press, 1998).

5 Vilfredo Pareto, quoted in Michael Hechter, *Internal Colonialism* (Berkeley: University of California Press, 1975), p. 311.

6 Anthony Smith, 'Chosen Peoples: Why Ethnic Groups Survive', *Ethnic and Racial Studies*, 15, 3 (July 1992), p. 450.

7 Cited in Alfred Pfabigan, 'The Political Feasibility of Austro-Marxist Proposals for the Solution of the Nationality Problem of the Danubian Monarchy', in Uri Ra'anan *et al.* (eds), *State and Nation in Multi-Ethnic Societies* (Manchester: Manchester University Press, 1991), p. 54.

8 Numerous other definitions dot the literature, including the following. According to Paul Brass, an ethnic group may be defined in three ways: in terms of objective attributes, with reference to subjective feelings and in

relation to its behavior (Paul R. Brass, *Ethnicity and Nationalism* (New Delhi: Sage Publications, 1991)). All the definitions that follow focus on at least one of those categories. An ethnic group, according to R. Narroll, is defined as a biologically self-perpetuating group that shares fundamental cultural values and differentiates itself from other groups (R. Narroll, 'Ethnic Unit Classification', *Current Anthropology*, vol. 5 4 (1964)). These cultural values may be embodied in language, religion or myth of origin. Which of these predominates is discussed by Uri Ra'anan: in 'eastern regions', ancestral language seems to be the dividing factor, while in 'southern regions' religion is the primary differentiating aspect of ethnicity Both of these are personal characteristics, as opposed to the western concept of nationality, which is closely tied to territory and state. (See Uri Ra'anan, 'Nation and State: Order out of Chaos' in Ra'anan *et al.*, *State and Nation*, p. 14.) Fredrik Barth focused his definition of ethnicity on the boundary that defines an ethnic group, rather than its cultural components (Fredrik Barth, 'Introduction' in Fredrik Barth (ed.), *Ethnic Groups and Boundaries* (Boston: Little, Brown & Co., 1969), p. 15). N. Glazer and D. P. Moynihan describe an ethnic group as 'any group of distinct cultural tradition and origin' (N. Glazer and D. P. Moynihan, *Ethnicity, Theory and Experience* (Cambridge, MA: Harvard University Press, 1975), p. 4). Ted Robert Gurr focuses on yet another angle: ethnic groups, which he refers to as communal groups, 'are psychological communities' underscoring the perception of collective identity that membership in a group connotes (Ted Robert Gurr, *Minorities at Risk* (Washington, DC: United States Institute of Peace Press, 1993), p. 3).

9 While the definitions provided in the text as well as in the above footnote may vary in focus, they all connote a group of people that are united (or perceive to be united) in some way. Such a lack of clarity fosters a wide range of interpretations so that the real-world applications of ethnic group boundaries result in a lack of comparable classifications. This confusion is best illustrated by the attempts to classify the various peoples inhabiting the Balkans. The unconventional official divisions of the Balkan populations have given rise to a plethora of groupings that belie the above classifications: peoples are distinguished by religion (the Bosnian Muslims, Bosnian Croats, and Bosnian Serbs, as well as the Bulgarians and the Pomaks), by levels of development (the Albanian Albanians and the Kosovo Albanians), and by language (the Albanian Tosks and Gegs). For the sake of simplicity, peoples of the Balkans will be referred to as ethnic groups throughout the text, even through they do not necessarily conform to the standard definitions of ethnicity.

10 Smith, 'Chosen Peoples', p. 450.

11 According to James Kellas, there is more to the difference: 'ethnic groups are essentially exclusive or ascriptive, meaning that membership in such groups is confined to those who share certain inborn attributes. Nations on the other hand are more inclusive and are culturally or politically defined' (James G. Kellas, *The Politics of Nationalism and Ethnicity* (New York: St Martin's Press, 1991), p. 4).

12 Indeed, representatives of 'indigenous' peoples across the globe recently demanded that their status be elevated to that of a 'nation' instead of their designation (by the International Labor Organization) as 'tribal populations'. The concept of the nation as the highest ranking is also evident in the classification of ethnic groups in former Yugoslavia: the federal government distinguished between nations (*narodi*), nationalities (*nacionalnosti*) and national minorities (*manjine*). Nations are those whose population centers are located

mainly within the Yugoslav federation (such as Serbs, Croats, Slovenes, etc.), while the latter refer to those ethnic groups that have their homelands in neighboring states (Albanians and Hungarians).

13 *Webster's Dictionary* (New York: Warner Books, 1979).

14 Smith, 'Chosen Peoples'.

15 Walker Connor, *Ethnonationalism* (Princeton: Princeton University Press, 1994), p. 41.

16 Kellas, *Politics of Nationalism*, p. 3

17 Paul Brass, *Ethnicity and Nationalism*, p. 48.

18 Uri Ra'anan, 'The Nation State Fallacy' in Joseph V. Montville, *Conflict and Peacemaking in Multiethnic Societies* (Lexington, MA: Lexington Books, 1990), p. 5.

19 What are the origins of such ethnic heterogeneity? In some countries it is the result of political boundaries that were drawn arbitrarily by the colonial powers. In many European countries it is the consequence of the inflow of people from the former colonies (Indians and Caribbeans in Britain; Africans and Arabs in France). In others still, multiethnicity comes from the fact that they are immigrant nations to which migrants have flowed (for example, the United States and Australia).

20 Walter Connor, 'Nation Building or Nation Destroying', *World Politics* 24 (1972), p. 320.

21 Editorial, *Nature Genetics* 24 (February 2000), p. 97.

22 Susan Olzak, *The Dynamics of Ethnic Competition and Conflict* (Stanford: Stanford University Press, 1992), p. 8.

23 Pierre L. Van den Berghe, 'Class, Race and Ethnicity in Africa', *Ethnic and Racial Studies* 6 (1983), p. 222.

24 Migration so clearly permeates all of these, and yet very often research is monodisciplinary and in one of these fields fails to cross-fertilize into others. Little consideration is made of efforts to understand and explain migration issues in other disciplines. Multidisciplinary efforts have been rare, but not nonexistent. See, for example, Tomas Hammar, Grete Brochmann, Dristof Ramas, and Thomas Faist (eds), *International Migration, Immobility and Development* (New York: Berg, 1997).

25 In this context, work refers only to work for pay. See the 1993 Work At Home Survey, conducted by LINK Resources and cited in the *Miami Herald*, 13 December 1993.

26 The most pervasive occurrence of slavery in the contemporary period has been found in Mauritania.

27 Lloyd Reynolds, 'Labor Mobility' in Clark Kerr and Paul D. Staudohar (eds), *Economics of Labor in Industrial Society* (San Fransisco: Jossey-Bass Publishers, 1986).

28 Campbell R. McConnell and Stanley L. Brue, *Contemporary Labor Economics*, 2nd edn (New York: McGraw Hill, 1986).

29 *New York Times*, 12 March 2000.

30 Workers compete for jobs, promotions, education, privileges, benefits, etc. While workers compete as individuals, among themselves, they also tend to compete collectively, in groups. Such groups are based on class, neighborhood, and/or educational ties. In multiethnic societies, groups are often based on ethnicity, race, or religion.

31 For a discussion of Marx's and Kuznets's views, see M. Zarkovic, *Issues in Indian Agricultural Development* (Boulder, CO: Westview Press, 1987), chapter 8; Shlomo Avineri, 'Marx and Modernization', *Review of Politics* (April 1969); Jay

Mandle, 'Marxist Analyses and Capitalist Development in the Third World', *Theory and Society* 9 (1980).

32 Arnos H. Hawley, *Human Ecology* (New York: Ronald Press, 1950).

33 Hubert M. Blalock Jr, *Toward a Theory of Minority Group Relations* (New York: Wiley, 1967), p. 73.

34 If there is no scarcity, then there is no problem. While there is scarcity in all goods in society, there must be limited access and attainability. Harmannus Hoetnik describes this condition as one that competition comes from scarcity that is both objective and subjective; it is not only are all economic goods scarce (in the objective sense) but members of society must perceive them as such (subjective). Harmannus Hoetnik, 'Resource Competition, Monopoly, and Socioracial Diversity' in Leo Despres (ed.), *Ethnicity and Resource Competition in Plural Societies* (The Hague: Mouton, 1975), p. 10.

35 Pierre L. Van den Berghe, "Ethnicity and Class in Highland Peru' in Despres, *Ethnicity and Resource Competition*, p. 72.

36 Hoetnik, 'Resource Competition, Monopoly', p. 9.

37 Elliot Skinner, 'Competition within Ethnic Systems in Africa' in Despres, *Ethnicity and Resource Competition*, p. 142

38 These rewards, and the lack thereof, are the subject of a study by Susan F. Feiner (*Race and Gender in the American Economy* (Englewood Cliffs, NJ: Prentice Hall, 1994)).

39 Donald L. Horowitz, *Ethnic Groups in Conflict* (Berkeley: University of California Press, 1985), pp. 8–12.

40 See Joseph Rudolph Jr. and Robert Thompson (eds), *Ethnoterritorial Politics, Policy and the Western World* (Boulder: Lynne Rienner, 1989), p. 47.

41 Theodore Wright in William C. McCready (ed.), *Culture, Ethnicity and Identity* (New York: Academic Press, 1983); W. Howard Wriggins and James F. Guyot, 'Demographic Change and Politics' in W. Howard Wriggins and James F. Guyot, *Population, Politics and the Future of Southern Asia* (New York: Columbia University Press, 1973); William Alonso and Paul Starr (eds), *The Politics of Numbers* (New York: Russell Sage Foundation, 1987).

42 Irving Lewis Allen, 'Variable White Ethnic Resistance to School Desegregation: Italian–American Parents in Three Connecticut Cities, 1966' in McCready, *Culture, Ethnicity*, p. 14.

43 Ibid., p. 15.

44 Milica Z. Bookman, *The Demographic Struggle for Power: The Political Economy of Demographic Engineering in the Modern World* (London: Frank Cass, 1998).

45 Such lines are not entirely rigid, as clear from the success of demographic policies that attempt to convert and assimilate populations.

46 Horowitz, *Ethnic Groups in Conflict*, p. 302.

47 Stephen O. Olugbemi, 'The Ethnic Numbers Game in Inter-Elite Competition for Political Hegemony in Nigeria' in McCready, *Culture, Ethnicity*, p. 266.

48 Tamils in Sri Lanka have been trying to defend their culture and ethnicity against the dominant Sinhalese. However, to the Sinhalese, the oppression of the Hindus that speak Dravidian languages from India is perceived as a major threat. Indeed, according to a Sinhalese politician, 'In this country, the problem of the Tamils is not a minority problem. The Sinhalese are the minority in Dravidistan. We are carrying on a struggle for our national existence against the Dravidian majority' (Sri Lanka, House of Representatives, Parliamentary Debates (Hansard), vol. 48, col. 1313, 3 September 1962, quoted in Robert Kearney, 'Ethnic Conflict and the Tamil Separatist Movement in Sri Lanka', *Asian Survey* 25, 9 (September 1985), p. 903).

49 Gurr, *Minorities at Risk*, p. 56.
50 According to Zenner, it is especially prevalent when the minority is in a middleman position: in the middle between the ruling elite and the masses and between the producers and the consumers. See Walter P. Zenner, *Minorities in the Middle* (Albany: State University of New York Press, 1991), p. xii.
51 A consensus was developed after independence because the political and economic powers were allowed to develop and sustain themselves separately: Basham claims that Malays were dominant in employment and development schemes, their language and religion (Islam) dominated, but the Indians and Chinese were allowed to flourish in economic and professional activities. However, each side viewed the other as controlling too much politics or economics, leading to the ethnic riots of 1969. See Richard Basham, 'National Racial Policies and University Education in Malaysia' in McCready, *Culture, Ethnicity*, p. 58.
52 However, they were present in large quantities and at lower levels, while the quality, elite, and powerful positions were not in their hands.
53 Goldberg and Harel have found that they are underrepresented in higher status positions: while they are 47% of the population, they account for only 16% of first degree students, 15% of members of Parliament, 6% of industrial managers. They do, however, account for 77% of production workers. See Albert I. Goldberg and Gedaliahu H. Harel, 'Sensitivity to Ethnic Discrimination: The Case of Israeli Production Foremen' in McCready, *Culture, Ethnicity*, pp. 141–2.
54 In Kenya there was the 'kikuyuization' of the country's bureaucracy after independence, as members of the Kikuyu tribe took over where the British vacated.
55 Horowitz, *Ethnic Groups in Conflict*, pp. 8–12.
56 J. S. Furnivall, *Colonial Policy and Practice* (Cambridge: Cambridge University Press, 1948), p. 304.
57 She said, 'when all else fails, "final solutions" are enacted'. Edna Bonacich, 'A Theory of Middleman Minorities', *American Sociological Review* 38 (October 1973), p. 592.
58 It is necessary in order to underscore the difference between economic growth and economic development, or long-term modern economic growth as some economists (including Simon Kuznets) have referred to it. Economic growth is simply defined as an increase in income per capita. It comes about from an increased use of resources, principally land, labor, and capital.
59 Additional ramifications often follow. In the more developed countries, ramifications of economic development include rising employment, increased labor productivity, higher real wages, and reduced inequality. This has not necessarily been the experience of the less developed countries.
60 Bradley Schiller, *The Macro Economy Today*, 8th edn (New York: McGraw-Hill, 2000), pp. 29–30. This transformation occurs because rising incomes associated with economic growth entail a change in the nature of demand, shifting as it did into those sectors with higher income elasticities such as manufactured goods and services. Moreover, some sectors have experienced more technological innovation than others, enabling higher rates of growth. Some US data aptly illustrate the structural transformation that occurred during the 19th and 20th centuries: At the turn of the 1800s, agriculture accounted for some 90% of the national income; 200 years later, that number was about 5%. Manufacturing, on the other hand, accounted for 5% and 20% respectively. Finally, services grew from some 2% to 75% of national income over 200 years.

61 Anna Kutka, 'Demographic Trends in the Labor Force' in Eli Ginsberg (ed.), *The Changing US Labor Market* (Boulder, CO: Westview Press, 1994), p. 17.

62 For example, in the United States, the structural transformation of the labor force can be traced to the post-Second World War expansion of higher education that enabled the development of the service sector, the large supply of female workers in the 1970s and 1980s that were necessary for the expansion of that sector, the leadership role that the US assumed after the Second World War enabled it to assume a dominant role for its services in fields such as international banking, air transportation, communication, advertising, marketing, etc. Eli Ginsberg, 'The Changing World of Work' in Ginsberg (ed.), *Changing US Labor Markets*.

63 Simon Kuznets, *Economic Growth of Nations. Total Output and Production Structure* (Cambridge, MA: Harvard University Press, 1971), chapters 4 and 6; Simon Kuznets, *Modern Economic Growth. Rate, Structure and Spread* (New Haven: Yale University Press, 1966).

64 Immanuel Wallerstein, *The Modern World-System: Capitalist Agriculture and the Origins of the European World Economy in the Sixteenth Century* (New York: Academic Press, 1974).

65 Lucie Cheng and Edna Bonacich (eds), *Labor Immigration Under Capitalism: Asian Workers in the United States Before World War II* (Berkeley: University of California Press, 1984).

66 Simon Kuznets wrote the second volume of Everett Lee, Simon Kuznets, and Hope Eldridge *et al.*, *Population Redistribution and Economic Growth, United States: 1870–1950* (Philadelphia: American Philosophical Society, 1960).

67 John Lansing and Eva Mueller, *The Geographic Mobility of Labor* (Ann Arbor: University of Michigan Press, 1967).

68 German–Italian labor recruitment agreement signed in 1955 was a program of guestworker recruitment to fill labor shortages. Later, similar agreements were signed with Spain, Greece, Turkey, and Portugal. While Germany's importation of foreign labor occurred through a regulated program, France's labor importation program relied on the market to determine levels of inflows. Both were aggressive importers of workers.

69 Indeed, more than 90% of south Asian migrants since the mid-1970s have gone to oil exporting countries of western Asia as these countries, unlike western Europe and North America, have been receptive to foreign labor. Tomas Hammar and Dristof Tamas, 'Why Do People Go or Stay' in Hammar *et al.*, *International Migration, Immobility*, p. 6.

70 Lansing and Mueller, *Geographic Mobility*, p. iii.

71 E. G. Ravenstein, 'The Laws of Migration', *Journal of the Royal Statistical Society* (1889), pp. 241–301.

72 Ethnic collective action is defined by Susan Olzak as 'a public action of two or more persons that articulates a distinctly ethnic (or racial) claim, expresses a grievance, or attacks members of another ethnic group (or their property). Such actions include protests ... and conflicts'. Olzak, *Dynamics of Ethnic Competition*, p. 6.

73 R. Park and E. Burgess, *Introduction to the Science of Sociology* (Chicago: University of Chicago Press, 1921), cited ibid., p. 29.

74 India was nevertheless included in this study because of clear evidence of interethnic competition, economic growth due to a liberalization process, and high rates of in and out migration.

75 World Bank, *World Bank Development Report 2000* (Oxford: Oxford University

Press, 2000), table 1; data for Yugoslavia are from the *Britannica Book of the Year* (1998), p. 745.

76 *Times*, 23 August 1999.

77 The ethnic composition of India is interesting insofar as it is predominantly a Hindu state while at the same time it is the second largest Muslim state in the world, after Indonesia. There are more Muslims in India than in Pakistan.

78 There is a difference between the Tosks and the Ghegs as well as between them and the Kosovo Albanians.

Interethnic Competition During Economic Decline

During the economic decline of the late 1980s the population of Serbia boycotted fruit juice produced in Slovenia (but not juice produced in other former Yugoslav republics). Economic hardship in Israel resulted in the laying off of Palestinian workers (but not Israeli workers). In periods of economic shortage, Sri Lanka dried up development funds in the Tamil regions (but not the Sinhalese regions). During the economic turmoil associated with independence, Estonia denied property rights on agricultural land to Russians (but not to Estonians). Examples of interethnic differences in the way broad economic fluctuations are experienced exist across the globe. As not all people are created equal, so too not all ethnic groups are affected by business-cycle gyrations in the same way.

In this chapter, I turn my attention to economic decline and its effect on interethnic competition and domestic ethnic hierarchies.[1] I introduce theories pertaining to the accentuation of interethnic competition during times of economic decline. Moreover, this chapter also includes evidence of polarization among ethnic groups that occurs during economic decline. Finally, I discuss several sources of economic decline, leading to the proposition made in chapter 1, namely that the source of economic decline is relevant in determining just how entrenched ethnic bifurcation has become.

INTERETHNIC COMPETITION DURING ECONOMIC DECLINE

Economic change (growth *or* decline) can accentuate feelings of ethnic loyalty and group distinctiveness, in other words, it can stimulate feelings of nationalism. Given that nationalism is the political expression of ethnic sentiments, its link to interethnic competition is indisputable. Nationalist feelings by definition contain elements of interethnic competition because of the underlying motivation to pursue ends that will enhance a group's overall well-being, position, and advantage within society. A group's well-being is simultaneously political, economic, and cultural. (Indeed, it is hard to distinguish between the desire for national control of resources among the inhabitants of diamond-rich Yakutia (in Russia) and the pride in their culture and the desire to see their people in power.) Thus, nationalism is simply a coherent manifestation of interethnic competition.

The literature on economic change and interethnic competition has largely focused on the relationship between nationalism and economic growth. While growth is discussed in chapter 3, the significantly sparcer literature on economic decline and ethnicity is discussed below. There is a consensus among scholars that the relationship between economic decline (or lack of development) and ethnic awareness is direct. In other words, the greater the underdevelopment, deterioration, and stagnation of an economy, the greater the efforts of minority ethnic groups to differentiate themselves from the majority or dominant group. Hroch found this in nineteenth-century Europe, Michneck in pre-break-up USSR, and Birch in Bangladesh.[2] In addition, Drake claims that economic decline and poverty of some regions and their populations, especially relative to others, 'was a major underlying cause of the civil war in Sudan, and it had a definite role in the break-up of Pakistan into Pakistan and Bangladesh. Within Indonesia, too, several of the regional rebellions experienced since independence have had economic grievances at their root'.[3]

Interethnic competition increases during economic decline for two reasons that are relevant for this study: the mere occurrence of economic change unsettles the status quo of interethnic economic relations; and economic change tends to affect different groups differently.

First, economic change, specifically economic decline, stimulates interethnic competition by upsetting the balance of employment, distribution of resources, education opportunities, and economic advantages that result from changes in economic variables. In the scramble for jobs, ethnic groups may cross over into other groups' jobs, causing niche overlap which, according to Olzak, further releases competitive forces.[4] When economic conditions deteriorate, interethnic competition becomes more ferocious and fuels nationalist ideology. Ethnic group differentiation and awareness go hand-in-hand with decline. Macro- and microeconomic problems become exacerbated as interethnic bickering imperils economic functioning and paralyzes economic institutions, contributing to further macro and micro failures. Therefore, it is during times of comprehensive change that political and social competition among ethnic groups for advantages of their members is most acute.

Second, when there is economic change, the effect across population groups is not the same. Economic change has redistributive effects, some of which are predictable and recurrent. Indeed, some groups within society tend to, repeatedly, lose more or benefit less from economic change. Most often the losers include minority ethnic groups, the elderly, women, and so forth. Haggard and Kaufman said that in the course of economic decline, the 'sharp deterioration in aggregate economic performance cuts across social strata and affects the income of a wide array of social groups'.[5] It affects social groups differently, just as it affects different regions within a state differently: transition-induced economic change in the Czech Republic affects female employment differently from male employment;[6] war-induced economic change affects Albanian businesses in Serbia differently from Serbian businesses; growth in the United States affects social services in affluent regions differently from poor regions.

Economic competition is even more pronounced where ethnic groups are concentrated in specific regions. Hechter said that 'the uneven wave of industrialization over territorial space creates relatively advanced and less advanced groups, and therefore acute cleavages of interest arise between these groups'. As a consequence, 'there is a crystallization of the unequal distribution of resources and power between the two groups'.[7]

The unequal distribution of resources described by Hechter is crucial in perpetuating interethnic competition because it leads to perceptions of economic injustice. Such injustice, perceived by ethnic groups who are not reaping the benefits of economic change, is due to two factors: the objective macroeconomic conditions (such as poverty) as well as policies aimed at rectifying those conditions. However, perception of unjust policies also occurs among ethnic groups who have been advantaged by economic change. Indeed, policies aimed at rectifying the unequal distribution of resources across ethnic groups/regions is often perceived as unjust because it can result in the following: above-average contribution to the national budget by some groups, insufficient benefit from the national budget by some groups; unfavorable terms of trade resulting from price manipulation (that affects some groups and not others); unfavorable regulation pertaining to investment and foreign inflows of resources (affecting selected regions and peoples); and so on. It is clear that perceptions of economic injustice may be experienced by groups in regions that are more *or* less developed relative to the nation, as is evident in India (the Punjab as well as Kashmir), the former Yugoslavia (Slovenia as well as Macedonia) and in the former USSR (Estonia as well as Turkmenia). The high-income, subnational regions such as Punjab, Slovenia, and Estonia have experienced tax revolts in their recent past, reflecting a dissatisfaction with what they perceived to be unfair drainage of their resources. At the same time, the less developed regions are lobbying for increased 'spread effects' of national development, as well as a change in the redistributive policy. Either of these motivate ethnic populations to mobilize their energies and increase interethnic competition for resources.[8]

Therefore, ethnic group competition is both absolute and relative. In other words, groups compete not only for who gets what, but also for who gets more. Their competition reflects the Christmas-present syndrome, according to which children are more focused on what their siblings receive than on their own presents. So too, interethnic competition occurs not only for economic and political power, but also for that power relative to other groups' power.

MANIFESTATIONS OF ETHNIC BIFURCATION

In the course of economic decline, competition between ethnic groups produces losers and winners. Those who lose become marginalized; those who win become empowered. This process of ethnic bifurcation is evident in economic, political, and social spheres. The former includes changes in labor force participation, in business ownership, in expenditure on social services, and so forth. In the political sphere, changes in political participation, the introduction of discriminatory policy, and alterations in ethnic voting patterns are among the indicators of marginalization and empowerment. Finally, in the social sphere, manifestations of ethnic bifurcation include changes in linguistic laws, in religious tolerance, and in incidents of crime.

During ethnic bifurcation, society becomes bipolar insofar as ethnic groups move into one of two opposing poles. At one pole, ethnic groups have economic and political power, they control the most lucrative positions, they enjoy the most privilege, and they have access to the best opportunities. In other words, they are empowered. They are the 'get-outta-my-way' group that has little regard for minority groups while making use of them in various economic capacities. At the other pole, the minorities enjoy fewer privileges, control fewer resources, and have fewer sources of power. They are marginalized ethnic groups. They are the 'kick-me' group, often subservient, fearful, and hesitant. It is as though they carry a sign that says, 'kick me in the behind, kick me around, kick me out, kick me into prison' etc. The two poles are characterized by two different sets of economic rules and regulations. These rules are both formal and informal, spontaneous and institutionalized. They dictate the terms of employment, the nature of schooling, the quality of livelihood, and the cultural life of their populations.

The indicators of marginalization and empowerment in the

economic, political, and social spheres are discussed below. The discussion in this chapter refers to the process as it develops within national boundaries (henceforth, internal) to be distinguished from its external variety, which is the topic of chapter 3.

Economic Indicators

Within the *labor market*, evidence of ethnic bifurcation during economic decline is clear as marginalized groups experience more short-term unemployment, long-term unemployment, underemployment and involuntary part-time employment than dominant groups (the Roma in the Czech Republic were first to lose their jobs during the downturn of the early 1990s, as were the Palestinians in Iraq during the same period). The incidence of discouraged workers is also higher among marginalized ethnic groups (as among the Palestinians seeking work in Israel). To the extent that discrimination on the basis of ethnicity is tolerated or encouraged, then marginalized ethnic groups become channeled into low-skilled jobs and occupations (witness Albanians hauling heating coal for Yugoslav city residents). At the same time, workers from empowered groups hold on to jobs longer during economic downturns. Not only do they tend to be concentrated in occupations and at skill levels that are less susceptible to business cycle fluctuations, but they also seem to recover and reorient more rapidly.[9] Moreover, during economic decline, necessity forces ethnic groups to spill into occupations they previously shunned. In the process, they engage in what Olzak has called niche overlap, according to which groups penetrate jobs previously held by workers.[10] Such overlap is also discussed by Money in her study of immigrants, where she claims that it accentuates interethnic competition: 'The native and immigrant labor forces compete more directly in times of economic recession than in periods of prosperity because workers are often willing to take otherwise unacceptable employment during periods of economic downturn.'[11]

Another indicator of ethnic bifurcation is the loss of *property rights* by marginalized groups. The denial of rights to business owners of a target ethnic group has been and remains a popular policy in multiethnic states (indeed, the Nuremberg Laws of 1935, permitting the wholesale expropriation of Jewish property, continues to have reincarnations across the globe). Such a policy is introduced by dominant groups to safeguard their economic position during periods of falling growth rates. As discussed in chapter 6, it serves to further empower the dominant group and to disadvantage the marginal group (as occurred in Malaysia when the government introduced legislation restricting business ownership by ethnic Chinese). Alternatively, loss of property rights may be the result of spontaneous interethnic group interaction (as in Kosovo, where businesses of opposing ethnic groups were the target of mass destruction). Whatever its source, the denial of property rights in business reduces the present income and potential future income of a marginalized ethnic group.

Discriminatory policy pertaining to property rights is not limited to business ownership but extends to land, real estate, or any other asset with income generating potential. Any change in a group's ability to own and manage such assets is equally damaging for the marginalized groups insofar as it affects the livelihood of their members. When Estonia denied property rights on land to Russian farmers on its newly sovereign territory (in 1991), the result was a marginalization of Russians and an empowerment of Estonians. When the Indians in Fiji lost their rights to own land, ethnic marginalization was clearly occurring.[12] It was also evident in Iraq in the aftermath of the imposition of a new environmental and resource policy which entailed the diversion of rivers in the southern marshlands and thereby directly decreased the income possibilities of the region's inhabitants (who, incidentally, were Shiite Muslims, not the dominant and ruling Sunnis[13]).

The unequal allocation of domestic investment and development funds by ethnic group is further evidence of ethnic bifurcation. In multiethnic states in which a dominant group determines policy, economic decline can trigger an alteration in 'who gets what'. Policies pertaining to capital flows and investments that discriminate by ethnic group are easier to carry out if ethnic boundaries coincide with administrative boundaries. Then, policy can more easily be masked as regional policy (such as the reduction in development funds for the Tamil regions of Sri Lanka). However, even when regional boundaries do not completely coincide with ethnic boundaries, policies can undermine the access of marginal groups to the benefits of investment (for example, in the former Yugoslavia, federal budget allocations to ethnically mixed regions such as Bosnia tended to favor the Muslim population, albeit not through federal policy but rather at the discretion of the republic level leaders).

The unequal distribution of foreign aid and foreign investment represent yet one more manifestation of ethnic bifurcation as marginal groups tend to benefit less and empowered groups more. When economic decline occurs, foreign aid and foreign investment tend to decline, prompting the dominant ethnic groups to reevaluate the recipients of those flows. They do this through their position in the central government that gives them the right to disperse foreign flows to sectors and regions of the domestic economy. Such was the experience of the former Yugoslavia. During the 1980s when economic decline was widespread, foreign investment flowed largely into

Slovenia and Croatia, while little of it was allocated to Kosovo and Macedonia.[14]

During economic decline, public expenditure for social services is often reduced. Expenditure for health and education may not be cut equally for all ethnic groups, providing yet one more indication of the process of marginalization.[15] As in the case of capital disbursements, such open discrimination in health and education expenditure is easier to achieve when target ethnic groups are localized in a specific area.[16] This requirement is usually met, since health and education provision takes place on the local level, and ethnic groups often tend to be concentrated by neighborhoods. (The city of Philadelphia is a good example: Italians tend to live in south Philadelphia; Russians tend to live in the northeast; Jews tend to concentrate in Jenkintown and blacks in West Philly. Neighborhood schools and clinics reflect that ethnic composition.) There is plenty of evidence in the United States that expectant mothers of different races do not get the same quality of prenatal care, so that the death rates among races differ.[17] Alternatively, when a territory is not ethnically distinct, discrimination may still take place albeit on an individual, micro level. Even in countries with universal health care, marginal ethnic groups receive care that is quantitatively and qualitatively different from what the dominant groups receive. A study of the Czech Republic, conducted by Helsinki Watch, indicates that Roma women are segregated and placed in overcrowded maternity wards and Roma schoolchildren are forced to sit in separate rows in the back or simply sent to mental institutions.[18] Such discrimination continues, despite its official repudiation.[19]

Political Indicators

Ethnic bifurcation manifests itself in the political arena in several ways, all of which entail the nature of ethnic group participation in the political process. First, *representation* of ethnic groups in political institutions is susceptible to the gyrations in the overall interethnic climate and (indirectly) to the business cycle. Changes in the number of parliament seats held by marginal groups, as well as changes in the number of slots in the administration that are allocated to them, represent the principal ways in which ethnic dominance manifests itself. During downturns in the business cycle, the ruling ethnic group is less likely to be generous in granting minority representation that might represent its group's economic interests and make demands. Despite the clear guidelines set forth by the Conference on Security and Cooperation in Europe that minorities have the right to run for political office,[20] examples of their low representation in government abound. In Estonia there has been a precipitous decrease in ethnic

Russians in public life since independence (which coincided with an economic downturn), despite the fact that many of them have learned the Estonian language and accepted Estonian citizenship.[21] A similar decrease in political participation of ethnic Russians occurred in the Russian republic of Bashkortostan, where, under electoral law, only a citizen who has a command of Bashkir is eligible to run for presidency[22] (while the central government in Moscow disputes this law, saying that there has to be equality in opportunity among candidates of all ethnic backgrounds, the local government stands by its ruling in order to limit the contenders who are only Russian speaking).

Where newly empowered ethnic groups come to power and dismantle previous electoral regulations, marginalization takes numerous forms. In some cases, the government simply imposes a ruling, as occurred in Indonesia where ethnic Chinese were virtually banned from politics (as well as the military and government service).[23] Alternatively, marginalization results from the electoral process. In the Czech Republic, the party of the former Charter 77 dissidents, who were also actively sponsoring human rights programs for minorities, received only 4.3 percent of the vote while the ultra-rightist Republican Party, with its proposal to expel Vietnamese and Cuban guest workers, captured over 6 percent of the vote.[24] The voice of the electorate was heard, as the party advocating human rights did not win seats in Parliament while the party advocating antiminority legislation won 11 seats. It was similarly heard in India, where the 1998 elections brought the Bharatiya Janata party to power. This party rallied Hindu nationalism on a platform of Hindutva (Hindu Rule), targeting primarily the Indian Muslims, some 100 million (12% of the population).[25] Moreover, in the Indian state of Gujarat, the Rashtriya Swayamsevak Sangh party has as its political agenda to make Hinduism the supreme religion, threatening the rights of Muslims and other religious minorities.[26] Both of these parties gained popularity during the persistent economic recession of the 1990s.

Second, ethnic bifurcation results from discrimination in state *constitutions*. Discriminatory specifications are discussed in chapter 6 below, suffice it to say here that some constitutions explicitly indicate equality or inequality among its ethnic groups (the current Israeli constitution, as well as the apartheid-era South African constitution, both promote the dominance of a select group). Moreover, constitutions sometimes even specify the ranking of those groups (such as the 1974 constitution of the former Yugoslavia). It is important to note that constitutions are dynamic documents that can be changed and amended to coincide with changing demands and characteristics of the policy. Such constitutional changes may be either minority-friendly or not. Clearly, the current South African constitution represents an improvement for previously marginalized groups because it has no encoded discrimination between its races (although there was still, in the year 2000, an ongoing struggle over the exact wording of equal racial rights[27]). Equally clearly, the new constitutions of the former Yugoslav countries, the Czech Republic, and Estonia are less minority-friendly than the old ones. The case of Yugoslavia is illuminating insofar as the communist, Titoist constitution, while ranking peoples, granted different ethnic groups more rights than any of the post-communist constitutions of the successor states (that have clearly demoted all but the titular majorities).[28] In the Czech Republic, imme-diately after the 1990s elections, the government undertook moves to *de jure* guarantee the Roma minority full human rights in the consti-tution.[29] However, *de facto*, such protection does the Roma little good, given the well-documented increased harassment they are suffering in the post-communist period. In Estonia, present-day leaders repeat-edly invoke the country's history (when it was 'the only state in interwar Europe to implement a full system of cultural autonomy for its national minorities'[30]) in an effort to crystalize the controversies pertaining to the position of the newly created and newly demoted Russian minority.

Third, the introduction of policies that adversely affect target ethnic groups is one more indication of dominant group empowerment. While such *discriminatory* policies are discussed in chapters 6 and 7 below, it is useful here to illustrate their role in marginalizing and empowering ethnic groups. Discriminatory policies are widespread across economies. They have been introduced in the production process (such as in the Punjab, where Sikhs have greater access to agricultural credit than non-Sikhs), in consumption (such as in the Czech Republic, where Romas cannot frequent the same cafés as ethnic Czechs), and in education (such as in Malaysia, where ethnic Malays are favored in the scholarship queue). Moreover, discrimina-tory policies have been observed in housing, media, and law. With respect to housing, the Czech Republic has been very forthright in its discrimination. By 1993, various cities passed legislation granting local authorities 'the right to evict troublesome Roma from their apartments (on grounds such as overcrowding, lack of hygiene etc.) and expel them from the cities without court orders'.[31] The Republican Party, with its primary emphasis placed on security, calls for new laws that would give the police extraordinary measures to act quickly – reflecting clearly its anti-Roma sentiment. The party's first president, Miroslav Sladek, publicly offered a new Alfa Romeo sports car to the first police force that could rid its town of Roma.[32] With respect to discrimination in the media, Yugoslavia provides an apt example: since the Roma have been demoted from 'nationality' to 'ethnic group', they therefore no longer have the right to their own independent media.[33] According to policy, they can only have limited time on state radio and television stations.[34] Finally, with respect to discrimination in law, different ethnic groups are treated differently by the legal system, creating or reinforcing ethnic bifurcation. Even in countries in which *de jure* the law is equal for all, evidence of *de facto* differences by ethnic groups exists. A recent study provides compelling evidence of how blacks in the United States are not subject to the same police treatment, as indicated by frequent police questioning of automobile drivers whose only crime is 'driving while black'.[35] In the Czech Republic, police protection is not the same for the Czechs as for the Romas: according to a Prague newspaper, police stood by and watched as unarmed Romas were beaten with clubs, chains and iron bars by disgruntled youths.[36] Latham provides evidence of unequal application of the law in Montenegro ('after a Roma allegedly assaulted a Montenegrin, members of the majority community burned down an entire Romani village. To date, there has been no attempt to punish those who were responsible'[37]). Given such evidence of ethnic inequality under the law even in countries that profess equality, minorities in countries with dual legal systems have reason for trepidation. For this reason, the recent election of Muslim parties and the concomitant imposition of Islamic law in Nigeria drew a violent response from Christian populations that interpreted such legislation as evidence of their decreasing relevance in political affairs, in other words, their marginalization.[38]

Fourth, ethnic bifurcation is also evident in the decreased *participation* of marginalized groups in the election process. Voter turnout is sensitive to factors such as intimidation by dominant groups (as has repeatedly occurred in the Indian state of Bihar). In the absence of intimidation, minorities sometimes collectively reject the electoral process, usually to make a political point (such as the Albanians in Kosovo, who refused to participate in Yugoslav elections during the 1990s[39]). Alternatively, ethnic groups may simply be barred from participating in the electoral process (indeed, overseas Chinese across Asia and Pacific have been prevented from voting in elections in their host countries[40]).

Social Indicators

Intolerance of minority *culture* is an indication of ethnic bifurcation within a society. The dominant group promotes its own culture by suffocating that of the marginalized group (for example, in Indonesia the Chinese are not allowed to celebrate their New Year;[41] in Japan, the Governor of Tokyo publicly referred to people of Chinese and Korean descent as *shangokujin*, a derogatory term with xenophobic connotations used as a sharp insult[42]). The dominant group exhibits cultural intolerance because it is emboldened by its empowerment (such empowerment was evident among ethnic Slovaks in Slovakia after the break-up of Czechoslovakia where, in an insulting effort to denegrade minority culture, Slovakian former president Vladimír Mečiar publicly called all Romas 'mental retards'[43]). Alternatively, cultural intolerance occurs because the dominant group is frustrated by what it perceives to be insufficient influence and power (in France, public outcry by the dominant ethnic French population followed the insistence of a schoolgirl on wearing an Islamic headscarf in a public school, calling into question the supremacy of French culture).

Language is closely related to culture. Since language is the glue that often holds groups together, language policy at the state level reflects the country's policy toward minorities.[44] Sometimes a policy is tolerant of minority languages, supporting diversity and heterogeneity (as was the case in Yugoslavia during Presdient Tito's era). Alternatively, a policy is intolerant of minority tongues and requires linguistic assimilation of its residents (in Bulgaria, the policy of Bulgarization of Turks during the 1970s prohibited the use of the Turkish language;[45] in Macedonia, the Bulgarian language was prohibited by the Serbian authorities during the interwar period;[46] in post-independence Macedonia, the Ministry of Education banned classes outside the state educational system and proceeded to close down Turkish-language schools in 1975[47]). It is intolerant policies such as these that leads Horowitz to claim that 'language is a symbol of domination'.[48] When dominant ethnic groups introduce discriminatory language policy and/or revoke the language rights of minorities, it indicates that ethnic bifurcation is taking place.

When the *religion* of dominant and minority groups differs, then ethnic bifurcation is manifested in religious intolerance. This may entail simple ridiculing of minority beliefs or interreligious differences in the allocation of funding, space, and media time. Religious discrimination may extend into the workplace, the housing market, and trade relations. Intolerance may escalate and result in the physical destruction of religious shrines and artifacts. In Bosnia, there was a three-way mutual destruction of religious edifices by Catholics, Orthodox Christians, and Muslims. In India, a dispute over the Babari mosque in Ayodhya (which Hindu nationalists long alleged was built on the birthplace of Lord Rama) led to the forcible demolition of the mosque in 1992, which incited riots and underscored the role of religious nationalism in interreligious conflicts.

All these manifestations of religious intolerance are deemed illegal in most Western democracies. Indeed, religious harassment by empowered groups can only persist unpunished in countries where the legal system fails to acknowledge and protect minority religious rights.

The experience of the Baha'is (a sect of Islam) in Iran is an example of multifaceted harassment. While there are 3 million Baha'i adherents in Iran and adjoining countries, their religion is not formally recognized by the Iranian authorities.[49] In 1983 it became a crime to be a Baha'i, and Baha'i-owned enterprises were confiscated.

Ethnic bifurcation is evident when observing the differential incidence of *crime*. The number of prisoners, juvenile delinquents, homicides, drug crimes, and rapes among marginalized populations is higher than among dominant groups. Poverty is positively related to crime and the marginalized populations tend to be poor. Examples of such differential crime rates are found in numerous multiethnic states. Former Yugoslav immigrants are increasingly responsible for crime in western Europe, with Italy leading in the statistics.[50] In South Africa there has been a dramatic increase in crime since the mid-1980s, most of which is committed by blacks. The murder rate is one of the highest in the world, and cases of robbery, rape, assault, housebreaking, and vehicle hijackings hit record highs in the early 1990s.[51] In the Indian state of Bihar, Harijans, formerly untouchables, have extremely high crime rates (possibly in response to the practice of 'Harijan hunting', a sport of landowners who intimidate these landless laborers).[52] In the Czech Republic, crime jumped during the 1990s to new levels: according to Hochenos, 'although Roma make up only 2 percent of the Czech population, they accounted for 11 per cent of all crimes and 50 percent of crimes such as pick-pocketing and burglary'.[53] (As a result, the skinheads that attack the Romas are viewed favorably by the majority population because they play the role of social protectors.) In the United States, crime rates by the Native American population tend to be higher, on a per capita basis, than among other groups. Finally, in Singapore, often called the Switzerland of Asia, on average one person is hung every nine days.[54] Most of the executed are not ethnic Chinese but Thais and Malaysians, indicating that there is a disproportionate crime rate among the minorities.

Marginalized populations tend to exhibit higher rates of *personal distress*, including suicides and divorces, than dominant groups. While the evidence is inconclusive, it seems most clear in countries with large numbers of internally displaced people living in temporary or permanent encampments. The Native American population comes to mind, as does the ethnic population of the far north of Russia.[55]

By way of conclusion, several points about ethnic bifurcation need to be made. First, in the long run, economic, political, and social marginalization and empowerment result in a growing gap in the personal incomes of ethnic groups. Over time, reduced access to health services, sanitation, safe water, and food will show up in decreased health indicators such as higher infant mortality rates, lower life expectancy, higher maternal mortality rates, and greater malnutrition among the marginalized population. Also over time, reduced educational and literacy expenditure for these groups will show up as decreased economic and employment potential of the group. Therefore, the personal income of the marginalized groups will fail to keep up with the income of the empowered group.

Second, ethnic bifurcation is characterized by circular and cumulative causation. Indeed, indicators of marginalization and empowerment are also the cause of further marginalization and empowerment. A circular, self-perpetuating spiral tends to emerge in multiethnic states during economic decline: as an ethnic group loses income, it loses power and becomes marginalized, since it is marginalized, it has less opportunity for employment and therefore endures further loss in income, and so on.

Third, none of the above indicators, on their own, provide the necessary or sufficient conditions to prove that marginalization has in fact occurred. Nor do all manifestations of ethnic bifurcation occur together. It is only when a large number of the indicators are present that they point to the likely existence of marginalization or empowerment. Given this inherent imprecision, the lines of demarcation between marginalization and empowerment are murky.

ECONOMIC COMPETITION, ETHNIC BIFURCATION, AND SOURCES OF ECONOMIC DECLINE

In an effort to understand how interethnic competition and ethnic bifurcation occur under different economic conditions, five sources of economic decline are studied. These are discussed below, following an explanation of the term *economic decline*.

In the text, economic decline is interpreted broadly. It encompasses decreases in income per capita that, over time, result in negative growth rates. It also includes rates of growth that, while falling, remain positive. Moreover, economic decline is used as an umbrella term that subsumes economic stagnation, namely, income per capita that fails to change over time. This stretching of the narrow definition of economic decline enables the inclusion of a broad range of economic changes into the study.

How does economic decline manifest itself? At the macro level, there is a drop in output, as the supply of goods and services falls. Such a production decrease often entails the unemployment of resources, including labor. This in turn translates into a decline in income, both at the personal level (due to a drop in wages and interest income) as well as the national level (due to a drop in tax revenue). The result is a decrease in the standard of living: personal income changes affect households directly while national income changes affect them indirectly (as social programs and benefits are reduced). Furthermore, these drops in income bring about a decrease in aggregate demand, fueling a recessionary downturn in the business cycle. The decrease in output may be preceded or followed by a decline in productivity of factors of production. Moreover, decreasing employment and, where relevant, increasing inflation, complicate the formulation and execution of expansionary government policy: indeed, monetary and fiscal interventions become unable to control events and reverse the trend of economic decline. Sometimes this leads to economic paralysis as institutions fail to perform and require massive intervention to prop them up. With respect to international economic relations, economic decline usually includes a deteriorating balance of payments, stagnation in foreign investment and inflow of capital, and disarray in international financial markets. The more a country participates in the global economy, the more it is susceptible to external shocks, and the more its decline reverberates to other countries.

The above characteristics of economic decline are universal, with minor alterations for specific conditions. Three points warrant elaboration. First, while characteristics of economic decline may in general be universal, the proximate source of the economic decline is not. Economic decline may be due to cyclical fluctuations or to structural imbalances; its source may be exogenous or endogenous. Economic shocks to the economy ripple through the entire system, reverberating across sectors and over time periods. During the 1990s, the countries under study experienced decline for a series of complex reasons, including a movement from communism to capitalism, a liberalization of capitalist economies (both are transformations of economic systems), the eruption of war, the imposition of international sanctions, and the execution of boundary changes (see table 2.1). Each of these resulted in short-run labor shortages, decreases in financial flows, decreases in labor productivity, and technological stagnation. Some effects even lingered in the long run. Each source of economic decline is discussed below, as well as the particular form of competition and ethnic bifurcation that it produces.

Second, the characteristics of economic decline manifest themselves differently in different countries. Clearly, the more developed a country (the greater its productive capacity and the more abundant its reserves of human and physical capital), the more it can sustain cuts in its income before exhibiting economic, political, and social strains.

Third, caution must be used when drawing conclusions about the causal links between an event such as war and economic decline. In this case, common sense, as well as theories based on empirical

Table 2.1
Principal Sources of Economic Decline

Country	Economic System	Sanctions	War	Boundary Change
Russia	C to C	N	Y	BU (Neg)
Yugoslavia	C to C	Y	Y	BU (W; Neg)
South Africa	Lib	Y	N	Neg
Israel	Lib	Y	Y	W
Brazil	Lib	N	N	none
India	Lib	Y	N	US
Estonia	C to C	N	N	BU (Neg)
Czech Republic	C to C	N	N	BU (Neg)

Notes: Y = yes; N = no
C to C refers to a change from communism to capitalism while Lib refers to economic liberalization within capitalism; boundary changes may be realized in the form of break-up (BU), war and occupation (W), negotiation (Neg) or unrealized in the form of active secessionist movements (US).

evidence, indicates direct causation. However, it may not be the only source of decline. Indeed, all too often multiple events combine to shock the economic system. The experience of Yugoslavia, a country that has endured each of the sources of decline described above, produced a lively debate among social scientists as to the main culprit of the plummeting growth rates. For example, Hinic and Bukovic pointed out that while sanctions had a dramatic effect on the economy, the decrease in economic activity was due more to the disruption caused by the break-up of Yugoslavia than by the sanctions.[56] Boarov wrote that the economy was in such a catastrophic condition anyway that it is hard to separate the impact of the sanctions from bad administration.[57] Dyker and Bojicic claimed that 'the impact of sanctions should be seen in terms of their incremental effect on an economic trend that had already been firmly established'.[58] A study of sanctions and stabilization measures conducted by the Belgrade Institute of Economic Sciences indicated that much of the downward trend began before the imposition of sanctions, and that their imposition simply solidified what was already occurring. Finally, Mladan Dinkic's scathing criticism of the role of the leadership lay the blame squarely on the shoulders of the rulers.[59] The above lack of consensus on the principal cause of economic decline is repeated in Russia, Israel, Estonia, and the Czech Republic; in other words, in all the countries that have experienced multiple simultaneous shocks to their economies.

Selected indicators of economic performance are presented in table 2.2. A comparison of the GNPs in 1997 shows that the size of the economies under discussion varies widely, ranging from tiny Estonia ($4.9 billion) to large Brazil ($784 billion). However, when per capita values are compared, the ranking of economies changes drastically (Estonia and the Czech Republic led in 1997, despite their recent histories of economic decline). With respect to growth rates during the 1990s, the decrease is the most pronounced in Yugoslavia.

According to table 2.2, Brazil, India, and Israel all experienced growth during 1990–97. Why then are these countries included in a study of decline? The answer lies in the inconclusiveness of the World Bank statistics in light of other sources. According to the Penn World Tables (containing data collected by Heston and Summers at the University of Pennsylvania), Brazil had a very patchy record of growth. Indeed, as is evident from table 2.3, during the late 1980s and early 1990s there were more years of negative growth rates than there were positive. Telescoping in on India also shows erratic growth rates during that period. Moreover, when the Indian data is supplemented by data from the Economist Intelligence Unit (EIU), then the patterns are even more inconclusive: during 1994–97, the EIU shows that growth in GDP decreased every year from 1994 to 1997.[60] With respect to Israel, the seemingly high rates of growth presented in table 2.2 (namely, 6.5% average annual change) might be due the use of current prices in the GDP per capita data (unlike the remaining statistics in the table). The Penn World Statistics indicate more erratic annual growth rates.

Table 2.2
Indicators of Economic Performance in Selected Countries, 1990 and 1997

Country	GNP, 1997	GDP/p, 1990	GDP/p, 1997	Growth
Russian Federation	394.9	4507	2742	–5.9
Yugoslavia [a]	NA	3000	300 (1993)	–12.9
South Africa	130.2	2468	2336	–0.8
Israel	94.4	10920*	15940**	+6.5
Brazil	784.0	1948	2107	+1.1
India	357.4	374	465	+3.4
Estonia	4.9	3683	2984	–2.7
Czech Republic	54.0	3680	3329	–1.4

Notes: GNP is given in billions of US $. GDP is given in 1987 US $. GDP/p refers to per capita GDP. Growth refers to average annual percent change.
* Given in 1990 US $; ** Given in 1998 US $.
Source: United Nations Development Program, *Human Development Report 1999*, New York: Oxford University Press, 1999, tables 6 and 11. Growth values are calculated by the author.
[a] *RFE/RL News Brief* 2, 23, 24–28 May 1993, p. 19.
* The World Bank, World Development Report, 1992, table 1.
** The World Bank, World Development Report, 1999/2000, table 1.

Table 2.3
Economic Performance in Israel, Brazil, and India, 1985–1992

	Israel		Brazil		India	
Year	GDP/p	Growth	GDP/p	Growth	GDP/p	Growth
1985	8310	—	4017	—	1050	—
1986	8559	2.9	4294	6.8	1092	4.0
1987	9041	5.6	4319	0.5	1123	2.8
1988	9070	0.3	4208	−2.6	1204	7.2
1989	8961	−1.2	4272	1.5	1235	2.5
1990	9289	3.6	4043	−5.3	1262	2.1
1991	9483	2.0	4010	−0.8	1252	−0.8
1992	9801	3.3	3886	−3.1	1284	2.5

Notes: GDP/p refers to real GDP per capita, in US $, at 1985 international prices.
Growth refers to annual percent change.
Source: GDP/p: Penn World Tables (www.pwt.econ.upenn.edu); growth: calculated
by the author.

Transformation of Economic Systems

The focus of economic inquiry reflects economic reality. The study of capitalism is a case in point. The global spread of capitalism[61] has preoccupied Karl Marx, Max Weber, Emile Durkheim, and other social scientists since the 1800s.[62] Following the Second World War, analysis focused on capitalism's negative externalities and their rectification, as embodied in the concept of the capitalist welfare state. At the end of the twentieth century, the emphasis turned to the transformation of capitalism. This emphasis emerged from evidence of widespread changes in economic systems. In some countries, we have witnessed the transformation (or transition) from communism to capitalism; in others, we find basic alterations in the nature of the pre-existing capitalism. During the 1990s, one of these two systemic changes occurred in the majority of world countries, affecting employment, public programs, and incomes of billions of people worldwide. In the course of both transformations, economic decline occurred. Such a decline was usually of short term duration. In the absence of structural imbalances, the transformations had positive long-term effects.

These transformations, as well as their effects on competition and ethnic bifurcation, are studied in the formerly socialist countries of Russia, Yugoslavia, Estonia, and the Czech Republic as well as the capitalist countries of Brazil and India.

Movement from communism to capitalism
The Berlin Wall collapsed in November 1989, taking with it an unpopular political and economic system that prevailed far beyond the

borders of East Germany. To fill the void, an economic transformation was ushered in, as formerly communist states in Eastern Europe, the Soviet Union, and Asia embraced economic and political changes at a pace that caught the world by surprise. This trend was clear irrespective of the level of development, the extent of previous economic reforms and the strength of the economic links to the Soviet Union. Even countries that have withstood change in the initial years of the economic transformation to capitalism, such as China and Cuba, are presently reconsidering their positions.

What does the process of transformation from communism to capitalism entail? From the proliferation of literature that has flooded the field during the 1990s, several basic tenets can be distilled.[63] The movement to capitalism involves the following: macroeconomic stabilization, price reform, and structural and institutional reforms.[64] Macroeconomic stabilization measures provide the background within which other measures can effectively be taken. Indeed, fiscal policies (aimed at balancing total domestic demand with domestic production and controlling the budget deficit) and monetary policy (aimed at controlling the growth of the money supply) provide the stability that is a precondition for successful reforms. Price reforms entail the dismantling of centrally planned and controlled prices in favor of market prices that reflect true supply and demand. The following are crucial elements of price reform: domestic price liberalization (to introduce the market as a determinant of prices), trade liberalization (to decontrol exports and liberalize imports by opening up international trade at world prices), and currency convertibility (to enable trading of the domestic currency in the international money market). With respect to structural and institutional reforms, the following are essential: the imposition of hard budget constraints for firms (thus resulting in the demise of unviable firms), the stimulation of the private sector (thus diminishing the role of state ownership), the reform of the legal system (including property rights protection and tax legislation), the reform of the banking and financial system (including the expansion of a capital infrastructure), and the development of a social safety net.

While these concomitants of the transition process are largely undisputed, what continues to be under discussion is the pace of change, the extent of change, the sequencing of change, and the political environment within which change takes place. With respect to the pace of change, some scholars (such as Sachs[65] and Kornai) have advocated the Big Bang approach, while others (such as Soos and Wanniski[66]) have advocated slower, gradual change.[67] The 'Big Bangers'[68] argue for sweeping, sudden, and simultaneous reforms across all sectors. While causing extreme pain in the short run, such reforms are deemed preferable to those that drag out and thereby also drag out the pain. Scholars advocating a gradual approach argue that the pain caused by rapid steps toward a market system would be unbearable, as unemployment, decreased output, inflation, and a deteriorating trade balance wreck the already precarious social and economic fabric. They argue for a sequencing of reforms, preferably the establishment of market institutions followed by the privatization of large holdings, a process that is bound to result in significant unemployment. Hence, the distinction between Big Bangers and gradualists may sometimes be reduced to a difference in sequencing.

With respect to the extent of change, again theory and practice are divided into radical and conservative approaches. Among the more radical reformers, there are efforts to obliterate all elements of 50 years of communist economic measures and embark on an unbridled capitalist path, complete with all its pitfalls. This approach, although popular and certainly supported by some Western leaders and economists, has not been adopted universally in the formerly communist states. In fact, advocates of a third way have emerged, proposing a path that mixes the best of socialism with the best of capitalism in order to move to the market while avoiding the pitfalls associated with capitalism.[69]

With respect to the political environment in which reforms occur, the crucial difference of opinion lies in the desirability and necessity of a politically free environment. The debate is between those who advocate a liberal political environment in which individual desires are communicated to the rulers and checks and balances are maintained through a multiparty system, and those who deem such a system neither necessary nor desirable. The principal examples of these two views in action are Russia and China. In the case of the former, the *glasnost* reforms accompanied *perestroika* reforms, simultaneously sending political and economic tremors throughout the society. In China, despite the introduction of capitalist economic reforms, the political atmosphere remained unaltered.[70]

What was the nature of the transformation in Yugoslavia, Russia, Estonia, and the Czech Republic, and how did it result in economic decline? Estonia and the Czech Republic have been most aggressive in pursing economic reforms, followed by Russia and finally by Yugoslavia.[71] The first two countries have adopted the Big Bang approach consisting of extensive reforms within a politically liberalized environment. Success was encapsulated by the European Commissioner, who noted in 1999 that 'Estonia is a functioning market economy where market forces play their full role'.[72] In 1998, Freedom House also ranked the Czech Republic and Estonia third and fourth respectively among 28 reforming economies.[73] The transition path of Russia has been more complicated, replete with stop-and-go efforts. Finally, the transition in Yugoslavia has been least successful, in part due to the lack of commitment by the leadership and in part due to the demands on the economy associated with war and sanctions (see below). There is no doubt that other successor countries of the former Yugoslavia, especially Slovenia[74] and to a lesser extent Croatia,[75] were much more successful in implementing liberalizing reforms.

Most reform activity took place in the early 1990s, although numerous measures continued to be implemented throughout the decade. Stabilization policies were introduced in all four countries. In Russia, this entailed an effort to balance the budget which, in 1992, under the leadership of Egor Gaidar (Yeltsin's economic adviser) took the form of restrictions on government expenditures and the imposition of new taxes. Similar stabilizing steps were taken by Estonia and the Czech Republic and were followed soon after by price liberalization. By 1992 virtually all prices in Russia were liberalized with the exception of government-controlled monopolies (including gas, electricity, transportation, and telecommunications). In the Czech Republic, prices began to be liberalized in early 1991 and by the end of the year, 85 percent of consumer and producer prices were determined by the market. Yugoslav price liberalization lagged behind that of other countries because, while most prices were freed in 1990, subsequent reimposition of government control extended to some 500 product prices. Trade was liberalized in all countries early on, since it was viewed as the conduit to economic revival.[76] In Russia, the trade sector remains the bright spot in its reform experience: since 1992, the country continues to employ relatively light trade barriers, producing a continuous boom in trade. The rouble became convertible and has been relatively steady until the Asian crisis of the early 1990s, when it came under severe pressure. None of the other currencies suffered during the 1990s. The Czech koruna was made convertible in 1991 and was ultimately tied to a combination of the US dollar and the German mark. Estonians imposed strict monetary reform to ensure the convertibility of its kroon, which has been pegged to the German mark.[77] The Yugoslav dinar has been pegged to the German mark since 1994, although its exchange rate has varied to account for inflation. With respect to institutional reforms, there is no doubt that the Czech Republic has been the most aggressive in its policy of speedy and radical privatization.[78] Large enterprises have been transferred to private hands through a voucher scheme – one round in 1992–93 and one in 1993–95, whereby over 1,500 enterprises were privatized and some 8.5 million citizens gained ownership rights.[79] By the end of 1996, almost 75 per cent of GDP had been produced in the private sector.[80] In Estonia, privatization has been carried out in three waves of small,

medium, and large businesses and residential property. The first, small
wave, was the easiest and took place during 1991–93. The large
enterprises are still being privatized at the time of writing. By 1997, 67
percent of the Estonian GDP was produced in the private sector.[81] In
Russia, some 70 percent of the GDP came from the private sector, while
in Yugoslavia this number remains a low 40 percent (however, 91% of
officially registered businesses are private; it is simply that they are
small and do not produce high output[82]). Reform of the banking
system has gone the furthest in Estonia, making the Estonian Central
Bank one of the most autonomous central banks in the world. In
Yugoslavia, the banking reforms have been miniscule, in part because
of the capital isolation imposed by international sanctions. In the Czech
Republic, banking is the least reformed sector. All countries opened
stock exchanges in the early 1990s: the Prague Stock Exchange
remains the highest capitalized equity market in the region, while
the Belgrade Stock Exchange is the least active. The tax systems in
all countries are not excessively reformed. In Russia it is said to be
'fragmented, contradictory, excessive, nontransparent, and rife with
delinquency'.[83] In Yugoslavia it was modified extensively in 1996 but
compliance remains hard to enforce since cash transactions have
become the norm. Finally, bankruptcy regulation, along with legislation pertaining to formation, dissolution, and transfers of businesses
have been introduced in all countries.

What effect did these reforms have on economic growth? As is
evident from table 2.2, all four states experienced economic decline
during 1990–97. However, the Czech Republic and Estonia both
turned their economic performance around. Indeed, according to
PlanEcon's disaggregated data for the Czech Republic, the real GDP
reached its lowest point in 1991, with a –11.5 growth rate. In 1992 it
had improved to –3.3, and by the following year was already positive
(0.6).[84] While a similar turnaround was witnessed in Estonia, Russia
and Yugoslavia have yet to achieve their desired growth rates. In
Russia, the transition has been described as 'difficult at best and a
disaster at worst'.[85] In each year until 1998, Russia experienced
negative growth rates. Until 1995 inflation exceeded 100 percent, the
informal economy increased in importance, the rouble devalued, and
exports performed dismally. Unemployment ranged, in the mid to late
1990s, between 9 and 20 percent. In August 1998 the financial system
collapsed: Russia devalued its currency, defaulted on $40 billion of
domestic debt, prices rose by two-thirds in the next seven months, the
spending power of Russians decreased 40 percent, and the value of
the rouble fell from 15 cents to 4.[86]

How did interethnic competition and ethnic bifurcation manifest
itself in the course of the above economic decline? Interethnic

competition was most pronounced in the labor market. When firms privatize and restructure, workers get laid off. Also, in the absence of government intervention, when firms cannot meet their hard budget constraints, they go bankrupt, thereby increasing unemployment. Moreover, the pursuit of profit maximization by the individual firm reflects an entirely different ideology than that associated with the socialist goal of full employment. Therefore, workers' jobs are more precarious in a market economy and their competition for work and at work is more acute than during communism, when job tenure relaxed the pressure on workers. Secondary evidence from the four countries shows that workers from the different ethnic groups were affected differently by the liberalizing reforms that their countries undertook (see below). Such inequality was enabled for a variety of reasons. The most important is the tilting of job competition in favor of the titular majority through a series of language and citizenship regulations. These are discussed in chapter 6, suffice it to say here that they were introduced in all the four countries under study.

As a result of the above liberalizing reforms and the particular contexts within which they took place, ethnic bifurcation occurred: in Estonia, the Russian population became marginalized while the Estonian peoples became empowered; in Russia, non-Russians became the target of discrimination; in the new Yugoslavia, preference was given to Serbs and Montenegrins in all economic, social, and political matters (the same pattern of empowerment of titular majorities occurred in Croatia, Macedonia, and Slovenia); and in the Czech Republic, the dominant Czechs became empowered while the Slovaks and the Romas became marginalized.

In Estonia, interethnic competition plays itself out in enterprise and work collectives that were formerly the site for integration and that, during privatization, became the site for differentiation. In his study of minorities, Vetik identified the dangers inherent in economic restructuring for the employment prospects of the new Russian minority.[87] In part, this occurs because legislation pertaining to citizenship and language proficiency has a profound effect on employment opportunities for those who, following independence, find themselves without the appropriate working papers. Interethnic animosities are playing themselves out with particular vigor in the Estonian industrial sector. Post-independence governments and the general population associate their dire environmental state with Russian industrialization policy. Auer noted that the question of closing down environmentally destructive plants has become grounds for interethnic accusations, since the industries deemed to be most destructive (namely oil shale and phosphorite ore mining, processing and 'energetics'), are also predominantly filled with Russian workers.[88]

In order to stem the tide of environmental disaster, ethnic Estonians are in favor of closing all such production. This is viewed as an anti-Russian proposal by the Russian population, provoking a further sense of isolation and stoking the fires of nationalism.

Under conditions of down-sizing and bankruptcy, unemployment is disproportionately borne by those newly demoted in the ethnic pecking order. In all the successor states of Yugoslavia, these tend to be the new minorities. However, the Roma are the most negatively affected because while diasporic Serbs, Macedonians, Croats, and others all have a home state to turn to (one in which they are the titular majority), the Romas have no such anchor and no such protective home base. Latham provided evidence that 'with collapsing economies, rampant unemployment, and faltering social safety nets, the largely unskilled and poorly educated Roma are unable to compete with other populations'.[89] In Kosovo, after a decade of reforms (albeit half-hearted ones) the unemployment rate among the Romas is close to 95 percent, forcing them to make their living on the black market.[90] In Macedonia, those Roma who used to work in state-run enterprises have lost their jobs. As a result, Romani unemployment is 80 percent compared with 45 percent for the general population.[91]

The Roma are no better off in the Czech Republic, where they have become even more marginalized in light of Czech empowerment following the break-up of Czechoslovakia. Their plight in the aftermath of transformation reforms is aptly described by Hochenos: 'The advent of economic shock therapy brought inflation and unemployment. The first to lose their jobs, of course, were the Roma. In some places, unemployment hit as much as half of the Roma population (the rate for all Czechs was 3% in 1992).'[92] Moreover, in her study of the effects of privatization on employment, Paukert shows that by 1995, there was an overall decline in overall employment in the Czech Republic of 10–12 percent. There was a transfer of workers into the private sector (that went from employing 1% of the labor force in 1989 to 80% in 1995[93]). However, minorities did not participate in that new employment. It is possible that this was due to legislation such as the Law on Employment of 1991,[94] which protected employers' rights in hiring and firing (which they did not have before) thereby increasing the possibility of ethnic discrimination. The primary targets of discrimination are the local Roma, who are bypassed for jobs even by Ukrainian immigrants.[95] While these Ukrainian workers are cheap, they are also illegal. Yet, they have greater employment opportunities than the Roma, who are considered more offensive.

In Russia, privatization generated both unemployment (13% unemployed and underemployed in 1996) and a decrease in wages – those that were still paid out were in arrears (in 1996, 75% of the total national monthly wage bill was overdue).[96] This led to increased incidents of strikes and protests, which were often dominated by one ethnic group (although their strikes were not ethnic in demand). Miners in the Tula region, oil workers in the Komi region, as well as residents of remote regions in the Russian far north, all experienced the effects of unemployment due to privatization.[97] This supports the study of unemployment in central Europe by Fretwell and Jackman, who argue that the closing of enterprises, following bankruptcy, has localized effects because manufacturing tends to be very concentrated.[98] Clearly, when bankruptcy occurs in a region populated with minority workers, they will experience unemployment more acutely.[99] Moreover, a study of Chinese migrants into the Primorskii Krai region of Russia shows that the rise in interethnic competition has clearly increased between local Russians and Chinese since 1991, when trade was liberalized and exchanges between China and Russia expanded. Alexseev shows that public opinion has become anti-Chinese due to their perception of 'economic aggressiveness of Chinese nationals'.[100]

Liberalization in capitalist economies
The capitalist system is not monolithic. There are as many varieties of capitalism as there are countries professing themselves capitalist. Indeed, French capitalism (replete with vestiges of indicative planning) differs from the highly *laissez-faire* capitalism prevailing in the United States, which in turn is unlike the highly interventionist Japanese version, which in turn differs from the welfare state of Germany. While all are successful, high-growth capitalist economies, their similarities often belie fundamental differences.

Capitalism is not stagnant. It is alive, vibrant, and dynamic. It transforms itself to adapt to the demands of social, political, and economic reality. The capitalism that existed in, for example, the United States in the year 2000 is fundamentally different from what existed 100 years ago. The fluctuations in business cycles are more subdued (due to government intervention in the form of monetary and fiscal policy), the concentration of monopoly capital is lower (due to government regulation and antitrust legislation), and worker conditions are better (because of social programs, social regulation, and unemployment insurance mandated by the government).[101]

Since capitalism is not monolithic, differences between countries manifest themselves in the degree of privatization, price liberalization, and regulation. Since capitalism is not stagnant, the proportion of private vs. public ownership changes over time, as does the degree of price manipulation and overall government involvement in the economy. While systemic changes in capitalist economies rarely get the media exposure that the movement from communism to capitalism gets, they are no less important in defining the parameters of economic behavior.

Liberalization of capitalist economies includes privatization, de-regulation, and the freeing of prices.[102] With respect to property rights, liberalization entails an increase in privatization resulting in an increase in the proportion of property owned by the private sector. With respect to the competitive environment, liberalization entails an increase in competition through the reduction of trade barriers, regulation, and expanded exemptions from antitrust laws. With respect to government intervention in the economy, liberalization entails an increased reliance on the market mechanism and prices to convey information to economic players and a decrease in government guidance of the economy. By the early 1980s a consensus emerged that a growing public sector was unlikely to bring about the desired growth in less developed countries. Buoyed by the electoral success of conservative governments in the United States and Britain, whose ideological underpinnings lay in increasing market forces, numerous countries across the world embarked upon their own liberalization processes. New Zealand is an example of a country that went from having the most regulated and closed high-income economy to currently ranking among the highest with respect to free market, low tax rates, widespread privatization, and low trade barriers. Due to the long-term success of radical reforms of the 1980s, New Zealand's experience is now touted as a model for other countries. Two such countries, Brazil and India, have embarked upon liberalizing reforms. They are presented in this chapter in an effort to identify links between economic events and interethnic competition and bifurcation. Liberal-ization affects competition and the ranking of ethnic groups because it tends to produce an unintended short-term effect, namely economic decline. While their adoption is aimed at stimulating the economy (by increasing production (and therefore employment) and by increasing profits (and therefore investment)), liberalization measures tend to produce short-term drops in economic growth in the course of the adjustment process.

As background to the study of reforms in India and Brazil, it is useful to mention the assessment of economic freedom conducted by the Fraser Institute.[103] According to its report on some 100 countries in 1999, India and Brazil rank sixty-first and sixty-eighth respectively with respect to a bundle of indicators that reflect economic rights and incentives (including legal protection of property rights, pervasiveness of government regulation and trade barriers, fear of confiscation etc.). Such a ranking may be viewed as both good and bad – good insofar as it is not even lower, and bad because it comes at the tail-end of years of economic reforms.

Both India and Brazil were characterized by strong government involvement in the economy following the Second World War. Industrial policy in the aftermath of the Second World War was based on promotion of heavy industry under government ownership and management.[104] Government controls of the economy were extensive, with the rationale that the market will not allocate resources to coincide with national goals (while both economies were capitalist by several defining indicators, lip service was paid to socialist goals, especially in India). Since the Industries Act of 1951, the Indian government controlled almost all manufacturing, mining, and power by the license system, whereby production quantities, allocation of resources, and prices of inputs and sometimes output were determined by the government by the granting of licenses. Moreover, the government regulates foreign exchange, trade, and the prices of basic agricultural products. In both countries, despite years of nationalization, most businesses were privately owned (in India, only 10% of industrial output was in government hands[105]). Under these conditions, the liberalizing reforms took the following form.

While India first implemented reforms under Rajiv Gandhi in the 1980s, only two of them were liberalizing, namely, relaxing industrial regulation to promote efficiency, and promoting exports (there was also increased priority for infrastructure and improvement of technological capacities).[106] It is only the reforms of 1991 that stand out as the first comprehensive attempt at reviving the economy by seriously decreasing the government's role and increasing that of the market (the motivation also included raising money from privatization in order to deal with the budget deficit which reached some 7% of GDP in 1999, while the public debt got close to 60% of GDP and interest payments amounted to 46% of revenue[107]). In this effort, large industries were targeted. The New Industrial Policy (NIP) of 1991 scaled down the industries reserved for the public sector from 29 to 8, industrial licensing was abolished in all but 18 industries, private sector competition was introduced in some areas, and the government announced a halt to nationalization.[108] It has been less a case of divestment in industry rather than a case of allowing the private sector to enter areas previously inaccessible. The most high profile case of privatization is the recent sale of 51 percent of a symbol of government ownership, Indian Airlines, in 2000.[109] Nevertheless, the economic survey issued by the Finance Ministry in 2000 said that further reforms were still required, calling for a slash in subsidies, privatization of state companies, and liberalization of financial markets as the only way to achieve growth and a dent in poverty.[110] (Views on these reforms differ: according to Ratnam, it was 'a low profile, selective and cautious affair';[111] according to Bhagwati, reforms were 'forceful and explicit ...

And are being unfolded in a *Blitzkreig* of successive moves'.[112] Perhaps it is a sign of the political sentiment that India's Finance Minister first used the word 'privatization' in public two years ago.[113])

The Brazilian experience is similar, including recent reforms that were insufficiently pervasive and only partially successful. The first timid steps were taken in 1979 with a lukewarm attempt at privatization. It was only in 1988 and then in 1990 that the National Privatization Program was created and subsequently extended. Between 1979 and 1990 the program was restricted to previously privately owned enterprises. After 1990 it was extended to include federally owned companies (with the exception of oil, gas, ore extraction, and shipping lines, monopolies enshrined in the constitution[114]). The goal was to sell off some government enterprises in order to stimulate their production and raise revenue. However, not only were key sectors conspicuously absent or only partially touched (including energy), but the results were less than optimal because 'of the absence of a comprehensive reform program and continued uncertainty regarding the legal and regulatory arrangements'.[115] With respect to deregulation, the federal administration reduced the number of ministries, closed some public bodies, eliminated posts and laid off public workers. However, the results were unimpressive since the decrease in government involvement was neither pervasive enough nor deep enough. Finally, liberalizing reforms also included the opening up of trade: in 1990, a market-oriented system of floating exchange rates was adopted, tariff protection was decreased and some import restrictions were lifted. The goal of the trade policy is harmonization with Brazil's neighbors' policies and thereby the stimulation of growth.

According to the data presented in table 2.3, India had a record of mixed economic performance during the years preceding the imposition of reforms (1985 to 1992): sporadic growth and sporadic decline, in other words, stagnation. Table 2.2 shows that there was net growth during the period 1990 to 1997. However, those data mask yearly fluctuations. To capture those, data from the EIU are introduced, according to which Indian growth in GDP decreased every year from 1994 to 1997.[116] It is exactly these years that would show an effect of economic reforms, to the extent that there was an effect. Although Brazil also had erratic growth rates, they tended to be negative more than positive (see table 2.3).

In assessing the effect of liberalization on interethnic competition and bifurcation, several points need to be made. First, given the limited change that liberalization of capitalism brings about, we should not expect to see as much ethnic bifurcation as in the transformation from communism to capitalism, where change was both fundamental and widespread. This weak effect is best observed in the labor market. While liberalizing policies such as privatization entail a loss of employment, that loss is tempered by the limited scope of reforms. Indeed, unlike the experience of the former communist countries, in which the majority of enterprises were privatized within a short space of time, Brazilian and Indian businesses were always largely private with the exception of large, government owned enterprises. In India, reforms only occurred in the organized sector, which affects only 10 percent of employment.[117]

Second, given the depth of its liberalization program, the experience of New Zealand is worth revisiting. There, the single most negative effect of liberalizing reforms has been the rising inequality within the population.[118] While inequality is evident among males and females, the rich and the poor, the rural and the urban, it is most pronounced between the 10 percent Maori indigenous population and the predominantly white newcomers.[119] Similarly, in both India and Brazil a rising inequality has emerged along several cleavage lines. While in the former, the two principal cleavages are ethnic and caste, in the later, the cleavage lines are most pronounced between races: the whites, the Indians, the browns, and the blacks.[120] Brazil is one of the world's most unequal societies (as measured by income distribution) while spending more heavily on social policy than many of its Latin American neighbors. According to Marx, 'Brazilian elites found that they could maintain their long-established social order of white privilege without enforcing racial domination.'[121] While displays of racial hatred are rare in Brazil, and the browns and the blacks do not live in segregated communities, that does not mean that there are no inequalities. Not only is the country governed, managed, and owned by whites, and blacks and browns are disproportionately poor and have greater difficulty getting employment, but the latter have also been more hurt by government policies. Some of these policies entail liberalization. According to Billette Hall, 'economic liberalization for Brazil, as for many other developing countries, has meant an increasing dependence on world export markets and international capital flows. That in turn has left it prey to the vagaries of the global economy.'[122] In the process of opening up markets to foreign investment, unemployment increased as foreign firms layed off workers in their quest for efficiency. As a result, blacks and browns lost more jobs than whites (in Salvador, for example, the unemployment rates for black and brown workers was 28.3% in December 1999, while it was 18.4% for whites[123]). And Amerindians are even worse off. This is repeated in the Sao Paolo area, where business closings due to privatization resulted in 20 percent unemployment, as well as in an increase between the rich and the poor (a cleavage that, incidentally coincides with race).[124]

In India, the effect of liberalizing reforms is under debate as data pertaining to poverty comes to light. According to new World Bank evidence, the percent of the population living in poverty decreased faster before economic reforms than with them (from 1973/4 to 1986/7 the percentage of people living in poverty dropped from 54 to 38, while during the years of reform it dropped only one percentage point).[125] Moreover, Indian National Sample Surveys show that consumption by the poor decreased in the 1990s because of the higher food prices (which are a result of the reforms).[126] How was this increased poverty distributed among the ethnic groups of India. Not surprisingly, Bihar and Uttar Pradesh were the most affected.[127] They contain the largest proportion of poor people, amounting to one fourth of the total Indian population. Given the concentration of ethnic groups in their titular Indian states (as discussed below), the link between poverty and ethnicity is easily made.

Third, there is a fundamental difference between India and Brazil that is rooted in their different center-state arrangements. India is a decentralized federation in which its substate administrative boundaries (called states, not to be confused with the way the term is usually used throughout the text, namely to refer to countries) largely coincide with ethnic boundaries. In other words, Gujaratis tend to live in Gujarat, Sikhs tend to live in the Punjab, Maharastris in Maharastra, and so on. It is states, rather than the central government, that have primary responsibility for sectors that are affected by reform, such as energy, irrigation, education, and health. Therefore, to the extent that state policies pertaining to employment or discrimination affect a population, they affect it simultaneously at the regional and the ethnic level. By comparison, Brazil is highly centralized. Reform decisions are made at the level of the center and what regional variation exists is not controlled in a decentralized fashion. Moreover, state boundaries do not coincide with ethnic or racial boundaries so ethnic bifurcation does not have regional-level support.[128] As a result of this difference, some liberalizing policies were experienced differently by ethnic minorities in the two countries. For example, deregulation in Brazil did not have the same effect that it produced in India. When businesses were liberalized from some regulatory practices in both countries during the 1990s, in India localized ethnic groups responded by creating growth centers that benefited them disproportionately (indeed, the transformation of Bangalore into India's Silicone Valley served to propel Karnataka into the realm of high growth states and placed Karnataks among the enviable ethnic groups, along with the Punjabis and the Bengalis[129]). No similar economic event was tied to an ethnic group in Brazil. Moreover, when controls on agricultural prices were relaxed, the highly agricultural Indian states benefited disproportionately. (By extension, the ethnic populations also benefited. This clearly occurred with the Sikh population in the Punjab.) No similar occurrence was witnessed in Brazil.

Fourth, India and Brazil also differed in the nature of the ethnic component in the political setting within which reforms took place. In India, the imposition of emergency rule in 1975, the placement of some states under presidential rule, corruption charges, political, and economic scandals all take place against a background of interethnic competition. Indeed, in 1978 and afterwards, corruption charges were followed by communal riots that split the Congress Party into Hindu and secular factions; in 1982 and again in 1987, Muslims and Hindus fought; in 1984 there was violence in Punjab directed against the Sikhs. In Brazil, no comparable expression of racial animosities has occurred.[130]

International Sanctions

Sanctions as a policy tool have waxed and waned, as have all fashions, throughout history. They were popular after World War One (as multi-lateral measures taken through the League of Nations) and then again during the Cold War (as unilateral measures taken largely by the superpowers to control states within their spheres of influence). Today, in the aftermath of the Cold War, sanctions are once again emerging as a tool to obtain a desired effect.

Economic sanctions may be defined as the government sponsored withdrawal of trade and financial relations. This translates into the limitation of exports, restriction of imports and a prevention of financial flows, as well as the freezing of assets abroad and the isolation of the country with respect to travel and communications. The purpose of sanctions is to affect a target country in the following ways: alter policies (with respect to human rights, terrorism or apartheid); desta-bilize governments (such as US efforts against Fidel Castro or Saddam Hussein); alter the outcome of a military adventure (such as the British efforts against Argentina over the Falkland Islands); or reduce the military potential of a belligerent state (such as during World Wars One and Two). The attainment of goals that underlie sanctions are more easily achieved under certain conditions, as has been studied and clearly enumerated by Hufbauer, Schott, and Elliot.[131]

Four countries under study have been targets of international sanctions: South Africa, Israel, India, and Yugoslavia. In all countries except for South Africa sanctions are ongoing at the time of writing. (In South Africa they were imposed in 1977, strengthened in 1986, and ended in 1991; in Israel, India, and Yugoslavia, sanctions began in 1946, 1998, and 1992 respectively. In Yugoslavia, they were partially

suspended in 1995 and continue in a modified form.[132]) Only the
Yugoslav sanctions involve the entire international community (they
were imposed by the United Nations Security Council,[133] while Israeli
sanctions merely entail the neighboring Arab countries;[134] in South
Africa and India, only the United States participated[135]). Only the
Yugoslav sanctions have been comprehensive, extending to all goods,
services, and flows of factors across boundaries[136] (in Israel, sanctions
entailed only a boycott and blocade;[137] in India they were partial; and
in South Africa they also involved partial sanctions with additional
disinvestment). In each case, sanctions were imposed as punishment
(for Yugoslavia's involvement in the Bosnian war;[138] for Israel's anti-
Arab position; for India's nuclear testing; and for South Africa's
apartheid policies).

The imposition of sanctions has a direct effect on the economy's
ability to function because it hinders trade, investment, production,
and consumption. Depending on their depth and breadth, sanctions
can be crippling and the subsequent economic setbacks profound. The
four countries under study were not affected equally by sanctions:
India suffered the least, the evidence from Israel and South Africa is
mixed but leaning toward minimal impact, while there is little doubt
that Yugoslavia was crippled by sanctions. Evidence follows.

According to Bhalla, sanctions did not have a big effect in India
since its large economy depends little on the US, the only participating
country. He estimates that the costs are at most some $3 billion or about
1 percent of the Indian GDP.[139] Similarly, the Arab boycott of Israel did
not produce significant pain. While it undoubtedly hampered trade
routes, decreased trade possibilities, increased inefficiencies, and prevented common regional development programs, the Israeli economy
took off and grew despite its neighbor's economic cooperation. Moreover, the impact of the boycott is marginal also because the Arab states
are neither major Israeli suppliers nor markets.

The evidence pertaining to the effect of sanctions on the South
African economy is mixed, despite the fact that one of the principal
economic goals of the post-apartheid government has been to reverse
the tide of sanctions and disinvestment. In the period between 1989
and 1993 the economy went into its longest recession, with negative
real economic growth. Gelb noted that there were low GDP growth
rates: 1.8 percent in the 1980s to –1.1 percent in the early 1990s. There
were also declining rates of gross fixed investment (which plunged to
a low of –18.6% in 1986 and stayed negative from 1990 to 1993), and
high rates of capital flight.[140] Balance of payments problems also
existed. A study by Muller shows that the lifting of sanctions had a
positive effect on trade, which picked up in the 1990s.[141] Her study
implies that the lifting of sanctions had a visible effect on the economy.

On the other hand, Marais claims that the improved economic performance cannot necessarily be attributed to sanctions, but rather to apartheid policies and their limiting effects on the labor market.[142] He points out that despite sanctions, South African exports experienced an upturn from 1987 onwards.[143] Gelb concurs with the view that sanctions were insignificant for the economy by claiming that foreign investment did not flock back to South Africa (as it was expected) after sanctions were lifted. Moreover, the business that did return after 1994 did not produce the desired employment results. This is largely because the firms that did return, returned not as heavy manufacturing, job creating, social spending entities, improving visibly the lives of local workers, but rather as partners in existing businesses, or as mergers and acquisitions.[144]

While the Indian, Israeli, and South African growth experience cannot be attributed solely to sanctions, the economic decline in Yugoslavia can conclusively be traced to broad-based and comprehensive sanctions. In the short term, the effect of sanctions was sharp and painful; in the long term, partial adjustments were made (the leadership introduced countermeasures policies, the population adapted, and sanction busters found substitute sources and channels for trade). After only one year of sanctions (mid-1992 to mid-1993), the loss of revenue in the new Yugoslavia is estimated to be some $25 billion, and the per capita national income dropped by an order of ten, from around $3,000 to $300. GNP dropped by $12 billion in that year, the value of foreign trade fell by $9 billion, industrial output fell by 40 percent in the first five months of 1993 over the same period in 1992, and one-half of the labor force is unemployed.[145] At the onset of sanctions, 5,000 dinars had a value of $550, while three weeks after sanctions were imposed, their value dropped to $2.70.[146] In 1993 inflation rose to 1,880 percent (at an annualized rate, it was 363,000,000,000,000,000 percent).[147] According to the Belgrade Economic Research Center, 97 percent of the population dropped under the poverty level.[148] In Montenegro alone, the sanctions were responsible for a loss in revenue of $277 million: businesses lost $130 million in exports, $90 million in tourism, and $57 million from shipping.[149] Clearly, with this kind of economic effect, sanctions also resulted in a humanitarian disaster as fundamental health care and nutrition was denied to the civilian population.[150]

To the extent that international sanctions aggravate economic conditions, they increase interethnic competition for increasingly scarce resources. In addition, the hardships associated with sanctions affect different ethnic groups in different ways, depending on their pre-existing advantages and on their ability to adjust. In Yugoslavia, the official empowerment of the Serbian population placed it in a better position to withstand the ramifications of sanctions than minorities such as Croats, Slavic Muslims, and Albanians. The boycott of Israel prevented the development and exploitation of overland trade relations with neighboring countries and in the process affected Palestinian businesses, who would have benefited from economic exchange with Arab countries. The officially empowered Jews had access to other sources of trade, ones that were less available to the Israeli Arabs. In South Africa, ethnic bifurcation continued and possibly even intensified after the imposition of sanctions.[151] The targeted population, namely the blacks, did not benefit as they were expected to.[152] The arms embargo only served to stimulate the rapid development of the local arms industry, which was owned and managed by whites. Disinvestment led to the abandonment of plants and industry in South Africa and the selling of productive assets to local whites. As a result, the lives of the black population deteriorated because domestic companies did not have to adhere to the Sullivan Principle (a code of conduct for US companies operating in South Africa) and therefore did not provide programs for housing, medical care, and education for their black workers.[153]

In the case of South Africa, sanctions did not help those they were aimed at helping (namely, the black majority) by displacing the apartheid government. In other countries, sanctions also did not achieve their stated effect. Their paradoxical effect, namely the pauperization of the general population in the face of unchanged governments, points to the need to reevaluate policy. With that goal in mind, the United Nations announced in early 2000 the formation of a committee to review sanctions as a policy tool, with implications well beyond Yugoslavia, into Cuba and Iraq, both countries in which the leaders that sanctions were meant to remove still remain firmly rooted among their impoverished populations.[154]

War

Barbera said, 'war is either productive, destructive, unpredictable, or irrelevant' to economic growth and development.[155] The first two of these are more common; at the very least, war affects economies insofar as it necessitates a choice between 'guns and butter'. Despite differences in war potential among belligerents, resources available to conduct war as well as the physical location of war, all sides experience some ramifications of war. Multiethnic societies may also experience increased competition and ethnic bifurcation. Some of the principal economic ramifications of war were identified by Neal and are discussed below.[156]

First, one of the primary changes in a war economy is the shift from civilian to military production (in order to make more war products available, especially iron, steel, and aluminum, as well as food and clothing). Clearly, the diversion of these goods from their prewar destinations in the production process has an impact on the economy. The extent of the diversion of the region's productive resources depends upon the existing state of armaments, the state of the enemy's armaments, the length of time before they will be needed, and the self-sufficiency of the economy (specifically, the availability of raw materials and industrial goods).[157] Second, if there was preexisting competition in the economy, it is of necessity disrupted. Government requirements cause disruption of the normal process of price determination, as the government enters the markets and sets prices to alter production and distribution. Third, during wartime numerous demands are placed upon the labor force. Mobilization requires the withdrawal of people from routine economic activities and their placement into war activities. Therefore, the supply of labor decreases. Moreover, increased military production may increase the labor requirements in those industries. Thus, labor-market disequilibrium occurs as the demand for labor increases and the supply of labor decreases.[158] Fourth, the war effort may get financed from public or private sources. The former entails the raising of taxes and the floating of loans, with the particular conditions dictating to what extent these activities will be engaged in. The latter entails the use of business capital, as provided by owners and investors, commercial banks, and internal financing. Fifth, the monetary and banking authorities take direct control of prices, which are under inflationary pressure due to increased government demand for goods and subsequent shortages. The pressure may also be alleviated by rationing and the restriction of personal consumption. During wartime, the banking system must exhibit flexibility and bend to government pressures.

In the post-World War Two era, Yugoslavia, Russia, and Israel have all engaged in warfare. Yugoslavia has been directly or indirectly involved in war since 1991 (first, covertly in Croatia and Bosnia, then overtly in Kosovo, and finally, on the receiving end of a NATO attack). Russia was at war in Chechnya in 1994–96 and again in 1999.[159] While the country has had skirmishes as well as nonviolent border disputes, none have reverberated throughout the economy and political system as much as fighting in Chechnya. In Israel, there have been four wars with one or more of its neighbors since its creation in 1948.[160] The economic effects of these wars differs in the three countries. In Yugoslavia, the decade of warfare, culminating with the crippling NATO bombing, has devastated the economy. In Israel, continuous wars have produced the institutionalization of crisis during which the economy, polity, and society struggle to adjust to constant or imminent war. In

Russia, Chechnya has become a major economic and political issue, one that underscors the inability of the post-Soviet army to put down an insurgency on its fringes.

The magnitude of Yugoslavia's economic devastation lends itself to Neal's framework for the study of war. With respect to war production, the Serbian government imposed austerity measures and government control over key sectors of the economy (food, medicine, energy etc.). In order to increase production of strategic goods, the government resorted to the accelerated printing of money. With respect to the displacement of competitive processes, increased state control is evident in the renationalization of some firms and banks (in July 1994 there was a comprehensive effort to renationalize[161]). At the same time, the privatization process that started with legislation in 1990, transferred some 20 percent of social ownership into private hands.[162]

With respect to war labor problems, there is no doubt that the Yugoslav wars have had a negative effect on the labor force, mostly due to the decrease in the supply of labor. This has occurred for several reasons. First, many workers were drawn into the conflict (more specifically, into the army or expanding police force), leaving their enterprises short of skilled labor. Second, the supply of labor has also decreased because of the emigration of workers out of the warring states, in order to escape both a possible drafting and dire economic conditions. Very significant has been the exodus of the skilled population (brain drain), which has affected Serbia especially harshly (it is estimated that some 100,000 to 150,000 professionals left Serbia in 1992).[163] Third, the war has created refugees, as people fled or were evicted from their homes. These population movements have caused shortages of labor in some locations, and an overabundance of labor in others. Fourth, given the deteriorating demand and economic production, workers have been laid off.

With respect to financing the war effort, the Serbian budget for 1993 was altered to include an allocation of 75 percent to the military[164] (compared to 6.5% in 1999[165]). In addition, the government froze individual and enterprise foreign currency holdings, which it 'borrowed' to finance the war. Estimates of this amount are hard to come by, although one source puts it at $12 billion in private hard currency accounts.[166] The Yugoslav government authorized the periodic printing of money to finance the war effort until it was stopped by Prime Minister Milan Panic in the summer of 1992. Moreover, Serbia announced a moratorium on repayments of its foreign currency debt, in part because of the need to retain the foreign currency reserves for the war.[167]

With respect to management of monetary and banking systems, there was a renationalization of some banks and a tightening of banking procedures. As noted above, Serbian hyperinflation exceeded all textbook descriptions. As a result, the dinar was *de facto* replaced by the Deutsche Mark, even if its official exchange is periodically adjusted. Barter has increasingly become the preferred method of exchange.

In Russia, also, budgetary allocations have been directed to the war effort. In the course of its second bout of Chechnya fighting, the government announced a 50 percent rise in military spending.[168] According to the CIA, estimates for military expenditure are not available, however, it is believed that in 1996 they were at one-sixth of peak Soviet levels in the late 1980s.[169] The magnitude of the involvement in Chechyna in terms of troops employed, fatalities suffered, and funds allocated is not as significant as in Yugoslavia, however. And while war does provoke nationalistic feelings among the population, while partial victory does produce collective shame, and while Chechnya has played a role in Vladimir Putin's election, it has not reversed the course of liberalizing reforms, it did not entail the renationalization of financial and banking sectors, and it did not cause labor imbalances.

Military allocations in Israel are high (9.5% of GDP in 1999, amounting to $8.7 billion[170]). As a result of its historical animosities with its neighbors, Israel has sustained high military expenditures over the years, leading Yehuda and Sandler to claim that the Arab–Israeli conflict is winding down in part because the costs of war have become staggering.[171]

Did the wars in Yugoslavia, Russia, and Israel result in economic decline? The most obvious case is that of Yugoslavia, where almost one decade of warfare brought on billions of dollars of damage, devastated lives, created some 2 million refugees, and resulted in a major economic setback for the entire Balkans region. Then, the 11-week NATO bombing inflicted some $60 billion further damage (this estimate is provided by the EIU; the Yugoslav estimate is $100 billion[172]). As a result, it is estimated that the economy will contract by 40 percent, bringing the real GDP to 30 percent of its 1989 level.

Did war exacerbate interethnic competition and did it result in ethnic bifurcation? The answer is yes for two reasons. First, war produces economic decline and by extension economic competition for the dwindling pie. Second, during wartime, the 'enemy' ethnic group is clearly identified. Thus, interethnic competition is facilitated by the clarity of ethnic divisions and is encouraged by the violence inherent in the war. Even in the former Yugoslavia, where interethnic marriages and the existence of the 'Yugoslav' identity obfuscated ethnic boundaries, war unleashed ethnic finger-pointing.

War has ethnic implications, as is evident from all three countries under study. Across the former Yugoslavia, the war underscored the marginalization of the Romas. In Bosnia, they were forcibly mobilized into different armies, depending on the territory where they happened to be living. That resulted in Romas killing other Romas. There are reports that Romas were used to clear the mines, a job rarely given to more desirable ethnic groups.[173] In Kosovo, Romas were sacked from their jobs to make room for incoming Serbian refugees resettled by the government.[174]

Serbs have developed mixed feelings about their long-time ethnic allies, the Montenegrins, as a result of their differing position on the NATO bombing as well as its subsequent introduction of the German mark as the national currency. Serbia retaliated by closing its markets to Montenegrin exports. It also denied it subsidized food. This was viewed by Montenegrians as evidence of their marginalized status within the Yugoslav federation. Serbs, on the other hand, viewed it as an appropriate diversion of food to Serbs who were starving as a result of the NATO-induced loss of jobs and property.[175]

In Russia, the war with Chechnya further marginalizaed the Chechen population as discrimination against them, always under the surface, has now come out of the closet. Egged on by the bombing of apartment blocks in Moscow, the Chechen invasion of neighboring Dagestan (in the summer of 1999), and splintered rule by armed gang leaders, popular opinion turned against the Chechens with vehemence that absolved random, anti-Chechen attacks both within the region and outside it.[176] The operationalization of anti-Chechen sentiment is exemplified by the ruling that failure to carry a Russian internal passport is grounds for detention.[177] Yet, this document has not been issued in Chechnya since 1996. Such a catch-22 for Chechens provides license for a wide range of discriminatory maneuvers against them.

What was the nature of the ethnic bifurcation in Israel? The creation of Israel, and the subsequent wars with neighboring countries, resulted in the marginalization of Israeli Arabs and the empowerment of Israeli Jews. The establishment of the Jewish state by definition relegated the Israeli Arabs to second-class citizens. Measures taken in the course of the decades denuded Arabs in terms of economic and political power and further subjected them to rampant discrimination. Over three-quarters of the pre-war population of 900,000 fled outside the new state boundaries. With the inflow of Jews from across the world, a land shortage developed and Arab property was confiscated to satisfy the Jewish demand. Remaining Arab farmers were limited in their access to water and electricity, credit, and marketing cooperatives.[178] Politically, they also experienced exclusion, with little representation in government and influence in decision-making.[179] There is evidence that the Israeli government imposed measures to control, weaken, and divide the Arab population (according to Lustick, these included censorship, restrictions on movement, and administrative detention[180]). Moreover, the Israeli Arab community was officially splintered into several groups, thereby diluting the effect of their aggregated population size.[181] Despite that, beginning in the 1970s, the controls were somewhat relaxed and the Israeli Arabs began participating in the democratic participatory system. They nevertheless remain a marginalized people within a bifurcated society.

Boundary Changes

The end of the twentieth century witnessed a flurry of changes in state boundaries. While a few of these entailed the joining of pre-existing states (as with North and South Yemen and East and West Germany), more often than not they entailed the break-up of states (as with the Soviet Union and Czechoslovakia). When boundaries marking the limits of state sovereignty change, the economy convulses as it adapts to its new limitations, possibilities, and relationships. At least in the short term, the adjustment process entails economic decline. This occurs for two principal reasons: (a) the disruption of established trade relations, and (b) the severance of positive interregional flows. With respect to the first, subnational regions are linked to each other, the center, and the international economy through a series of complex economic relationships. One of these consists of the exchange of goods, services, and factors of production across regional borders, which fosters trade dependency. Trade dependency of a region refers to the importance of extraregional markets for the satisfaction of its market demands or the sale of its output.[182] Clearly, regions that do not conduct a large portion of their trade within their states are characterized by a low level of dependency *on the state* and either a high level of self-sufficiency or a high level of dependency on the global economy. The regions that have lower trade dependency will experience less economic disruption and decline in the aftermath of border alterations.

With respect to interregional flows, only two types exist, but only one is relevant for this study: public flows mandated by the government as an integral part of its regional development policy.[183] Public interregional transfers occur through the tax system, the central budget and its various funds, subsidies and loans, a controlled price system (including the foreign exchange), as well as manpower and investment policies. Measures include reduced import duties, selective credits by the national bank system, preferential participation in institutional borrowing abroad, tax preferences to foreign partners in joint ventures, and so forth. Regions that receive less net flows from other parts of the country will suffer less economic disruption and decline when boundaries are redrawn.

The economic pain attributed to redrawing boundaries can be inferred by assessing the degree of trade dependency and the direction of net interregional public financial flows. Russia and the Czech Republic suffered less than Estonia and Yugoslavia from the redrawing of boundaries because they had the lowest trade dependency and had net financial out-flows. An explanation follows.

The Soviet Union has been classified as high in trade dependency across its constituent republics. This occurred because development policy has dictated a geographical diversification of the economy and economic policy has attempted to reap the benefits of specialization and economies of scale. Together, these policies resulted in a high degree of interdependence among regions. According to Havrylyshyn and Williamson, 'in the Soviet Union the planners' infatuation with scale economies and the underpricing of transport may well have nurtured an artificial volume of inter-republic trade'.[184] One crucial exception to this trade dependency is Russia. Evidence indicates that regional dependency on the union was lowest in Russia, highest in Belorussia, and relatively high in Estonia. These republics exported the following percentages of their production to Soviet markets: 29.3, 69.6, and 66.5 respectively.[185] Despite such pre-independence trade dependency, Estonia managed to cut its ties to Russia more effectively than its Baltic neighbors, Latvia and Lithuania. It was quick to develop trade ties with the European Union (Estonia exported 6,000 units of industrial production to the European Community while only 1,410 to Russia and its Baltic neighbors; it imported 7,566 units from the EU while only 2,296 from Russia and the Baltic states[186]). Moreover, Estonia forged trade ties with Sweden and Finland and financial and technical assistance ties with Germany and Denmark. For these reasons, it was better equipped than other former Soviet states to withstand the Russian crisis of 1997–98.[187]

Contrary to the Soviet experience in trade dependency, Yugoslav republics had highly fragmented markets (especially from 1974 to 1991). Empirical studies by Bicanic, Ocic, Ding, and Bookman all indicate extremely low levels of interregional trade.[188] Former Yugoslav republics had trade relations with foreign countries independent of the center. In some cases this accounted for 30 percent of its trade. Therefore, while the break-up did disrupt trade relations, all new states were able to adjust (and would have done so even more successfully in the absence of war and sanctions). As a result of its sanctions-induced isolation, 85 percent of Montenegro's trade is with Serbia, reversing the earlier lack of trade dependency.[189]

The decrease in trade between the Czech Republic and Slovakia since their split in 1993 resulted in a drop of some 30–40 percent in the first three months.[190] Slovakia was at a disadvantage since its economy was largely based on raw materials (while final production was concentrated in the Czech lands) and a military industry (which became obsolete when President Havel imposed a ban on the export of military goods).

With respect to interregional flows, those regions that were net recipients suffered more from the redrawing of boundaries than those that were net losers. The Czech Republic benefited from the redrawing of boundaries if for no other reason than that federal outflows from Prague ceased: according to Dean, Slovakia contributed approximately 25 percent of the national income of the federation, less than proportional to its population of 31 percent, and as a result, it persistently drained more than it contributed.[191] After the break-up, it is Slovakia that must struggle with the loss of between $700 million to $1 billion in annual support from the federation.[192] A similar difference between republics emerged in Yugoslavia and the Soviet Union. In the former, the less developed regions (Kosovo, Montenegro, Bosnia, and Herzegovina) contributed less to the center than they received; Slovenia, Croatia, and Serbia proper contributed more. A study by Bookman found that in fact Serbia contributed the most to the Federal Fund,[193] while Kosovo and Montenegro contributed the least.[194] Ding appraised the fiscal burden of each republic relative to the strength of its economy, and found that by this measurement, Serbia ranked the highest.[195]

The disruption of trade relations and the cessation of interregional flows associated with boundary changes most often induces economic decline. How long it takes economies to bounce back depends on their previous degree of dependency, the direction of their net flows, and their ability to develop alternative trade relations. Such economic decline accentuates interethnic competition and ethnic bifurcation. In addition, ethnic empowerment and marginalization is further induced by changes in numerical majorities and minorities that follow boundary alterations. When a minority becomes a majority, there tends to follow a change in the political and legal status of ethnic groups, as well as their pecking order. Hence, ethnic bifurcation can be traced to constitutional or policy changes that new governments enact.

In Estonia, it came as no surprise that the post-independence popular sentiment became vehemently anti-Russian. While ethnic Estonians voted overwhelmingly in favor of independence, only 25 percent of ethnic Russians expressed support for leaving the Soviet Union.[196] This resulted in retaliatory procrastination by Estonian authorities in granting citizenship rights to minorities. As noted by Vetik, in 1998, six years after the adoption of the Citizenship Law, some

60 percent of non-Estonian residents were still without citizenship.[197] Such a lack of citizenship rights, coupled with the language policy described above, serves to relegate Russians to a marginalized status.

Given Russia's dominance in the former Soviet Union, the collapse of the federation was a personal blow to Russians. Hochenos describes this: 'The startling electoral success of the Greater Russian nationalist Vladimir Zhirinovsky in December 1993 ... [points to] a population smarting from the loss of power and prestige that accompanied the collapse of the Soviet Union.'[198] Russia's inability to conclusively quell the insurgency in Chechnya added insult to injury. Ilishev notes that 'in the wake of the Chechen war, Moscow is desperately trying to reassert its right to greater control over ethnic regions'.[199] The prevailing sentiment was two pronged: a sense of Russian empowerment coupled with a new marginalization of those ethnic groups who were held responsible for the break-up. In the absence of communist-era legislation, Russians became less willing to accommodate non-Russians in their midst. Politicians in Moscow became increasingly sensitive about the federation, the existing center-state relations, and the relationship between ethnic and administrative boundaries in Russia. Such sentiments on the part of ethnic Russians were further stimulated by the inflow of Russian migrants from the countries that emerged from the Soviet Union, as well as reports of mistreatment of their fellow Russians that stayed behind (across the former Soviet Union, more than 9 million people moved between 1990 and 1996, that is 1 in 30 people[200]).

Across the states borne from the former Yugoslavia, boundary changes and independence reduced accountability of ruling governments, eliminated the mandatory respect of Titoist minority legislation, and gave license to the new nationalist governments to introduce measures that enshrined ethnic bifurcation. The political rights of minorities were also curtailed with the demise of the former communist constitution. Indeed, all the new states, with the exception of Slovenia and Macedonia, introduced legislation according to which the Roma became demoted in the ethnic pecking order (previously they were considered a nationality, but under the new post-communist constitutions, they became an ethnic group). In Serbia, the absence of communist housing policies resulted in 'Romani ghettos' and the 'the life expectancy among Roma in two locations in Serbia was similar to that for the poorest Asian and African nations'.[201] In a Romani community in Kosovo today, Romas live in separate communities on the edge of town, and, according to Latham, garbage is collected only once every six months.[202] In another community, there are no street lights and the roads are terrible. (Incidentally, minorities are no better off in Croatia. The homes of Romas (who had lived for years in

Germany and Austria and dutifully repatriated their earnings) were confiscated under the Tudjman government.[203])

Ethnic bifurcation in the Czech Republic is most clearly evident in the empowerment of ethnic Czechs and the marginalization of Romas. However, there has also been a marginalization of Jews who, while not a popular ethnic group during communism, were nevertheless protected by legislation that extended to all minorities. Numerous Jews departed (as they did from all East European states), leaving a sentiment that Hochenos called 'Semitism without Jews'. Hatred is directed at Jewish history and artifacts of their past existence in the area. One poll shows strong anti-Semitic attitudes among 23 percent of Czechs.[204]

THE SOURCE OF ECONOMIC DECLINE

Does the source of economic decline matter? In other words, if the economy is contracting by 2 percent per year, does it matter if the decline is due to war, boundary alterations, or insufficient capital investment? It is argued that the source does matter because different sources of decline affect interethnic competition and ethnic bifurcation in different ways. Some sources of decline encompass exogenous shocks that 'happen' to an economy; other sources are embodied in endogenous structural imbalances. Not all sources produce effects of the same duration, depth, and breadth. Some are temporary and acute, yet leave no long-lasting damage on the social, economic, and political fabric. Others continue to linger, leaving permanent damage in their wake. Some sources of economic decline foster ethnic bifurcation that is both too deep and too entrenched to be easily reversed. The following variables are relevant in determining the effect of the source of decline on bifurcation.

First, the speed with which a given source of economic decline works itself out of the system and the speed with which the economy turns around are important in determining just how deep the interethnic animosities become. Clearly, the movement from communism to capitalism in Estonia, completed within less than a decade using the Big Bang approach, is less damaging to interethnic relations than one that takes a longer time to complete (such as in Russia). Second, a country that reinforces ethnic bifurcation with discriminatory policy will experience longer lasting interethnic animosities than one in which marginalization and empowerment play themselves out in the absence of supporting government intervention. Third, the more open the interethnic animosities (such as in war), the deeper the antipathy toward the enemy ethnic group becomes. Fourth, the greater the involvement of outside states, the more serious the internal ethnic bifurcation. Outside involvement tilts the precarious domestic balance between ethnic groups (as was evident with German involvement in the secessionist efforts of Croatia).

When the source of economic decline lingers over the long run, discriminatory policies reinforce bifurcation, interethnic animosities are open, and the international community becomes involved in a destructive manner, then the conditions are present for explosive interethnic conflict (as is discussed in chapter 8).

NOTES

1 It is necessary to distinguish between economic decline in highly developed regions (such as the United States and Canada) and in less developed regions (such as India and Brazil). While this distinction is elaborated below, suffice it to say here that interethnic competition following economic decline will manifest itself differently in a largely service economy, in which the majority of people enjoy a high standard of living and where they have democratic freedoms than in a country where those conditions are absent.

2 Miroslav Hroch, *Social Preconditions of National Revival in Europe* (Cambridge: Cambridge University Press, 1985); Beth Michneck, 'Regional Autonomy, Territoriality, and the Economy', paper presented to the American Association for the Advancement of Slavic Studies, Washington, DC, October 1990; Anthony Birch, *Nationalism and National Integration* (London: Unwin Hyman, 1989).

3 Christine Drake, *National Integration in Indonesia: Patterns and Policies* (Honolulu: University of Hawaii Press, 1989) p. 145.

4 Niche overlap releases competitive forces. At the same time, competition causes niche overlap. Frederick Barth (1969) shows how interethnic competition caused changes in the niches that two groups exploited in Pakistan. Barth is cited in Susan Olzak, *The Dynamics of Ethnic Competition and Conflict* (Stanford: Stanford University Press, 1992), pp. 26–7.

5 This applies to economic change that is of crisis proportions. See Stephen Haggard and Robert R. Kaufman, *The Political Economy of Democratic Transitions* (Princeton: Princeton University Press, 1995), p. 8.

6 Sharon Wolchnik, 'Gender Issues During Transition' in *East-Central European Economies in Transition*, study papers submitted to the Joint Economic Committee of the US Congress, Washington, DC, November 1994.

7 Michael Hechter, *Internal Colonialism* (Berkeley: University of California Press, 1975), p. 39.

8 Unless they take another path: when perceptions of economic injustice influence the valuation of relative costs and benefits of belonging to a national union, and when costs outweigh benefits, economic factors are then mingled with ethnic, religious, or cultural factors to form a set of demands that may include leaving the union (namely, secession).

9 See the comparison of management styles with respect to job loss during economic downturns in Lester Thurow, *The Management Challenge: Japanese Views* (Cambridge, MA: MIT Press, 1988).

10 Olzak, *Ethnic Competition*, chapter 1.

11 Jeannette Money, *Fences and Neighbors. The Political Geography of Immigration Control* (Ithaca: Cornell University Press, 1999), p. 57.

12 Land has been reserved for Fijians, despite the fact that some one half of the population is composed of Indians. According to Adrian Mayer, land could be leased to Indians but only at exorbitantly high rents, thus effectively preventing their long-term sustenance from the land. Adrian C. Mayer, *Indians in Fiji* (Oxford: Oxford University Press, 1963), p. 62.

13 *New York Times*, 16 November 1993.

14 Milica Zarkovic Bookman, *The Economics of Secession* (New York: St Martin's Press, 1993), chapter 4.

15 For a discussion of how this affects the political scene, see Linda J. Cook and Mitchell A. Orenstein, 'The Return of the Left and its Impact on the Welfare State in Poland, Hungary, and Russia' in Linda J. Cook, Mitchell A. Orenstein and Marilyn Rueschemeyer (eds), *Left Parties and Social Policy in Postcommunist Europe* (Boulder, CO: Westview Press, 1999).

16 Examples of worsening health and education conditions of marginalized groups are more common than not. Some rare exceptions to this trend warrant mention. For example, there are refugee camps for Palestinians run by the United Nations and nongovernmental organizations where the health care and nutrition and prenatal care is so good that the population growth rate is very high (indeed, the high fertility of some 7 children per woman is not countered by high death rates due to malnutrition and bad health, as it is in Somalia and Uganda). *New York Times*, 24 February 2000.

17 *Miami Herald*, 20 January 1994.

18 Paul Hochenos, *Free To Hate* (New York: Routledge, 1993), pp. 217–18.

19 This is similar to the persistence of forced sterilization policies directed towards the Roma during the communist period, despite its public repudiation.

20 Donna E. Arzt, *Refugees Into Citizens* (New York: Council on Foreign Relations, 1997), pp. 113–14.

21 *Economist*, 13 March 1999, p. 60.

22 Ildus G. Ilishev, 'Russian Federalism: Political, Legal, and Ethnolingual Aspects – A View from the Republic of Bashkortostan', *Nationalities Papers* 26, 4 (1998), p. 737.

23 *New York Times*, 7 February 2000.

24 Hochenos, *Free To Hate*, p. 222.

25 See Surjit S. Bhalla, 'Domestic Follies, Investment Crises: East Asian Lessons for India' in Karl D. Jackson (ed.), *Asian Contagion* (Boulder, CO: Westview Press, 1999), pp. 137–8.

26 They have been very instrumental in the election outcome in state elections in February 2000. *New York Times*, 28 February 2000.

27 This far-reaching bill would outlaw discrimination on the basis of race, ethnicity, and sex. *New York Times*, 29 January 2000.

28 Robert Hayden, *Blueprints for a House Divided. The Constitutional Logic of the Yugoslav Conflicts* (Ann Arbor: University of Michigan Press, 1999).

29 Hochenos, *Free To Hate*, p. 218.

30 David J. Smith, 'Retracing Estonia's Russians: Mikhail Kurchinskii and Interwar Cultural Autonomy', *Nationalities Papers* 27, 3 (1999), p. 456.

31 Hochenos, *Free To Hate*, p. 221.

32 Ibid., p. 226.

33 According to the Yugoslav constitution of 1974, nationalities are composed of people who are the titular majority in a Yugoslav republic. Ethnic groups,

lower in the pecking order, have no territorial homeland within the federation.

34 Judith Latham, 'Roma of the Former Yugoslavia', *Nationalities Papers* 27, 2 (1999), p. 208.

35 David Cole, *No Equal Justice: Race and Class in the American Criminal Justice System* (New York: New Press, 1999).

36 Hochenos, *Free To Hate*, p. 213

37 Latham, 'Roma', p. 213.

38 In February 2000, the largest protests were in Kaduna. However, it seems likely that the sharia law will spread to other regions of the country, imperiling the daily lives of the Christians. *New York Times*, 23 February 2000.

39 Albanians have refused to participate despite the fact that their numbers were so great that they would have brought about a change in local politics through the electoral process. They also refused to participate in the census, both in Kosovo as well as in Macedonia.

40 Thomas Sowell, *The Economics and Politics of Race* (New York: Morrow, 1983).

41 The celebration has been banned since 1967. *New York Times*, 7 February 2000.

42 Adding insult to injury, the comment was made in reference to the Governor Shintaro Ishihara's perceived need to ready the military and riot police because these immigrant groups were likely to riot in the aftermath of a major earthquake. *New York Times*, 11 April 2000.

43 *New York Times*, 3 April 2000.

44 Sometimes other factors are responsible for holding groups together. In Switzeralnd, the glue seems to be money, in Ireland, religion plus the memories regarding the behavior of the English have been the primary factors of nationalism, etc. See Joshua Fishman (ed.), *Handbook of Language and Ethnic Identity* (Oxford: Oxford University Press, 1999).

45 The Bulgarization of Turks extended to name changes. The Bulgarian government engaged in compulsory name changes of Turks. Those who resisted were encouraged to emigrate. This policy led to the expulsion of up to 300,000 Turks. See Milica Z. Bookman, *The Demographic Struggle for Power* (London: Frank Cass, 1998), p. 112.

46 After the Treaty of Bucharest in 1913, Macedonia was split between Bulgaria (19%), Greece (about half) and Serbia got the rest. According to Palmer and King, 'The Serbian government began a religious, educational, and political campaign in Vardar Macedonia to reorient the pro-Bulgarian Macedonians.' Even after World War One, Bulgarian speech was forbidden. Stephen E. Palmer and Robert R. King, *Yugoslav Communism and the Macedonian Question* (Hamden, CT: Archon Books, 1971), p. 8

47 *OMRI Daily Digest*, 113, 12 June 1995.

48 Donald Horowitz, *Ethnic Groups in Conflict* (Berkeley: University of California Press, 1985), p. 219.

49 From 1978 to 1985, the government actively persecuted members of the sect. Moreover, children born to Baha'is were deemed illegitimate. Ted Robert Gurr, *Minorities at Risk* (Washington, DC: United States Institute of Peace, 1993), p. 243.

50 Indeed, Milan has become a hotbed for both mobsters and petty criminals, whose ethnicity has come to be associated with crime. *Economist*, 16 January 1999), p. 47.

51 Hein Marais, *South Africa Limits to Change* (London: Zed Books, 1998), p. 109.

52 The crime rates are so high as to have warranted paramilitary intervention from the central government. This is not just a class war, this is inter-

caste also. See *Economist*, 20 February 2000, p. 40.

53 Hochenos, *Free To Hate*, p. 221.

54 *Economist*, 3 April 1999, p. 53.

55 Cook *et al.*, *Left Parties*, p. 52.

56 Branko Hinic and Rajko Bukovic, 'Efekti Mera Ekonomske Politike i Ocekivana Privredna Kretanja u Narednom Periodu', unpublished paper (Belgrade, 1992), figures 1 and 3.

57 Dimitrije Boarov, the economics writer for *Vreme*, quoted in the *Miami Herald*, 26 August 1992.

58 *FRE/RL Research Report* 2, 21, 21 May 1993, p. 50.

59 Mladan Dinkic, *Ekonomija Destrukcije* (Belgrade: Stubovi Kulture, 1996).

60 Data presented in the *Economist*, 29 April 2000, p. 37.

61 Capitalism is characterized by private ownership of factors of production, labor that is free to sell its services in the labor market, decentralized decision-making that is coordinated by the market system. The motivation of economic actors is based on material incentives.

62 See discussion by Michael G. Peletz, 'The Great Transformation' in Robert W. Hefner (ed.), *Market Cultures* (Boulder, CO: Westview Press, 1998), p. 173.

63 In the late 1980s economists bemoaned the lack of theory describing the transition from socialism to capitalism. Indeed, while theory describing the process of moving from capitalism to socialism existed, scholars were caught unprepared for the reverse real-world events of the late 1980s. However, the early 1990s witnessed the proliferation of writings on the extent, pace and feasibility of reforms aimed at introducing capitalism to formerly socialist states and thereby incorporating them into the world economy. The end of the Cold War and the professed desires of former Soviet bloc states to embrace capitalism signified to many the victory of democracy and capitalism and thus the end of the need to study this region separately. (This view is embodied in Francis Fukuyama, *The End of History and the Last Man* (New York: Free Press, 1992).) Yet the rapidly changing events associated with the rise of nationalism, with economic hardship, and political realignments following the Cold War all point out that, to the contrary, the attention of research must once again be focused on these changing states and their emerging systems.

64 This organization of the elements of transition to a market economy is offered by Susan M. Collins and Dani Rodrik, *Eastern Europe and the Soviet Union in the World Economy* (Washington, DC: Institute for International Economics, 1991), p. 11. This paragraph draws heavily on their analysis.

65 Jeffrey Sachs, 'Poland and Eastern Europe: What Is to Be Done?' in Andras Koves and Paul Marer (eds), *Foreign Economic Liberalization* (Boulder, CO: Westview Press, 1991).

66 Karoly Attila Soos, 'Liberalization and Stabilization' in Koves and Marer, *Liberalization*; Jude Wanniski, 'IMF's Economic Massacre in the Balkans', *Wall Street Journal*, 10 August 1993.

67 These slower changes are associated with Hungary. Poland began reforms with a big bang; however, by early 1992, it had lost its nerve and adopted Hungary's more gradualist approach of privatization.

68 *Transition* 3, 5 (May 1992), p. 8.

69 These views, adhered to by people such as Alexander Dubchek, Mihailo Markovic, Istvan Czurska, and Vladimír Mečiar, were once popular in the West during the Cold War (when they were welcomed as dissident views chipping away at the communist hegemony), but they are now perceived in the West as reactionary. Before the demise of communism, Dubchek and

Markovic were popular in the West for their views which were perceived as anticommunist. Actually, these people were Marxists in search of a humane socialism to be applied to their societies. After the demise of communism, they remained true to their ideas, but the world changed, and they were no longer seen as opponents of communism but rather the embodiment of communism itself. They are countered by Janos Kornai, who said that a third way between communism and capitalism is impossible (see the *Economist*, 24 April 1993, p. 54). Czurska rejects both capitalism and communism as models for Hungary, and opts instead for the 'third road' (see *FRE/RL Research Report* 1, 40, 9 October 1993, p. 28). Western critics have said that the application of the third way will result in large economic costs and must therefore be discouraged (although some, like Sean Gabb, view the costs of the application of the third way in Slovakia as significantly lower than those of the increased Germanization of the Czech Republic ('Czechs, not Slovaks, Headed for Trouble', *Prague Post*, 1–7 September 1992, p. 15)).

70 *New York Times*, 9 October 1992. Some loosening was evident in mid-1993, as China attempted to win a bid to host the Olympic Games in the year 2000.

71 Following the Soviet–Yugoslav split in 1948 Yugoslavia led East European countries with respect to the number and scope of reforms. Indeed, it had applied the concept of market socialism throughout its economy and was a pioneer in industrial democracy through the system of self-management. Its dramatic reforms of 1965 and 1974 introduced a system that was the envy of the Eastern Bloc and amazing feat as seen by the West. Its trade was highly liberalized and much took place with western Europe. Western loans were forthcoming and the standard of living rose dramatically during the 1960s and 1970s.

72 This pertains to a discussion of Estonia's application for membership to the European Union. Quote from the *EIU Viewswire*, 'The European Commission's Report', 15 October 1999.

73 Adrian Karatnycky, 'Introduction' in Adrian Karatnycky, Alexander Motyl and Charles Graybow (eds), *Nations in Transit 1998* (Washington, DC: Freedom House, 1999), p. 7.

74 In the spring of 1991, the government introduced an economic program that entailed a macroeconomic program that established fiscal measures (including a modernized tax system and the elimination of the link between fiscal policy and money creation), the introduction of a convertible currency and structural reform consisting of privatization and financial restructuring of commercial banks and enterprises. With respect to the monetary changes, aimed at both establishing sovereignty over its economy and insulating the economy from the inflationary pressures from the rest of Yugoslavia, the following was done: a central bank was created to introduce monetary and exchange rate policies; legislation was adopted to establish a market for foreign exchange and thus eliminate the black market; the tolar was established as legal tender, convertible on a one-to-one basis from the dinar, against which it would float freely, as with international currencies, in 1991. See Boris Pleskovic and Jeffrey Sachs, 'Currency Reform in Slovenia: The Tolar Standing Tall', in *Transition* 3, 8 (September 1992), pp. 6–8.

75 Croatia first introduced the Croatian *dinar* (later replaced by the *kuna*), with a flexible exchange rate, in December 1991. The Croatian National Bank, the central bank, pursued a policy of tight monetary control, thus avoiding the inflationary collapse in adjoining Serbia, and it has restructured the inherited banking system. Moreover, in 1992, the Zagreb Stock Exchange opened in an effort to raise capital for the economy.

76 See Koves and Marer, *Liberalization*, p. 100.
77 'Estonia Country Guide: Economy and Trade, Money, and Finance' (13 November 1999).
78 See Thomas W. Hazlett, 'Bottom-up Privatization: The Czech Experience' in Terry L. Anderson and Peter J. Hill (eds), *The Privatization Process* (Lanham, MD: Rowman and Littlefield, 1996).
79 Rolph van der Hoeven and Gyorgy Sziraczki, 'Privatization and Labour Issues' in Rolph van der Hoeven and Gyorgy Sziraczki (eds), *Lessons From Privatization* (Geneva: International Labor Organization, 1997), p. 6.
80 Karatnycky *et al.*, *Nations in Transit*, p. 219.
81 Ibid., p. 251.
82 Ibid., p. 670.
83 Ibid., p. 504.
84 PlanEcon, *Czech Economic Monitor* (30 January 1998), pp. 5–6, cited in Paul R. Gregory and Robert C. Stuart, *Comparative Economic Systems*, 6th edn (Boston: Houghton Mifflin, 1999), p. 471.
85 Timothy J. Yeager, *Institutions, Transition Economies, and Economic Development* (Boulder, CO: Westview Press, 1999), p. 93. The following discussion on Russia draws on pp. 96–7.
86 *New York Times*, 1 May 2000.
87 Raivo Vetik, 'Nation Building and National Integration in Estonia', paper presented to the meetings of the Association for the Study of Nationalities, New York, April 1999, p. 8.
88 Matthew R. Auer, 'Environmentalism and Estonia's Independence Movements', *Nationalities Papers* 26, 4 (1998), pp. 664–6.
89 Latham, 'Roma', p. 207.
90 Ibid., p. 212.
91 Ibid., p. 219.
92 Hochenos, *Free To Hate*, p. 220.
93 Liba Paukert, 'Privatization and Employment in the Czech Republic' in Van der Hoeven and Sziraczki, *Privatization*, p. 161.
94 John Ham, Jan Svejnar and Katherine Terrell, 'Czech Republic and Slovakia' in Simon Commander and Fabrizio Coricelli (eds), *Unemployment, Restructuring and the Labor Market in Eastern Europe and Russia* (Washington, DC: World Bank, 1995), p. 104.
95 It is estimated that some 80,000 Ukrainian workers are working in the Czech Republic, most of them illegal. They get day jobs on the black labor market and earn the equivalent of some 2 dollars per day (before the Ukrainian mafia takes its cut), versus the average Czech monthly income of $350. *Economist*, 8 May 1999, p. 52.
96 Cook, *Labor and Liberalization*, p. 16.
97 Ibid., pp. 51–2.
98 David Fretwell and Richard Jackman, 'Labor Markets: Unemployment' in Nicholas Barr (ed.), *Labor Markets and Social Policy in Central and Eastern Europe: The Transition and Beyond* (Oxford: Oxford University Press, 1994), pp. 167, 169.
99 The Czech Republic postponed the bankruptcy law until 1993, putting off unemployment in the short run.
100 Mikhail A. Alexseev, 'Are Chinese Migrants at Risk in Primorskii Krai? Monitoring Inter-Ethnic Relations with Opinion and Event Data', paper presented to the meeting of the Association for the Study of Nationalities, New York, April 2000, p. 12.

101 The most glaring example just how fundamentally capitalism has changed over time comes from reading its strongest critic, Karl Marx, and comparing his descriptions to the present reality. Marx described the business cycles associated with capitalist production, and predicted that they would only get bigger and bigger; he described the process by which capital was concentrating in the hands of a few capitalists who were surviving the competitive struggle, and predicted that such a trend would continue until all production and distribution was controlled by a small number of monopolists; and finally, Marx predicted that the ensuing hardship endured by the working class would lead workers of the world to 'unite and throw off their chains'. While Marx painted a realistic picture of the world in the mid- to late 1800s, he was wrong on each of his predictions. But he was at least partially wrong because the capitalism that he wrote about was not the capitalism that existed one century later. Indeed, the *laissez-faire*, unregulated capitalism was replaced by a hands-on, regulated variety. Business cycles did not get out of control because monetary and fiscal policy was introduced to hamper them; capital concentrations were kept in check by antitrust policies; worker hardship was alleviated by social policy that provided a safety net, health and education programs, transfer payments etc.

102 In addition to these, liberalization also takes place in income redistribution and worker participation, but these are minor and will not be addressed in this study.

103 Fraser Institute, *Economic Freedom of the World*, www.freetheworld.com, April 2000.

104 Indeed, by 1950, steel, heavy machinery, chemicals, power, fuel, com- munications, transportation and life insurance were nationalized. Large banks, copper industry, wholesale grain trade and some coalmines were nationalized in the 1970s.

105 Gregory and Stuart, *Economic Systems*, p. 353.

106 John Echeverri-Gent, 'Economic Reform in India: A Long and Winding Road' in Richard E. Feinbert, John Echeverri-Gent and Friedemann Muller (eds), *Economic Reform in Three Giants* (New Brunswick: Transaction Books, 1990), p. 103.

107 *Economist*, 20 February 1999.

108 C. S. Venkata Ratnam, 'Adjustment and Privatization in India' in Van der Hoeven and Sziraczki, *Privatization*, p. 57.

109 *Economist*, 29 January 2000, p. 78.

110 *Wall Street Journal*, 29 February 2000.

111 Ratnam, 'Adjustment and Privatization, p. 66.

112 Jagdish Bhagwati, *India In Transition* (Oxford: Clarendon, 1993), p. 84.

113 *Economist*, 29 January 2000, p. 78.

114 Carlos Alberto Longo, 'The State and the Liberalization of the Brazilian Economy' in Maria J. F. Willumsen and Eduardo Giannetti da Fonseca (eds), *The Brazilian Economy: Structure and Performance in Recent Decades* (Miami: North South Center Press, 1997), p. 37.

115 Paul Hennemeyer, 'Energy Reform and Privatization: Distilling the Signal from the Noise' in Federico Basanes, Evamaria Uribe and Robert Willig (eds), *Can Privatization Deliver? Infrastructure for Latin America* (Washington, DC: Inter-American Development Bank, 1999), p. 292.

116 Data presented in the *Economist*, 29 April 2000, p. 37.

117 Ratnam, 'Adjustment and Privatization', p. 50.

118 *Economist*, 10 April 1999, p. 68.

119 Since the signing of a treaty with the British newcomers in 1840, the Maoris been a minority. The Treaty of Waitangi was an agreement between the Maori population and the Crown, which the British interpreted as the ceding of Maori sovereignty. See Natacha Gagne, 'Cultural Identities and the Nation-State in a Globalized World: The Case of New Zealand' paper presented to the meetings of the Association for the Study of Nationalities, New York, April 2000, p. 3.

120 *Economist*, 9 October 1999.

121 Anthony W. Marx, *Making Race and Nation* (Cambridge: Cambridge University Press, 1998), p. 15.

122 *New York Times*, 17 January 1999.

123 *Economist*, 22 April 2000, p. 31.

124 *New York Times*, 7 December 1999.

125 *Economist*, 29 April 2000, p. 37.

126 Ibid.

127 Ibid., p. 38.

128 See, for example, Maria J. F. Willumsen, 'Regional Disparities in Brazil' in Willumsen and Fonseca, *The Brazilian Economy*.

129 The creation of conditions for investment and production that made the city of Bangalore India's Silicone Valley have also enabled high rates of economic growth. Brad Wetzler says Bangalore 'is now home to 300 high tech companies that employ 40,000 people. Combined, there enterprises ... pumped out software and computer related services to the tune of $4 billion last year'. Brad Wetzler, 'Boomgalore', *Wired* (March 2000), p. 154.

130 See Rebecca Reichmann (ed.), *Race in Contemporary Brazil* (University Park: Pennsylvania State University Press, 1999).

131 The political conditions include companion policies (such as covert or military activity), the number of years economic sanctions were in force, the extent of international cooperation, the presence of international assistance to the target country, the political stability and economic health of the target country, and the warmth of prior relations between sender and target countries. In the economic sphere, the following conditions are included: the cost imposed on the target country (measured in terms of absolute, per capita, and percent of GNP), commercial relations between sender and target countries (measured by trade between them as a percentage of target country's trade), the relative economic size of the countries (sender and target), the type of sanctions used, and the cost to the sender country. Gary Clyde Hufbauer, Jeffrey J. Schott, and Kimberly Ann Elliot, *Economic Sanctions Reconsidered* (Washington, DC: Institute for International Economics, 1990), p. 40.

132 UN sanctions were suspended in December 1995, however, an outer wall of sanctions remains. It excludes Belgrade from international financial institutions. Moreover, an investment ban and asset freeze was imposed in 1998 (www.cia.gov, June 2000).

133 On 30 May 1992, the United Nations, under the instigation of the United States, voted to impose sanctions on the new Yugoslavia under UN Security Council Resolution 757. In April 1993, again under US sponsorship, a further tightening of sanctions was approved by the United Nations, and these were put into effect on 30 April when the Bosnian Serbs refused to sign the Vance–Owen peace plan.

134 Since 1979, Egypt is no longer among the boycoting countries.

135 In 1963 the UN Security Council called for a voluntary arms embargo against South Africa, which became mandatory in 1977. In 1986 the US government

passed the Comprehensive Anti-Apartheid Act which prohibits new loans to the South African government and new investments, forbids trade in selected goods, and terminates direct air flights. The Disinvestment movements calls on institutions to purge their portfolios of stockholding in companies that do business in South Africa. See Walter Williams, *South Africa's War Against Capitalism* (New York: Praeger 1989), pp. 134–5. With respect to India, under the US Glenn amendment, any country that explodes an atomic bomb is subject to unilateral sanctions.

136 The text of the UN resolution imposing sanctions on the new Yugoslavia included the following measures: all trade in all commodities was to cease; all foreign assets of the new Yugoslav federation were to be frozen; all air traffic was to be suspended; all repair, service, and insurance for the aircraft of Yugoslavia was to be arrested. After some six months of these sanctions the United Nations voted to tighten the embargo in the following ways: First, it empowered monitoring ships to inspect cargo passing into the Adriatic Sea and the River Danube and to interdict those vehicles that engage in sanction busting. Second, cargo vehicles were banned from crossing the country with oil, machinery, steel, tires, and other critical goods. These new measures included prohibiting the transport of any goods through Serbia and Montenegro; prohibiting the entrance of any ship into former Yugoslav rivers or sea; the restriction of truck and train passage to a few border points; and the seizure of all ships, freight trucks, trains and aircraft outside of the country. Trade was banned for all goods except medicine, food, and relief supplies and services. In addition, public and private financial assets in foreign banks were frozen. The sanctions against the new Yugoslavia extend into the political sphere as well. Yugoslavia suffered from a lack of international recognition. While other states born of the former Yugoslavia have received swift recognition (notably, Slovenia and Croatia in the few days following 15 January 1991), the new Federal Republics of Yugoslavia have to date not been formally recognized, with the exception of a *de facto* recognition by China, Russia and Romania. Moreover, the new Yugoslavia, composed of Serbia and Montenegro, was not automatically granted the Yugoslav seat at the UN in the way Russia assumed the Soviet Union's seat in January 1992. Instead, the Security Council passed a resolution on 22 September 1992, that Serbia and Montenegro will not inherit the Yugoslav seat and will have to apply for membership in the future. Yugoslavia was expelled from the United Nations' principal bodies in 1992.

137 The goal of the Permanent Boycott Committee was 'to frustrate further Jewish economic development in Palestine'. Donald Losman, *International Economic Sanctions* (Albuquerque: University of New Mexico Press, 1979), p. 47. Arab countries refused diplomatic and commercial ties with Israel. Moreover, they pressured countries they do business with to cease their trade relations with Israel.

138 The purpose of these sanctions was primarily to influence the outcome of the war in Bosnia-Herzegovina, to 'take a stand against aggression', to send a message that borders cannot be changed by force, to punish perpetrators and to aid in the toppling of the Milošević government, which is viewed as responsible for the war.

139 Surjit S. Bhalla, 'Domestic Follies, p. 140.

140 Stephen Gelb, 'Development Prospects for South Africa', paper presented to WIDER Workshop on Medium Term Development Strategy, Phase II, Helsinki, 15–17 April 1994, cited in Hein Marais, *South Africa Limits to Change* (London: Zed Books, 1998), p.1000.

141 After sanctions were lifted, South Africa also adopted a policy of export promotion. Marie Muller, 'South African Economic Diplomacy in the Age of Globalization', paper presented to the International Studies Association meetings in Los Angeles, 15 March 2000.

142 Marais, *South Africa*, p. 31. He also claimed claimed that, while foreign investment had been revived by 1996, it had only limited benefit for the South African economy because it was overwhelmingly used as a springboard for trade in neighboring African countries.

143 According to Hein Marais, 'the main value of sanctions appeared to lie in their negative effect on foreign investment flows and on the governments ability to secure financial assistance to offset balance of payments difficulties'. Ibid., p. 67.

144 *Wall Street Journal*, 11 February 2000.

145 *FRE/RL News Brief*, 2, 23, 24–28 May 1993, p. 19.

146 *New York Times*, 26 June 1992.

147 *Economist*, 9 October 1993, p. 60.

148 *FRE/RL News Brief*, 2, 26, 14–18 June 1993, p. 10.

149 *FRE/RL Daily Report*, 28 May 1993, p. 8.

150 X-rays were not done, anesthesia was unavailable, antibiotic supplies were dwindling and vaccines for children were in shortage. As a result, nearly 50 percent of Belgrade's schoolchildren were anaemic, 26 percent of the children in Nis were undernourished, and 17 percent of army recruits were rejected because of undernourishment. *FRE/RL Daily Report*, 15 September 1993, p. 6.

151 Another form of bifurcation occurred in South Africa between immigrant ethnic groups and the domestic population. As a result of labor shortages in the aftermath of the Second World War the country encouraged migration from adjoining countries. Ronald Libby, *The Politics of Economic Power in Southern Africa* (Princeton: Princeton University Press, 1987), pp. 30–40. In the post-apartheid period, the labor shortages no longer exist, yet South Africa remains a haven for migrants: it is estimated that some 2.5 to 8 million (one tenth of the population) are undocumented immigrants. Peter Slater, *Workers Without Frontiers. The Impact of Globalization on International Migration* (Boulder, CO: Lynne Reinner, 2000), p. 97. This surplus of labor, coupled with minimum wage regulations, has increased the resentment of local blacks towards black newcomers (a minimum wage law for domestic workers has the unintended effect of reducing the demand for domestic workers. When the majority of black women are employed in private homes, the effect can be devastating. *Economist*, 27 March 1999, p. 46.

152 This paragraph relies on Walter Williams, *South Africa's War Against Capitalism*, pp. 135–7.

153 Moreover, it seems that the target black population did not even support sanctions: in a series of opinion polls, black workers were overwhelmingly against disinvestment (indeed, in 9 out of 14 surveys, an absolute majority of black respondents was against disinvestment and sanctions). Ibid., p. 137.

154 The investigation was called by Kofi Annan as a result of widespread criticism of the Security Council's practices with respect to international sanctions. *New York Times*, 18 April 2000.

155 Henry Barbera, *Rich Nations and Poor in Peace and War* (Lexington, MA: Lexington Books, 1973), p. 3.

156 These are derived from Alfred C. Neal (ed.), *Introduction to War Economics* (Chicago: Richard D. Irwin, 1942).

157 In a market economy, an alteration of prices may be used to bring about a change in production. However, if the time is short, or if the economy is of a command nature, then prices may be set by the government. The government may also simply buy up a needed input, prohibit its use for other things, establish a system of licensing, or simply take over the source of supply.

158 This has two results: first, boosting of wartime morale to draw volunteers (such as women and retirees) into the market, and second, a conscious wage policy that necessarily differs from a peacetime policy.

159 See Anatol Lieven, *Chechnya: Tombstone of Russian Power* (New Haven: Yale University Press, 1998).

160 Israel was created in 1948 following the partition of Palestine by the United Nations. Numerous wars have been fought with its Arab neighbors, including those of 1948–49, 1956, 1967, and 1973.

161 Shale Horowitz, 'Rebuilding Ships at Sea: Post-Communist Economic Reform in War-Torn States', unpublished paper, p. 11.

162 This led Bozidar Cerovic to call the privatization process in Yugoslavia 'privatization by spoonfuls'. *Interviju*, 6 August 1993, p. 16.

163 *FRE/RL News Brief*, 28 December–8 January 1993, p. 14.

164 *FRE/RL Daily News*, 16 June 1993.

165 This amounts to $911 million (CIA factbook, www.cia.gov, June 2000).

166 Sabrina P. Ramet, 'War in the Balkans', *Foreign Affairs* 71, 4 (fall 1992), p. 91.

167 This was done in March 1992, and at that time, the foreign debt was on the order of $2.5 billion. Meanwhile the regional responsibility for the payment of the former Yugoslav debt was to be assessed, since it did not seem logical that Serbia should carry the entire weight of the former Yugoslav debt burden.

168 *Economist*, 1 April 2000, p. 23.

169 CIA Factbook, www.cia.gov, June 2000.

170 Ibid.

171 Hemda Ben Yehuda and Shemuel Sandler, 'The Winding Down of the Arab–Israel Conflict: Interstate and Ethnic-State Crises, 1947–1998', paper presented to the International Studies Association meetings in Los Angeles, March 2000, p. 31.

172 *Times*, 23 August 1999.

173 Latham, 'Roma', p. 213.

174 Ibid., p. 211.

175 *Economist*, 19 February 2000, p. 49.

176 Chechnya has been *de facto* independent since the Russian army was thrown out in 1996. However, they have had a twilight status, as no one knows who is in charge except the war lords, armed gangs who combine radical Islam and crime to extract money for kidnappings.

177 *Economist*, 19 February 2000, p. 50.

178 Daniel Byman, 'Immoral Majorities: A First Look at a Neglected Source of Communal Conflict', paper presented to the International Studies Association meeting in Los Angeles, 15–19 March, p. 22.

179 Numerous scholars have studied this process of economic and political loss of power. See, among others: Baruch Kimmerling and Joel S. Migdal, *Palestinians: The Making of a People* (Cambridge: Cambridge University Press, 1993); Elia T. Zureik, *The Palestinians in Israel* (London: Routledge and Kegan Paul, 1979); Ian Lustick, *Arabs in the Jewish State: Israel's Control of a National Minority* (Austin: University of Texas Press, 1980).

180 Lustick, *Arabs in the Jewish State*.

181 The Arab community was divided into Druze, Bedouins and Christians as well as the larger Sunni Arab community. See ibid. and Gabriel Ben-Dor, *The Druzes in Israel* (Boulder, CO: Westview Press, 1979).

182 The description of trade dependency by the author appeared in 'The Economic Basis of Regional Autarchy in Yugoslavia', *Soviet Studies* 42, 1 (1990).

183 Private flows consist of voluntary interregional movements of resources in response to economic opportunity.

184 Oleh Havrylyshyn and John Williamson, *From Soviet Disunion to Eastern Economic Community*, Policy Analyses in International Economics 35 (Washington, DC: Institute for International Economics, October 1991).

185 Havrylyshyn and Williamson, *Soviet Disunion*, p. 20.

186 *EIU Viewswire*, 26 October 1999.

187 'Baltic States Move Steadily Towards EU Membership', *National Financial Law Review* (London, July 1977).

188 Bookman, 'Regional Autarchy'; Ivo Bicanic, 'Fractured Economy' in Dennis Rusinow, *Yugoslavia, A Fractured Federalism* (Washington, DC: Wilson Center Press, 1988); C. Ocic, 'Integracioni i Dezintegracioni Procesi u Privredi Jugoslavije', *Marksisticka Misao* 4 (1983). The study by Ding uses data compiled from the Yugoslav press to show that trade with other republics accounts for roughly one-third of Slovenia's trade. Wei Ding, 'Yugoslavia: Costs and Benefits of Union and Interdependence of Regional Economies', *Comparative Economic Studies* 33, 4 (1991), p. 22.

189 Such high trade dependency made Montenegro especially susceptible to political policies such as the trade ban imposed by the Belgrade government in 1999 (in order to undermine Montenegro's westward leaning president, Milo Djukanovic). *New York Times*, 2 April 2000.

190 Ham *et al.*, 'Czech Republic and Slovakia', p. 110.

191 Robert Dean, *Nationalism and Political Change in Eastern Europe* (Denver: University of Denver Press, 1973).

192 To offset this loss, the Slovak economy will receive a boost from a change in policy pertaining to arms sales: while President Havel imposed a ban on arms exports, severely hurting the Slovak economy, Premier Mečiar lifted it immediately upon independence. Moreover, Slovakia *might* benefit from the creation of the Visegrad Free-trade Zone, created on 1 March 1993 (with Hungary, Poland, and the Czech Republic), which opens up markets with 64 million consumers. *New York Times*, 12 February 1993.

193 This fund is part of the federal spending, which also included military spending, administrative spending, and miscellaneous expenditures. Payment into the fund comes from individual republics, which is one of the three sources of funds for the federal government (the other two are federal sales taxes and import duties).

194 See Bookman, *Secession*, chapter 4.

195 In per capita terms, this translated into the following: Slovenia $360; Croatia $188; Vojvodina $178; and Serbia $132. Ding, 'Yugoslavia', p. 8. Ding also studied interregional transfers and found that with respect to federal revenue collected during 1988, Croatia and Serbia both contributed 25 percent, while Slovenia contributed 20 percent. Singleton and Carter analyzed regional transfers in their study of Yugoslavia, and found that, in fact, the more developed regions received a greater quantity of investment funds from the central budget: 'during the period 1947 to 1963, ... with the exception of Montenegro, the less developed republics received a lower than average per

capita investment than did the more developed. Slovenia, for example, received three times more per capita than did Kosovo.' Fred Singleton and Bernard Carter, *The Economy of Yugoslavia* (London: Croom Helm, 1982), p. 220.

196 Vetik, 'Nation Building', p. 2.
197 Ibid., p. 3.
198 Hochenos, *Free to Hate*, p. 298.
199 Ilishev, 'Russian Federalism', p. 736.
200 Slater, *Workers Without Frontier*, p. 95. Just in the new Central Asian states, the exodus of Russians was remarkable. The proportion of Russians fell between 1989 and 1998: in Kazakhstan, from 37 to 31; in Kyrgizstan, 21 to 14.6; in Tajikistan, 7.6 to 6; in Turkmenistan, 9.5 to 7; and in Uzbekistan, 8.3 to 6.5. *Economist*, 3 April 1999, p. 36.
201 Latham, 'Roma', pp. 208–9.
202 Ibid., p. 211.
203 Ibid., p. 217.
204 The poll was taken by the American Jewish Committee, cited in Paul Hochenos, *Free To Hate*, p. 270.

3

Interethnic Competition During Economic Growth

Numerous scholars who have studied ethnic relations during economic growth have identified an inverse relationship between growth and nationalism.[1] They have found that economic growth and development reduces ethnic group identities and therefore dissipates strong political tendencies among radical ethnic groups.[2] According to both Deutsch and Huntington, modernization causes ethnic groups to assimilate, thereby decreasing the possibility of ethnically based demands on the polity, society, and economy.[3] In this vein, Bauer claimed that modernization raises the educational and cultural levels of the population, thus making people think and act as members of civic societies not based on ethnic communities.[4] As a result, their ethnicity ceases to have the importance it had prior to economic growth.

However, the proliferation of ethnic self-assertion activity of the mid-1960s in west European industrialized countries such as France, Britain, and Belgium weakens the arguments of those who claim an inverse relationship between growth and nationalism. In response to these events, another group of theories emerged claiming that the relationship between economic growth and nationalism was in fact positive: in other words, growth and development, especially when resulting from industrial capitalism, was conducive to ethnic protest and that the political arena that accompanies modernization provides a vehicle for nationalist self-expression.[5] Connor suggested that with modernization and the increasing ability of a population to communicate, self-awareness increases and the distinction of the ethnic group is enforced.[6] Wallerstein argued that the higher income populations that reside in higher income regions are more likely to make strong demands of their political institutions.[7] To the extent that these demands are associated with a specific ethnic group, they are nationalist by definition. Moreover, Kellas claimed that 'nationalism seeks to defend and promote the interests of the nation,'[8] and added that nationalist sentiment and aspiration often comes from a sudden change in economic and political division of labor among ethnic groups (as is caused by the onset of economic development).[9] Also,

Gellner argued that rapid change such as that caused by economic
development which, among other things, causes or forces people to
move to cities, alters traditional roles that people had and forces them
to place themselves in new social relationships.[10] The most logical place
to begin to look for such relationships is to identify oneself as a member
of a larger entity, based upon those attributes that one carries around
with oneself, namely one's language, historical place, race, religion,
and so on. These then are the basis of a new identity. Modernization
implies the search for this new identity, and hence the importance of
nationalism. Finally, Brass identified a positive relationship between
interethnic competition and modernization. He said: 'Ethnicity and
nationalism are ... political constructions. They are creations of elites
who draw upon, distort, and sometimes fabricate materials from the
cultures of the groups they wish to represent in order to protect their
well-being or existence or *to gain political and economic advantage for their
groups* as well as for themselves [italics mine].'[11] It follows that advantages for one group bias the nature and the outcome of interethnic
competition.

The above overview underscores the lack of a consensus in the
literature pertaining to the relationship between growth and nationalism. As a contribution to this ongoing debate, it is suggested in this
chapter that interethnic competition occurs both during economic
growth as well as economic decline, although the focus of interethnic
animosities is different.

THE REDIRECTION OF INTERETHNIC ANIMOSITIES

Interethnic competition during economic decline was described in
chapter 2 as a struggle, along ethnic lines, for a slice of the dwindling
economic pie. Yet, during economic growth, the pie is growing: the
quantity of available goods and services is increasing, greater numbers
of people are employed to produce those goods and services, they are
receiving income for their labor, and they are consuming and saving
with that income. How does that cycle of expansion, that upswing in
the business cycle, alter the nature of economic competition among
ethnic groups? While the process of ethnic bifurcation is likely to take
place, as it does when the economy is shrinking, it is argued that
the predominant composition of the marginalized group is not the
domestic minority. Instead, animosities become redirected to the most
recent outsiders, the most different outsiders, namely, the newest
immigrants. Four explanations are offered for the refocusing of ethnic
animosities during economic growth: the common perception of
economic prosperity, extensive participation in the global economy,

the logic of ethnic discrimination in capitalism, and the ethnostabilizers built into liberal democracies.

Perception of Economic Prosperity

At the micro level, ordinary individuals assess the health of the economy in a subjective way. In other words, irrespective of what growth statistics indicate, it is one's own reality that signals to people the existence of economic growth. Questions such as 'Am I employed?', 'Does my job pay well?', 'Can I buy sufficient goods and services with my income?', and 'Am I better off today than I was five years ago?' underscore the importance of personal experience in the perception of economic reality. Moreover, expectations about future economic performance, the subjective assessment of one's own opportunities in the economy, and hope for ever-increasing material satisfactions all combine to form a generalized view of the economy. When economic growth has been sustained over time and when it has spread throughout the population, then the popular mood is upbeat and the perception of prosperity is common. It is during such long periods of sustained economic growth, especially the ones that significantly improve overall standards of living, that a social transformation occurs as the population outgrows the visceral concern with mere survival. Having satisfied their basic needs, their attention turns to loftier concerns. It is at such a time of prosperity, real and perceived, that literature, art, and music find a place in the lives and wallets of a population.[12] Museum attendance rises, the travel industry expands, and leisure activities flourish.[13] Moreover, volunteering activities draw the excess time and energy of those who perceive they have more than they need. Voluntary philanthropy (as distinguished from the involuntary kind that is enforced by religious decree, as in Islam[14]) redistributes money, goods, and time from one segment of the population to another.

Assuming that improvements in standards of living are experienced by a broad segment of the population, the resulting overall satisfaction is likely to dampen the *economically induced* animosity among ethnic groups. It will, therefore, decrease the propensity for interethnic competition and will diminish the need to identify a scapegoat on whom to lay the blame for economic ailments. As long as people are employed and have hope for future employment, they are less motivated to blame their own unemployment or lack of work opportunities on other ethnic groups. If people are generally satisfied with their government services and benefits, they are less likely to complain that other religious groups dominate the central government and siphon off 'too many' resources. If the stock market is active and its index rising, stockholders will tend not to care about the ethnicity of their fellow stockholders. Instead, the overall satisfaction emanating from sustained and pervasive economic growth predisposes people to greater interethnic economic cooperation and heightened interethnic tolerance than during adverse economic times. The more sustained the growth over time, the more broadly based and entrenched these characteristics become. Thus, the warning echoed to President Clinton during his electoral campaign, 'It's the economy, stupid!' can also be applied to interethnic relations. When people feel good about the economy and their own place in it, that feeling permeates work relations, social relations, and overall interethnic relations. People become more accepting of differences since the economy has shown its ability to accommodate and absorb those differences and still succeed. The sense of 'If I'm OK, you're OK' prevails. Such tolerance is subtle and discreet (unlike interethnic conflict, interethnic harmony rarely makes headline news).

Therefore, the economic basis for animosity and intolerance among domestic ethnic groups, so evident during acute economic decline, tends to fade in the course of growth. It is precisely because of the potent role played by economic growth in diffusing interethnic hostility and fostering tolerance that scholars and policy makers have pursued policies of economic growth as part of establishing peace (this is discussed further in chapter 8, suffice it to say here that the example of the Dayton Peace Accords, which has a heavy economic component, is a case in point).[15]

Participation in the Global Economy

The growth and development of countries has been tied to the international economy for centuries (witness the role of global trade in eighteenth century imperialism, dependency relations in the twentieth century, export promotion policies of the 1980s and 1990s etc.).[16] What are new in the current era of globalization are the volume and the nature of international economic interaction.[17] Not only has the sheer magnitude of flows of capital, goods, services, and labor increased, but the speed, pervasiveness, and impermanence of international transactions have also become apparent. Moreover, advances in technology and the spread of information have altered the very nature of exchange, specialization, and communication between economic entities. In the course of globalization, a concentration of power in the hands of corporations has undoubtedly occurred (indeed, if the top 100 economies are ranked, 51 are corporations, not countries; the top 200 largest corporations account for 28% of world economic activity; and the 500 largest corporations account for 70% of world trade[18]). At the same time, participation in the global economy decreases the power of state governments to control their own economic destinies as the total economic destiny becomes global. More than ever before, the world truly seems small, with shrinking distances and expanding interdependencies. Those who needed convincing were duly convinced by the Asian financial crisis of the 1990s, when external shocks reverberated quickly across the globe and the social and economic consequences were fast, painful, and all too easily transmitted across countries.

In the late twentieth century, high rates of economic growth have tended to be associated with a global presence and participation in the international economic relations. Countries that trade, exchange, and invest across state boundaries, and countries in which the governing policies are receptive to manifestations of global culture, all have populations that are more likely to have been exposed to different cultures, different economic systems, different races, and different religions. Such exposure to foreigners outside state boundaries underscores the difference between local diversity and international diversity. In other words, exposure to ethnic groups that are 'more different' increases the tolerance for those who are 'less different', local, and by comparison seem reassuringly familiar merely because of their proximity. Interaction in the global economy thus tends to accentuate the closeness of what is closer to home and the distinctiveness of what is farther away. It follows that interethnic tolerance of neighboring groups increases as interethnic *in*tolerance of distant groups increases. Several examples follow. At the turn of the twentieth century, German Jews and Russian Jews in New York did not interact. The arrival of other immigrants, more foreign to both groups, served to obliterate their own differences and solidify their ties.[19] Similarly, when African and Albanian immigrants began arriving in Italy, the popular attitude toward the German-speaking minority in the Sud Tyrol improved dramatically.[20] Finally, one effect of the European Union is the emergence of a stronger bond between Europeans (Germans, French, Spanish etc.) at the expense of others. Indeed, the more international Europeans have become within Europe, the stronger the Eurocentrism that, according to Cesarani and Fulbrook, is 'a sort of higher xenophobia directed against Muslims and the modern version of the Mongol hordes – East Europeans'.[21]

Capitalism and Discrimination

Countries that participate in the globalization process and that sustain high rates of economic growth over the long run tend to be capitalist. Theory has suggested and empirical evidence has consistently shown that sustained economic growth is most likely in a capitalist system.[22] This is because several characteristics of capitalism make it conducive for the proliferation of technological change.[23] Indeed, in a capitalist system, business owners are pressured into adopting the most technologically innovative techniques in order to survive in a highly competitive environment.[24] If they cannot, they will be subsumed by those who can.

In a capitalist economy, the goal of profit maximization underlies production, hiring, and investment decisions. In their quest for profits, employers, lenders, and renters are unlikely to indulge in ethnic discrimination unless it coincides with profit maximization. In other words, minimizing costs and maximizing revenues are more relevant considerations than the ethnicity, race, or religion of the factors of production, *ceteris paribus*. Becker's pioneering study of the labor force introduced discrimination into neoclassical economic analysis and shows that employers' taste for discrimination is subservient to the drive to minimize costs.[25] In Becker's tradition, Williams claimed that discrimination in policy subverts the operation of capitalist forces: 'market allocation tends to exact a penalty from those who engage in racial discrimination' (this was the experience of South African businesses that hired more expensive white workers).[26] Left on its own, the market has no use for race or ethnic differences. This absence of discriminatory practices in capitalism is evident in multinational corporations, where hiring and firing occurs largely in the absence of the exertion of racial or ethnic preferences. Indeed, in his assessment of Asea Brown Boveri Ltd (ABB), Kaplan says: 'Unlike the multiculturalism of the left, which masks individual deficiencies through collective (that is, ethnic or racial) self-esteem, a multinational corporation like ABB has created a diverse multicultural environment in which individuals rise completely on their own merits.'[27]

In multiethnic states, discriminatory policies are often introduced to make one group better off at the expense of another. In effect, this is government interference in the market and as a result, it introduces inefficiency into the economy. Discriminatory policy is addressed in chapter 6, suffice it to say here that in a capitalist system, which shuns inefficiency, there is little room for discrimination. This is not to suggest that discrimination does not exist in capitalist societies – it clearly does – rather, that the discrimination is not economically motivated or justified.

Does this assertion contradict chapter 2, where it was argued that countries in transition from communism to capitalism are in fact experiencing an increase in open discrimination against new minorities? There are three reasons why it does not. First, discrimination occurs because of political as well as economic reasons, hence evidence of discrimination in transition countries can be attributed to sources other than economics. Second, in chapter 2 the discussion focused on the process of transition to capitalism, not the state of capitalism as it is in theory or in reality when fully developed. Indeed, during the process of transition, employer and manager mentality is not fully atuned to capitalism, the supporting institutions are not yet fully evolved, and therefore capitalism is not yet fully developed. Third, in discussing capitalism and discrimination, we are talking about a system that is vibrant, dynamic, and producing economic growth. By contrast, the capitalism discussed in chapter 2 was producing economic decline. It is the decline as much as anything else that is responsible for the increased interethnic animosities.

Ethnostabilizers

A free market economy tends to go hand in hand with liberal Western-style democracy. While there are exceptions, notably highly developed and politically repressive Singapore and South Korea, academic literature as well as empirical evidence has supported the link between a *laissez-faire* economic organization and a democratic political system (chapter 8 explores this link in depth).

Liberal democracies have based their institutions on civil and human rights (not to be confused with the more recent phenomenon, minority rights). These rights are protected by law and prevent discrimination on the grounds of personal characteristics such as race, ethnicity, religion, gender, and age. Rules pertaining to these rights govern the housing market, the job market, the capital market, and the product market. The explicit expression of civic and human rights, such as the Bill of Rights in the United States, serves an important role in liberal democracies: it is the ultimate equalizer. Since all people have the same rights by law, the legal system can be viewed as an ethnostabilizer. Such ethnostabilizers are built into the political system and prevent the institutionalization and the formalization of discrimination against ethnic groups when competition between groups escalates and pressures for discriminatory policies mount. Ethnostabilizers, then, are background rules and regulations that are dormant when not needed but that automatically become activated to protect citizens of all ethnic backgrounds if and when interethnic animosities emerge.

The existence of domestic ethnostabilizers implies that interethnic competition is less likely to be deep and persistent among ethnic groups that are equally protected by the law. These ethnostabilizers serve to dissipate animosities between people who, while hierarchically ranked in income, education, and so on, are equal under the rule of law.

Therefore, as a result of subjective perceptions of economic prosperity, participation in the global economy, discrimination in capitalism and ethnostabilizers, ethnic animosities among domestic groups tend to be less strong during economic growth than during economic decline. During growth, animosities become refocused and aimed at those ethnic groups that find themselves at the political fringes. These are illegal aliens and recent immigrants, in short, the noncitizens. From their fringe position, they cannot participate formally in society, they are not protected legally, they suffer in the economy, and they are inadequately sheltered politically. It is the noncitizens who become the most likely targets of ethnic discrimination and the target of refocused ethnic animosities during sustained economic growth. Few ethnic groups have avoided this targeting when they were recent arrivals and at the bottom of the pecking order.

The concept of 'immigrant community' is broadly interpreted in this book. Since immigrants in the host country retain strong ties with their homelands (enabled by cheap transportation and communication), animosity directed at new immigrants (namely, noncitizens) often extends to their communities in their home countries. In that way, even potential immigrants are targeted and their home countries viewed as hotbeds of further immigration.

Yet it is exactly this link between the immigrant in the host country and the potential immigrant at home that connects the domestic economy to the global economy. It connects domestic interethnic competition to the pushes and pulls that stimulate and enable international migration. For the purposes of this book, the relevant link is immigration policy. It determines who gets to enter, work, and live in a coveted country and who does not, in other words, who goes and who stays. Immigration policy is the response to domestic economic, social, and political circumstances, and as such reflects the sentiment of domestic producers and consumers.

Immigration policy is also the embodiment of interethnic competition in host countries. Policy (as discussed at length in chapter 7), is based on the national mood toward immigrants, and the principal economic variable that determines that mood is employment. Competition for jobs is often acute and visceral, rarely matched by the competition for assets (indeed, with the exception of high profile cases such as the Rockefeller Center in New York or Harrods in London, it is rare that popular opinion is swayed by foreign ownership to the same degree as it is swayed by promotions to save domestic jobs (witness the US call to 'buy American')). Recent and potential immigrants have the ability to disrupt the employment status quo, and for that reason attract an antiethnic sentiment among residents. In other words, recent immigrants are perceived to have the power to reverse the growth trend, to upset the economic balance, and to alter the 'I'm OK, you're OK' reality. They do all this by taking jobs away from those who have them. They force down overall wages by accepting lower wages; they negatively alter the nature of the workplace by introducing diverse methods of interacting and their participation in the workforce produces a deskilling of local labor. The presence of immigrants is tolerated as long as they are limited to certain jobs, ones that members of the domestic labor force will not perform (such as street sweeping in Switzerland). The immigrants' contribution to the economy is deemed acceptable only if it is *Pareto optimal* (in other words, no one is made worse off, and someone is made better off).

While antiimmigrant sentiment is directed at all immigrants, animosity is particularly strong when their ethnicity is distinguished from the mainstream in the host country. In that case, their presence is tolerated if their distasteful ethnicity is successfully camouflaged. For example, they can be made invisible in uniformed unskilled jobs (Swiss street sweepers don bright orange one-piece overall uniforms – the brighter they are, the more successfully they draw attention away from their undesirable race and identity). Such uniforms serve to make immigrants palatable, to mask their diversity and to accentuate their phantom status within the host country. However, if immigrants are of the same ethnicity as the dominant host group, minority ethnicity status and noncitizen status do not coincide. In that case, there is less animosity.

MANIFESTATIONS OF ETHNIC BIFURCATION

Ethnic bifurcation takes place in growing economies when interethnic competition induces empowered domestic groups to orient their animosities toward recent, noncitizen immigrants. While it is common for recent immigrants in all host countries to suffer short-term discrimination and marginalization, the sheer volume of contemporary population movements into high-growth countries has highlighted the ramifications of bifurcation. Even in industrial Western countries, where protection of civil rights is touted domestically and human rights are supported internationally, evidence of marginalization of its noncitizens is clear.

The indicators of economic, political and social marginalization and empowerment are described below.

Economic Indicators

The most obvious economic indicator of ethnic bifurcation is the emergence of a dual labor market. The composition of workers in each of these two labor markets is different: one consists of legal workers (namely, citizens or aliens with working permits) while the other includes illegal workers. Different rules and regulations apply in the two markets, as do different wages, benefits, and working conditions.

The emergence and persistence of this duality reverberates throughout the economy as a result of linkage effects. These linkages are illustrated by the following example. An illegal alien stuck in a low skilled job receives low wages so his ability to purchase goods and services is low and his ability to satisfy his basic needs is low. As a result, his overall standard of living is low. Moreover, his ability to amass and exert economic power within society is low. Since illegal workers operate on the economic fringes, they have no redress to employment and income laws that govern the legal sector. At the same time, workers who are citizens become empowered as they participate in the growing economy and reap its benefits. The disparity between the two groups, as measured by income, opportunities, and power, grows over time in tandem with the growth of the economy.

The composition of the dual labor market is dynamic. When illegal immigrants become citizens, they gain the concomitant rights and privileges. They also gain opportunities and possibly even power. Shain described this dynamism of the labor force. He said that when immigrant groups first arrive in a host country, they tend to be at the end of the job queue but that changes as new immigrants arrive. Indeed, the political and economic clout of the Irish, Italians, and Jews grew when new groups, such as the Koreans, Chinese, and Croats arrived in the US.[28]

Political Indicators

Within politics as within economics, duality is based on citizenship. The political power of citizens is different from that of noncitizens. Not only do noncitizens lack voting rights to indicate their preferences, but they also lack representation to present their demands and protect their interests. Legal institutions only rarely cover them and public services are selectively accessible to them. While domestic organizations exist to look out for the welfare of noncitizens and illegal aliens (such as the Civil Liberties Union in the United States), and international organizations' tenants pertaining to human rights reach across state borders (such as the United Nations' covenants), far too many undocumented workers fall through the cracks.

This is not to imply that all citizens have power. To the contrary, there is evidence of highly dispersed, tiny communities that, while holding the passports of the host country, are too small, too weak, or too unorganized to play any significant political role (for example, the

Sorbs (not Serbs) in Germany; the Vlahs in Bulgaria etc.). However, political empowerment is at least possible upon the granting of citizenship rights. Indeed, ethnic minorities that are citizens have recourse to the system which enables them to express their power.

Social Indicators

Social indicators of ethnic bifurcation during economic growth are similar to those that emerge during decline. They include manifestations of intolerance of minority culture, religion, and language as well as increased incidents of crime and personal distress among the marginalized groups. In the course of economic growth, the marginalized groups are composed largely of recent, noncitizen immigrants. Given the similarity in the manifestations of intolerance, it is not necessary to repeat what was discussed in chapter 2. Instead, the debate pertaining to the eradication of such intolerance toward immigrants is presented below. This debate, ongoing in many host countries across the globe, is rooted in the differing concepts of assimilation and multiculturalism, both of which describe the relationship between a migrant and his or her host society. Host governments have two choices: they may induce assimilation by diverse ethnic groups into the dominant host culture or they may encourage the coexistence of numerous varied cultures. Immigrant countries, such as the United States and Australia, have all favored assimilation into the dominant white, Anglo-Saxon culture at some point in their histories, only to embrace multiculturalism in the 1990s. Canada is most clear at the present time in its effort to promote and accommodate its multiple cultures, races, languages, and ethnicities. It is the nonimmigrant countries, such as Germany, Italy, and France, that are most obviously having difficulty with the institutionalization of diversity. The public outcry over Muslim headscarfs in France is just one of numerous indications of the intolerance of diversity. As noted by Noiriel, each new wave of immigrants is found to be 'nonassimilateable' ('practically every new wave of migrants – from Italy at the end of the nineteenth century, Poland between the wars, North Africa since the 1960s – has met with the same prejudices and pessimistic evaluations of its "assimilability"'[29]).

The distinction between policies of assimilation and multiculturalism and the way in which they are received by resident populations of host countries sheds light on how difficult the eradication of interethnic bifurcation is likely to be. Immigrant countries have proven to be more tolerant of the diverse cultures, religions, and languages in their immigrants' baggage than nonimmigrant countries (this subject is revisited in chapter 8).

ECONOMIC COMPETITION, ETHNIC BIFURCATION, AND
SOURCES OF ECONOMIC GROWTH

Economic growth, as measured by the increase in income per capita,
entails the expanded production of goods and services. This expansion is usually enabled and/or accompanied by the increased
employment of resources, it translates into an increase in both personal
income (as factors of production reap their rewards) as well as public
sector income (as governments collect more revenue). Together, an
expansion of personal and public income enables a rise in the standard
of living as households increase their consumption and savings and as
the public sector increases its social programs and benefits. This expansion of aggregate demand fuels further production and economic
activity.

The pattern of economic growth described above has been experienced by several countries under study: Singapore, Hong Kong,
Australia, Canada, and the United States. With the exception of
Singapore and Hong Kong (that were briefly affected by the Asian
crisis of the 1990s), all countries under study have experienced
continuous growth during the past decade (see table 3.1). In fact, at
the time of writing, the United States is experiencing the most
sustained period of growth in its post-war history: eight straight
quarters of growth, reaching 5.5 percent at the end of 1999. In 1998,
Australia had one of the Western world's fastest-growing economies,
with GDP growth of 4.9 percent.

The speed and breadth of economic growth that occurred in
industrial, Western societies during the twentieth century has been
unprecedented in history. Understanding why countries grow and
why some grow more than others is a primary goal of economists.
Numerous economic theories have claimed that only technological

Table 3.1
Indicators of Economic Performance in Selected Countries, 1990 and 1997

Country	GNP, 1997	GDP/p, 1990	GDP/p, 1997	Growth
Singapore	101.1	10200	15467	7.4
Hong Kong	163.8	9897	12439	3.7
Australia	382.7	13070	15186	2.3
Canada	595.0	15895	16525	0.6
United States	7783.1	19652	21541	1.4

Notes: GNP is given in billions of US $. GDP is given in 1987 US $. Growth refers
        to average annual percent change.
Source: United Nations Development Program, *Human Development Report 1999*,
        Oxford: Oxford University Press, 1999, tables 6 and 11.

change is capable of avoiding diminishing returns in the long run and thus sustaining growth.[30] In other words, in the absence of innovation, the capacity to produce goods and services will fail to grow over time. Yet, it is too simplistic to focus only on technological change, since numerous other factors are also relevant. Indeed, Barro claims that while technological change theories are important for understanding growth as a global phenomenon and growth in countries 'at the technological frontier', they are less applicable in most regions of the world. There, a return to more classical approaches is preferable, ones that incorporate 'government policies (including institutional choices that maintain property rights and free markets), accumulation of human capital, fertility decisions, and the diffusion of technology'.[31] To accommodate both the importance of technology as well as other factors, this chapter discusses the following sources of economic growth: the capacity to generate technological change, the capital with which to apply it, the appropriately skilled labor force to support innovation, the access to markets in which to buy and sell products, and the environment (political, institutional etc.) to enable all this to occur.

An explanation of the qualitative difference between the sources of growth (discussed below) and decline (discussed in chapter 2) is warranted. Economic growth and decline could be viewed as emanating from the same sources, differing only by their presence or absence. For example, growth occurs when there is sufficient human capital and decline occurs when it is absent. Such a simplistic, binary analysis might serve to explain some fluctuations of the business cycle. It might even be used to explain the effects of structural imbalances on economic performance. However, it disregards the potent role played by triggering events in producing economic change. These events, such as war, sanctions, and the transformation of economic systems, are exogenous to the economies and, while rarely perpetual in duration, have the capacity to spin the economy into a downward spiral. In order to include the role of triggering exogenous events into this book, two separate chapters addressed two qualitatively different kinds of sources of economic change.

Technological Innovation

The economic impact of discoveries such as the spinning machine and the steam engine are well documented, as is the benefit of assembly line production processes. Today, information technology, embodied in cheap communications, powerful computers, and the Internet, is expected to have the same momentous effect, hurtling the world into a 'post-industrial revolution' in which tangible goods are becoming less important than ideas. The diffusion of information technology occurs with a lag, as did electricity, the transistor, and the automobile before it. Therefore, we have yet to see the full impact of information technology on societies and economies. Nevertheless, it is already being touted as nothing less than a revolution, producing a full-scale historic and social transformation.

As mentioned in chapter 1, technological change entails new, improved, and cost-saving ways of producing old products, or the production of entirely new products. Sometimes, technological change results in higher output using the same quantity of inputs. More often than not, it entails labor-saving progress in which higher levels of output can be achieved with less labor: computers, mechanical threshers, automated looms, and high-speed electric drills are all examples of products that are more productive than manpower. Indeed, labor-saving technology has drastically increased worker productivity, as the average Western European today is some 20 times more productive than in 1800.[32] Societies with an abundance of entrepreneurs and inventors are the ones most likely to develop, introduce, and profit from such productive technological innovation.[33]

Scholars across disciplines have studied the effect of technological change on economies and societies, as well as the most likely conditions for its proliferation. Kuznets focused on the crucial role of technological change in long-term growth,[34] while Marx touted capitalism as the most growth-promoting mode of production because it is most likely to stimulate technological change.[35] Rosenberg's study of the industrial revolution yielded a framework for the study of the incentives leading economies to innovate technologically,[36] while Mandle supplemented that framework by analyzing the capacity of countries to innovate.[37] However, the connection between technological innovation and interethnic competition has thus far escaped the attention of scholars.

The mechanism by which the proliferation of technological change throughout the economy produces ethnic bifurcation is two-pronged. First, since innovation entails more efficient, labor-saving production methods, labor often becomes displaced. The question of which ethnic group gets displaced is then relevant in assessing ethnic marginalization and empowerment. Second, technological change tends to alter the characteristics of the labor force needed by the economy. While 50 years ago a high school student might have been capable of producing widgets, sophisticated methods of production have increased the qualification standards demanded by today's economy. The question of which ethnic group is best suited to participate in the changing economy is relevant in the study of ethnic bifurcation.

Ethnic differences in labor displacement and economic participation point to unequal benefits of technological change. While evidence pertaining to such inequality exists (such as when Sikhs in the Indian Punjab participated more fully and suffered less displacement from the Green Revolution than Hindus[38]), it tends to be concentrated in the agricultural or manufacturing sectors. However, the evidence pertaining to information sectors and high-tech industries is not clear. The media and popular literature point to the high concentration of Chinese, Indians, and other Asians in the high-tech industries in North America. As long as they are proficient in the English language (the *lingua franca* of the Internet era), they share labor-market advantages with dominant ethnic groups. The increasing proportion of highly skilled Asian immigrants entering the United States, Canada, and Australia (discussed in chapter 7) seem to indicate that an analysis of ethnic bifurcation must take into consideration skills levels as well as ethnicity.

Capital Accumulation

Capital accumulation occurs when some portion of present income is saved and invested in order to augment future output and income. Capital accumulation includes all new investments in land, machinery, and physical equipment. While investment in these is directly related to output, investment in infrastructure (such as roads, sanitation, and communications) indirectly facilitates economic activity.

Economists since the early 1900s have focused on the important role of capital accumulation for economic growth. The Harrod–Domar model of the 1950s formally linked economic growth to the accumulation of capital, and subsequent scholarly research has expanded and strengthened this link.[39] According to the original model, the savings rate is crucial since it is positively related to capital accumulation, which in turn is positively related to output (indeed, evidence from countries with high savings rates, such as Japan, show unequivocal benefit from this source of capital). A deficiency of private savings is compensated for with public savings and debt. If private and public domestic savings are still inadequate for the desired levels of capital accumulation, then international sources of capital can fill the gap. Indeed, multilateral and bilateral flows of capital have compensated for domestic deficiencies and promoted economic growth in Eastern Europe, South America, and so on. Singapore's phenomenal growth is often attributed to the successful encouragement of such capital inflows in the form of direct foreign investment.[40]

It is this external source of capital accumulation that contributes to ethnic bifurcation. Positive and negative externalities of foreign investment and multilateral loans are not borne equally by the host population in general and ethnic groups in particular. When scarce foreign investment flows into a multiethnic country, more often then not it is the dominant ethnic groups that benefit the most, further reinforcing their empowerment. Indeed, they are better positioned to appropriate the in-flowing funds. To the extent that foreign investment involves the employment of domestic workers, the dominant ethnic groups are again better positioned to become employed and stay employed (through better access and more opportunities) than marginalized groups.

Human Capital and Appropriately Skilled Labor

In order to grow, economies require sufficient quantities of labor as well as an appropriate quality of labor. With respect to quantity, it is necessary to identify the optimal size in order to avoid a surplus or shortage of workers. During a surplus, there are too many workers and the economy cannot absorb them. They become redundant and their overabundance acts as a drag on the economy. As a result, workers are forced to emigrate (the concept of FILTH (Failed In London, Try Hong Kong), describing highly skilled Chinese expatriates drawn home for employment, lends a humorous slant to the serious issue of surplus labor[41]). In the case of a worker shortage, supply bottlenecks develop in the production process and economic growth becomes endangered. Due to this potentially limiting effect of labor shortages, leaders enhance their workforce by increasing the size of their populations in two ways. First, they pay attention to their population's fertility rates by introducing pronatalist policies (for example, in light of decreasing birth rates and population replacement rates, the government of Italy has formally expressed concern while the government of Germany has offered financial compensation to induce procreation. In Kazakstan recently, in response to precipitously falling birth rates, television commercials implore viewers to procreate[42] and the government offers 'real money for real children'). However, waiting for pronatalist policies to take effect is often not a viable short-term solution for labor-deficient countries. Instead, they resort to receptive immigration policy. By opening their doors to migrants from other countries, leaders satisfy their country's manpower demands. However, not all leaders are comfortable taking that route. When assessing the costs and benefits of immigration (discussed in chapter 7), they come up with different results. While some are willing to invite guest workers (such as Switzerland), others are reluctant (such as Singapore, a country with one of the most tightly controlled immigration systems in the world[43]).

With respect to the quality of labor, there has been a clear

transformation in the demands of the global economy. In the production processes currently defining the leading world economies,
brainpower is more important than manpower, horsepower, and
material power. Competitive advantage comes from ideas, not things.
Therefore, characteristics of the worker that aid in developing brainpower are now of quintessential importance. Education, skills, and
training, all embodied in a loose definition of human capital, are
relevant insofar as they determine the extent to which a worker is
adaptable to new conditions, willing to think creatively, take risks,
follow instructions, respond to incentives etc.). The skills in demand
change in tandem with the changing demands of the economy. While
the need for low skilled workers was high during the early stages of
industrialization, the demand for highly skilled workers is stronger
today. How do countries acquire human capital? They can train
workers or they can import them. Training takes time and benefits are
realized only with a lag, because 'the economy transforms itself a lot
faster than the educational and training system does'.[44] Indeed,
technological change is so broad and rapid that it sometimes outstrips
the ability of a country's educational system to keep up with its manpower demands (a study conducted by the Information Technology
Association of America predicted that employers in the United States
would need some 1.6 million additional information technology
workers by January 2001 and that they would not come close to filling
those jobs because there simply were not enough skilled workers
available). Alternatively, countries open their doors to skilled immigrants. Because skilled workers will be skimmed off the top wherever
they are in the world, Stalker predicts that there will be more labor
mobility in the twenty-first century because of the revolution in
information and communication technologies that will need more and
different workers in order to sustain itself.[45]

However, simply amassing highly skilled human capital is not a
sufficient condition for economic growth. The human capital must be
appropriate for local conditions otherwise its productivity enhancing
properties cannot be fully exploited. Indeed, not all economies, at all
times, require a highly qualified labor force. As education economist
Mark Blaug pointed out, in countries at low levels of development,
the economic benefits of primary education are higher than university education.[46] Even the high-growth economies such as Canada,
Australia, and the United States need a wide variety of skills to satisfy
the wide range of manpower demands. They often have to import low-
skilled workers because the domestic economy fails to produce enough
of them. The German post-war experience shows clearly that low-
skilled workers were required for the economy at the reconstruction
stage of development (a demand satisfied by the importation of labor

through the *Gastarbeiter* program).[47] Moreover, Canada,[48] and more recently Spain,[49] also import low-skilled labor (while at the same time, they require highly skilled workers for their economies' needs).

Efforts to achieve the appropriate quantity of labor (through pronatalist policies and immigration) as well as the appropriate quality (through investment in human capital and immigration) may sometimes inadvertently induce and/or reinforce ethnic bifurcation in the following ways. First, pronatalist policies aimed at inducing procreation may discriminate against the marginalized ethnic groups and favor the empowered ones. The goal of such a two-tier policy is to increase the size of the desirable population and decrease the relative size of the undesirable one. Evidence of such behavior is plentiful. Not only did Nazi Germany explicitly promulgate the expansion of the Aryan race through a variety of pronatalist policies, but more recently, Romania allowed a birth control program to be enforced among the Roma population that was banned among the Romanians, who were encouraged to procreate.[50] In India, the forced sterilization program instituted by Sanjay Gandhi in 1976 was interpreted by the Muslims as a direct attack on their polygamous lifestyles (which then resulted in interreligious riots and contributed to the fall of the government in 1977).[51]

Second, the economic, political, and social position of the local marginalized population may deteriorate as a result of immigration. Competition with incoming workers may further perpetuate their marginalized status. Not all immigrants are a threat, only those whose skills are in direct competition or who indirectly displace local marginalized workers. Olzak studied blacks in the United States and showed that job opportunities of African Americans decreased as the occupational mobility of white immigrants improved.[52] Also, in Canada the indigenous population residing in Manitoba has suffered in the labor market due to the high supply of immigrants: it has been said that Winnipeg's 'business establishment prefers its Indians from New Delhi rather than Dakota Tipi, a village 50 miles down the Trans-Canada Highway'.[53]

Third, investment in human capital is not the same across ethnic groups. There is ample evidence that discriminatory practices in access, opportunity, and financial incentives for education and training tilt the ethnic composition of potential participants. In the process, the preexisting ethnic bifurcation is further reinforced. This topic is discussed in chapter 6, suffice it to say here that while marginalized groups may have different admission requirements than the empowered groups, they may be charged different amounts, they may be denied certification of competency, or they may simply be denied basic education. Such impediments to the accumulation of human capital by members of a marginalized ethnic group serve to further diminish their economic and political participation in society.

Fourth, ethnic bifurcation is reinforced by inequality in the welcome that ethnic groups in host countries receive. To the extent that discrimination against some undesirable groups exists in immigration policies, their inflows are curtailed. A low position in the immigration pecking order also reflects (and at the same time further reinforces) that group's marginal economic, political, and social status. While the ethnic component of immigration policies is discussed in chapter 7, a few examples here illustrate this issue. In Hong Kong, Chinese immigrants from the mainland are viewed as undesirable (ostensibly they are unwelcome because they strain social services, although it has also been said that they are unwelcome because they are perceived as 'unwashed'[54]). As a result, their immigration is restricted. In Canada, the points system of qualification for entry during the 1970s was inherently biased toward immigrants from rich countries.[55] By extension, non-European nationals were not as welcome as white Europeans. Even in its census forms, Canada uses the term 'visible minorities' to distinguish those who are visibly different.[56] Moreover, in the Canadian province of Quebec, an explicit pro-French language bias exists in immigration policy (due to a special arrangement with the federal center, Quebec has its own immigration policy, entirely independent of the center). Finally, due to an influx of non-European immigrants, Western European countries are tightening immigration policy to stem the flows from North Africa and sub-Saharan Africa. As a result, African residents of Western Europe have become even more marginalized as the antiimmigrant bias reaches them, despite their residence, work permits, and even citizenship.

Access to Markets

In order to ensure sustained economic growth, a country must have access to markets both for the sale of its output and the purchase of its inputs. Those countries with sufficient domestic demand for output and domestic supply of inputs need not actively search for international markets. In reality, it is rare that countries do not reach out into the global economy for the most low-cost alternatives and the most lucrative sales. Economists have long argued that international trade and participation in the international financial markets are positively related to economic growth.[57] Some short-term exceptions to this lead countries to erect trade barriers, restrict the flow of foreign investment, curtail the activities of multinational organizations, restrict immigration and emigration, limit exposure to foreign cultures, restricted tourism, and so on. Recently, the phenomenal growth experienced by four Asian countries – Taiwan, Hong Kong, South Korea, and Singapore – reignited the hope that export-oriented policies are the panacea for small countries.[58] Such promotion of exports of manufactured goods (rather than primary products) during the 1970s and 1980s increased foreign exchange earnings, improved the trade balance, and stimulated growth in these four countries. Clearly, domestic policies of export promotion were aided by the high demand for their exports faced by these countries, as well as high personal savings rates, low interest rates, and low deficit spending.

The effect of market access on ethnic bifurcation is similar to the effect of capital accumulation and the development of human capital described above. One unique effect follows directly from increased international trade and its concomitant emphasis on the cost consideration: namely, the lower the price of labor, the more competitive the product it produces, *ceteris paribus*. In theory, a strict adherence to cost considerations implies that the lowest-cost labor will be employed. However, in reality, that does not mean that marginalized, low-income, unskilled ethnic groups will benefit from globalization. Some may, but the evidence is that production simply moves away to regions where wages are lower and benefits, as prescribed by law, are smaller. A poignant example is Singapore. Its population is said to be the best educated in the world. As a result, labor costs are high, prompting businesses to shift production to other places (Singapore produces in south China as well as in Johore (Malaysia) and the Riau archipelago (Indonesia)). A similar reasoning led Hong Kong to move its base of production to Guangdong province in south China. In both cases, industrial production shifted abroad while service production stayed at home (inducing Rosencrance to call these countries 'virtual states'[59]).

To conclude this section on the sources of economic growth and ethnic bifurcation, a return to chapter 1 is warranted. There, it was suggested that interethnic competition is altered by economic change. Indeed, the established ways in which ethnic groups compete for scarce resources is discombobulated when rapid or abrupt growth or decline occurs. During this process of change, some ethnic groups become empowered and others become marginalized, as is evident in the economic, political, and social spheres. But more than mere change is relevant. Both the direction and the source of economic change shed light on the complexity of interethnic competition. This chapter shows that the direction of change, namely growth or decline, is important in determining the composition of the marginalized groups and the focus of the interethnic animosities on the part of the dominant groups. In other words, during economic decline, when the overall economy is shrinking, interethnic competition becomes accentuated while, during economic growth, when the economy is expanding, animosities turn to the outside and manifest themselves in feelings toward recent immigrants.

Moreover, the sources of economic growth and decline are also relevant because they determine how deep and how entrenched the bifurcation between ethnic groups is. As argued in chapter 2, the source of growth matters because different sources have different effects on the economy. In the discussion of economic decline, it was mentioned that issues such as the speed of recovery, discriminatory policy, lack of international pressure, duration of event, and outside involvement are relevant in determining the depth of ethnic bifurcation. In a discussion of economic growth, another variable is important, namely expectations about the future. Continuity, reliability, and predictability of the source of growth are all embodied in this term. Will the source of growth continue into the future? Is its supply predictable? Can we base future expectations on its reliability? And, can we predict its continued presence? These are all questions that, if answered in the affirmative by economic participants, can stimulate growth. How do countries differ in their future growth outlook? A country that has a proven capacity to innovate and produce technological change and apply it to the market has greater chances of long-term growth than a low-income country that, through an agreement for technology transfer, is able to put its hands on some (outdated) innovation. A country that has the capacity to generate capital for investment is more likely to have continuous growth than one that relies on the vagaries and fickleness of foreign aid or direct investment. A country that has the ability to produce its own human capital or attract it from the global labor markets has greater prospects for future growth, and so on. When the source of growth is unreliable and when its future cannot be predicted, then the soothing effect of growth on interethnic animosities is less likely. The source of economic growth or decline is therefore important.

ETHNIC VERSUS REGIONAL ECONOMIC COMPETITION

In multiethnic societies in which substate divisions are drawn according to ethnic, religious, or linguistic lines, the distinction between ethnic and regional economic competition is often blurred. In other words, it is difficult to determine just how much competition between peoples is due to their ethnicity and how much to their regional affiliation. For example, when Slovenes and Punjabis (in Yugoslavia and India, respectively) competed for resources with other constituent regions in their federations, it was hard to decipher if they were competing on the basis of their regional or ethnic affiliation. Similar situations arose in the Soviet Union, Czechoslovakia, Canada, and Spain. Why is it important to identify the basis of the competition? The answer is because when ethnic or religious distinctions coincide with regional administrative boundaries, then the soil is fertile for the emergence of a nationalist and perhaps even separatist movement.

When ethnic and administrative boundaries do not coincide, then interethnic competition is merely regionalism. In that case, competition cannot spill over into demands that are nationalist in origin or aspiration (in the United States and Italy, for example, there is no nationalist sentiment because there is no association between ethnic identity and the region).

Irrespective of whether ethnic and regional boundaries coincide, competition is influenced by the regional level of development. When regions are at different levels of development, then interregional animosities may emerge in both the less as well as the more developed regions. In the former, dissatisfaction with the central government emerges because residents perceive they are getting too little (this was the case of Slovakia before the break-up of Czechoslovakia); in the latter, dissatisfaction occurs because residents perceive that the central government is siphoning too much (in some regions, the result is limited to a simple tax revolt; in others, a major social and political movement grows, as it has in Italy). The relevance of regional inequality for interethnic competition is underscored by the example of the former Yugoslavia, in which economics have so clearly become associated with nationality. Simmie and Dekleva claim that the pre-break-up distribution of economic resources underlies the chaos of the 1990s since the basis of interethnic conflicts is the 'economic wars between the richer northern republics and the poorer southern ones'.[60] The former Yugoslav republic of Slovenia (inhabited almost exclusively by the Slovenes) was 7.5 times wealthier than Kosovo (inhabited mostly by Albanians).[61] When economic development becomes an ethnic issue, it provides a conduit between nationalism and economics.

NOTES

1 While the discussion below explores the effects of the economy on nationalism, Aleksander Gershenkron instead explored the role nationalism plays on economic development. He claimed that nationalism enables a society 'to break through the barriers of stagnation in a backward country, to ignite the imaginations of men, and to place their energies in the service of economic development'. This view helps us understand his definition of nationalism as 'an ideology of delayed industrialization'. Aleksander Gershenkron, *Economic Backwardness in Historical Perspective* (Cambridge, MA: Harvard University

Press), p. 29. Nationalism is further seen as a conduit for economic growth insofar as it enables, according to Ernest Geller, communication through a literate, educated culture, and serves as a bond among like peoples. Ernest Geller, 'The Dramatis Personae of History', *East European Politics and Societies* 4, 1 (1990), p. 132.

2 See Anthony Smith, *The Ethnic Revival* (London: Cambridge University Press, 1981), pp. 1–3.

3 Karl Deutsch, *Nationalism and Social Communication*, 2nd edn (Cambridge, MA: MIT Press, 1966), and *Nationalism and its Alternatives* (New York: Knopf, 1969); Samuel Huntington, *Political Order in Changing Societies* (New Haven: Yale University Press, 1968).

4 This view is attributed to Otto Bauer, and discussed in Alexander J. Motyl, 'From Imperial Decay to Imperial Collapse: The Fall of the Soviet Empire in Comparative Perspective' in Richard L. Rudolph and David F. Good (eds), *Nationalism and Empire: The Habsburg Empire and the Soviet Union* (New York: St Martin's Press, 1992), p. 28.

5 This view is held by Michael Hechter in *Internal Colonialism* (Berkeley: University of California Press, 1975), and Tom Nairn in *The Break-Up of Britain* (London: New Left Books, 1997).

6 Walter Connor, 'Nation Building or Nation Destroying?', *World Politics* 24 (1972), p. 344.

7 Immanuel Wallerstein, *Africa: The Politics of Independence* (New York: Vintage, 1961), p. 88.

8 James G. Kellas, *The Politics of Nationalism and Ethnicity* (New York: St Martin's Press, 1991), p. 3.

9 Ibid., p. 164

10 Ernest Gellner, *Thought and Change* (Oxford: Basil Blackwell, 1964), pp. 147–78.

11 Paul Brass, *Ethnicity and Nationalism: Theory and Comparison* (New Delhi: Newbury Park, 1991), p. 8.

12 This trend is described by numerous futurologists, as well as by Alvin Toffler in his popular book *The Third Wave* (New York: Bantam Books, 1991).

13 In the United States, spending on leisure activities grew from 2 to 3% of GDP in the early 1900s to some 10% at the end of the twentieth century. *Economist*, 11 September 1999, Twentieth-Century Survey, p. 11.

14 Such involuntary philanthropy is discussed in chapter 4 below.

15 See, for example, Milica Z. Bookman, *Economic Decline and Nationalism in the Balkans* (New York: St Martin's Press, 1994).

16 It must be noted, however, that the degree of global integration has not grown constantly over the past century. Indeed, high trade barriers of the 1920s and 1930s prevented that, along with immigration controls, bans on foreign investments in some countries, bans on cultural exchanges. Many of these interferences, politically induced, reduced the potential of international exchange during this century.

17 See Peter Stalker, *Workers Without Frontiers. The Impact of Globalization on International Migration* (Boulder, CO: Lynne Rienner, 2000), pp. 6–8.

18 Robert Kaplan, *The Coming Anarchy* (New York: Random House, 2000), p. 81.

19 Stephen Birmingham, *Our Crowd: The Great Jewish Families of New York* (Syracuse: Syracuse University Press, 1996).

20 This region, annexed by Italy from Austro-Hungary in 1911, is populated by German speakers who have developed a relationship of autonomy within Italy. In a study by Jens Woelk, he shows that their position has changed with the arrival of immigrants. Jens Woelk, 'The Case of South Tyrol: A Model for

Conflict Resolution in the Balkans', paper presented to the meeting of the Association for the Study of Nationalities New York, 13 April 2000.

21 David Cesarani and Mary Fulbrook, 'Introduction', in David Cesarani and Mary Fulbrook (eds), *Citizenship, Nationality and Migration in Europe* (London: Routledge, 1996), p. 3.

22 For a good discussion of the growth promoting tendencies of capitalism and a review of literature, see Jay Mandle, *Patterns of Caribbean Development* (New York: Gordon and Breach, 1982), chapter 2. For empirical evidence of growth, see Jay Mandle, 'Basic Needs and Economic Systems', *Review of Social Economy*, 38, 2 (1980).

23 These characteristics include the private ownership of the means of production, a free labor force that hires out its labor for pay, the progressive concentration of capital, and production for the market.

24 For a discussion of the role of technology in capitalism, see M. Zarkovic, *Issues in Indian Agricultural Development* (Boulder, CO: Westview Press, 1987), chapter 8.

25 See Gary S. Becker, *The Economics of Discrimination*, 2nd edn (Chicago: University of Chicago Press, 1971).

26 Walter Williams, *South Africa's War Against Capitalism* (New York: Praeger, 1989), p. 70.

27 Robert Kaplan, *The Coming Anarchy*, p. 82.

28 Yossi Shain, *Marketing the American Creed Abroad* (Cambridge: Cambridge University Press, 2000).

29 Review of *The French Melting Pot: Immigration, Citizenship and National Identity* by Gerard Noiriel, *Foreign Affairs* 75, 6 (1996), p. 156, cited in Jeannette Money, *Fences and Neighbors. The Political Geography of Immigration Control* (Ithaca: Cornell University Press, 1999), p. 215.

30 See Gene Grossman and Elhanan Helpman, *Innovation and Growth in the Global Economy* (Cambridge, MA: MIT Press, 1991); Paul Romer, 'Endogenous Technological Change', *Journal of Political Economy* 98, 5 (1990); Phillipe Aghion and Peter Howitt, 'A Model of Growth Through Creative Destruction', *Econometrica* 60, 2 (1992).

31 Robert J. Barro, *Determinants of Economic Growth* (Cambridge, MA: MIT Press, 1988), p. x.

32 *Wall Street Journal*, 28 December 1999.

33 What conditions give rise to entrepreneurs? See section on Schumpeter in Benjamin Higgins, *Economic Development: Principles, Problems and Policies* (New York: Norton, 1959), pp. 88–105.

34 Simon Kuznets, *Economic Growth of Nations* (Cambridge, MA: Harvard University Press, 1971), chapter 1.

35 See discussion on Marx, technological change and economic development in Mandle, *Patterns of Caribbean Development*, chapter 2.

36 See Nathan Rosenberg, *Perspective on Technology* (Cambridge: Cambridge University Press, 1976), especially chapters 6 and 8.

37 Jay Mandle, *The Roots of Black Poverty* (Durham: Duke University Press, 1978).

38 For a discussion of labor displacement, see Zarkovic, *Indian Agricultural Development*, chapters 3 and 4.

39 The Harrod–Domar model is named after two economists, Roy Harrod and Evesey Domar, who concurrently but separately developed the theory in the 1950s.

40 The (anticommunist) countries of East Asia were also the recipients of United States economic and military aid which unequivocally fueled their growth. Dictatorial regimes there provided the 'best business climate' for Japanese and

American capital. See Kwang Yeong Shin, 'The Political Economy of Economic Growth in East Asia' in Eun Mee Kim (ed.), *The Four Asian Tigers* (San Diego: Academic Press, 1998), p. 18.

41 Stalker, *Workers Without Frontiers*, p. 113.

42 *Economist*, 3 April 1999, p. 35.

43 Singapore has imposed a monthly levy on employers who hire foreign workers. This means to reduce incentives to use foreign labor was not very successful, since in 1996 immigrants were still some 20% of the labor force. Stalker, *Workers Without Frontiers*, p. 84. It is noted that in the past, Singapore tried to fuel its economy without taking the 'easy option' of importing cheap foreign labor. For a while, it found that a regulated pool of foreign workers could serve well in a recession, as long as they could be laid off and sent home.

44 *Wall Street Journal*, 10 April 2000.

45 Stalker, *Workers Without Frontiers*, p. xi.

46 Mark Blaug, *Education and the Employment Problem in Developing Countries* (Geneva: International Labor Office, 1974).

47 The expansion of the West German economy, or the *Wirtschaftswunder* (economic miracle) was enabled by the expansion of its labor force which was not domestic in origin. Indeed, while the internal birth rate did indeed grow and even mirrored the US baby boom in a smaller scale, it was insufficient to satisfy the manpower demands during reconstruction and expansion. During the 1950s Germany instituted the *Gastarbeiter* system according to which temporary workers would be allowed into Germany on a temporary basis.

48 In Canada unskilled immigrants are demanded by the economy in a wide range of functions. There is evidence that simply knowing native tongues is sufficient for some types of jobs: Toronto has residents from 169 countries speaking over 100 languages. This enabled Ontario to establish over 3,000 call centers, in which companies such as American Express and IBM handle inquiries from all over the world.

49 Spain's economy currently has a shortage of low-skilled workers. Yet, it has trouble filling the gap because of EU regulations that ban work permits for outsiders from the community (a source of much disagreement between members since the more developed, northern Europe was able to import its labor legally when it needed it in the 1970s). *Economist*, 2 January 1999, p. 41.

50 Bookman, *The Demographic Struggle for Power* (London: Frank Cass, 1997), p. 84.

51 Ibid., p. 98.

52 Susan Olzak, *The Dynamics of Ethnic Competition and Conflict* (Stanford: Stanford University Press, 1992), p. 135.

53 Business leaders have been desperate to attract migrants to the area in order to fill jobs, offering attractive incentives. *New York Times*, 25 December 1999.

54 *Economist*, 6 March 1999.

55 He also claimed that Canada admitted proportionately twice as many European immigrants as the United States. William Watson, *Globalization and the Meaning of Canadian Life* (Toronto: University of Toronto Press, 1998).

56 This refers to the 1996 census, which also lists over 200 countries for possible birth of immigrants.

57 See, for example, Hla Myint's pioneering work *The Economics of the Developing Countries*, 4th edn (London: Hutchinson, 1973).

58 For some recent assessments of the success of the Four Tigers, along with the effects of the financial crisis of 1977, see Victor Mattel, *The Trouble with Tigers: The Rise and Fall of South-East Asia* (New York: HarperCollins, 1999); Robert

Garran, *Tigers Tamed: The End of the Asian Miracle* (Honolulu: University of Hawaii Press, 1998); Ross McLeod and Ross Garnaut (eds), *East Asia in Crisis: From Being a Miracle to Needing One?* (London: Routledge, 1998).

59 By employing Chinese firms to produce for them, they are avoiding dealing with hiring and bringing in new labor when there are shortages (they are also avoiding buying land, building buildings, and installing machinery). Rosencrance, *The Rise of the Virtual State* (New York: Basic Books, 1999), p. 109.

60 James Simmie and Joze Dekleva, *Yugoslavia in Turmoil: After Self-Management?* (London: Pinter Publishers, 1991), p. xvii.

61 Egon Zizmond, 'The Collapse of the Yugoslav Economy', *Soviet Studies* 44, 1 (1992), p. 110.

4

Voluntary Migration: Capacities and Incentives

A white South African family foregoes plans for emigration because restrictions on the export of capital prevent the expatriation of its assets. A 32-year-old Czech engineer is lured by the high salaries in the West and plans to leave his home town. A middle-aged Russian doctor is discouraged from emigrating to the United States because of the seemingly insurmountable obstacles associated with obtaining the appropriate occupational license. A Japanese worker from Osaka cannot even contemplate moving to Tokyo because the costs associated with the loss of seniority are unlikely to be offset by the benefits of new employment. Finally, an impoverished share-cropper in rural India considers his cousin's invitation to join him in Queens as the only way to save his children from a life of *de facto* indentured servitude.

These examples underscore the broad range of pushes and pulls that influence potential migrants. While some are shared equally by all citizens, most pushes and pulls are not experienced equally by the population. Although this inequality may be based on gender, education, location of residence, and wealth, for the purposes of this book it is the inequality based on ethnic, racial, religious, or linguistic orientation that is relevant. Such inequality manifests itself in the differing ability of different ethnic groups to respond to economic stimuli to migrate as well as in their ability to overcome impediments to their mobility. This chapter addresses this interethnic inequality.

The above examples also underscore the broad range of what is considered voluntary migration. While the South African family and the Indian share-cropper may believe that they lack free choice in staying or leaving, their dilemmas are qualitatively different from what they would be during involuntary migration. The difference between voluntary and involuntary flows is discussed below, although only the former is studied in this chapter while the latter is addressed in chapter 5.

FREE CHOICE IN MIGRATION DECISIONS

While there is little doubt that population movements have been a persistent component of world history, there is disagreement about classifying movements as voluntary or involuntary. Some movements clearly fall into one of those categories, such as the forced resettlement of Cossacks during the Stalin era and the economically motivated immigration from Italy to America at the turn of the last century. However, most migrations fall in the shady area between these two extremes, making it very difficult to distinguish between voluntary and involuntary movements. For example, when residency permits of 46,000 Vietnamese workers in the Czech Republic were suddenly withdrawn at the stroke of a pen, is the resulting out-migration voluntary?[1] The answer is unclear, indicating that involuntary migration includes not only forced departures at gunpoint but also more subtle forms of coercion such as revoking licenses and denying property rights. Thus, migration should be viewed as a continuum with purely voluntary migration and purely involuntary migration at the two ends of the spectrum.[2]

Voluntary population movements result from a personal cost/benefit analysis that indicates relocation will maximize utility. The choice to migrate is assumed to be rational; the process of assessing costs and benefits is assumed to be an informed one. Most voluntary migrations are motivated by expected economic benefits, namely a better job including higher wages, improved working conditions, greater status, more possibility for advancement, increased job satisfactions, and so forth. Sometimes the voluntary migrant bases his/her decision on nonpecuniary considerations, such as family bonds, political inclinations, and so forth. Whatever the motivation, the migrant exercises free choice in the migration decision.

During forced (or involuntary) migration, the decision to migrate is imposed on the individual. Involuntary migration includes both the forcible physical removal of individuals as well as the exertion of pressures that make survival in the present location untenable. Either way, people are evicted or transferred. The practice of forced population transfers has gained notoriety in the 1990s because there has been a global increase in involuntary migrants: in 1992 more than 20 million refugees fled from communal conflicts.[3] Within the territory of the former Yugoslavia alone, there are over 4 million displaced persons.[4] While these numbers pale in comparison to the number of Afghani or Palestinian refugees (4.6 million and 2.7 million respectively), they nevertheless represent a significant demographic shift of a pre-war population of 22 million.[5]

While the odds for involuntary immigrants are largely against their staying, they nevertheless make a rational assessment, in which death may factor as a cost. Benefits may be calculated as continued living, the possibility of refugee status in a host country, and the hopes for a new beginning elsewhere. Alternatively, in cases when there is a possibility of a population exchange, then migrants have the hope of resettlement in the home of a reciprocally undesirable individual from another region (such as in the case of Muslims and Hindus in Punjab in the aftermath of Independence, or Greeks and Turks in 1922–23).

The above bimodal division of population migration into voluntary and involuntary movements does not distinguish between ethnic groups. Yet, for the purposes of this study, this distinction is important. In voluntary migration, ethnicity often determines the capacity and incentive to migrate (as discussed below). In involuntary migration, ethnicity is again important because expelled populations are often targeted specifically by their ethnicity (as discussed in chapter 5). Indeed, the forced Muslim exodus from Myanmar was the result of a policy aimed specifically at the Muslim population; the Armenian expulsion from Turkey was not intended to include Turks.

INCENTIVE AND CAPACITY TO MIGRATE

Hirschman proposed a micro-level framework for analyzing individual choice in order to explain behavior. He said that when an organization fails to meet its expectations, individuals can express their disappointment in the form of exit (namely, stop buying the products) or voice (namely, protest in hopes of changing the objectionable practices).[6] Ahmed applies this framework to migration:[7] an individual will migrate if the location of residence fails to live up to its economic, social, and/or political expectations.

When the home country does not meet the economic expectations of a potential migrant (especially with respect to employment and income), such failure is a push that induces emigration. At the same time, economic expectations pertaining to opportunities in the host country exert a pull on the migrant. Potential migrants calculate, implicitly or explicitly, their chances of finding employment that is preferable to their current one (in terms of salary, benefits, future prospects, working conditions etc.). While numerous economists, including Hicks, Lewis, Ranis and Fei, Harris and Todaro, and Todaro, have focused on these economic considerations in migration, others have stressed that migration decisions cannot be viewed strictly in economic terms.[8] Instead, the decision to migrate is made on the basis of economic and noneconomic considerations. While determining which of these is the single most important can only be realistically done on a case-by-case basis, some broad outlines of economic and noneconomic considerations that determine the propensity to migrate are described below.

To enable an assessment of capacities and incentives to voluntarily migrate, four variables are introduced: institutions, infrastructure, personal characteristics, and government policy. These variables also determine labor mobility insofar as they describe what facilitates mobility, what contributes to the push and pull of workers, and what smoothes out their relocation process. At the same time, these four variables also encompass the obstacles to mobility. As such, each of them determines the capacity as well as the incentive to migrate. Not all features of all four variables are relevant in all countries, and certainly not all are relevant across all ethnic groups and professions. They are discussed below, with the exception of government policy which is discussed separately in chapters 6 and 7.

Institutions

An institution is a set of norms, rules of conduct, and generally accepted ways of doing things. Social institutions are well-defined, formal organizations of society that govern the way that society operates (examples include the class system and the system of property rights). Political institutions are the systems that govern the operations of the government of a particular society (including formal power structures, political parties, and mechanisms for obtaining power).[9] The principal institutions that affect workers' capacities and incentives to migrate are the religion that they practice, the culture in which they live, the family they are a part of, and the labor market within which they seek their livelihood. Clearly, an institution that values and rewards independence, creativity, hard work, innovation, and change is more likely to instill in its members the incentive to push off into new lands and new opportunities.

Religion
Undoubtedly, religion has an influence on economics, and by extension, also on migration. Given that religions prescribe acceptable rules of human interaction, it follows that economic behavior and people's roles as buyers, sellers, and otherwise participants in the economy are influenced by their religious values. Three features, relevant for economic behavior, are universal across religions: first, religious rules cannot be disputed, since doing so is viewed as disputing the teachings of God. Second, religious rules are based upon voluntary adherence because people fear God and are therefore motivated to follow God's prescribed path for them. Doing so results in rewards in the afterlife;

failing to do so results in punishment. Finally, rules governing human behavior were established during an earlier historical period and were amended only rarely. It is with difficulty and much accommodation that they are applied to twentieth-century economies (for example, the Islamic rules of taxation, which determine a man's wealth by the size of his land holdings, are no longer relevant in an industrial society in which women (as well as men) possess wealth and in which land is not the primary taxable asset).

Selected religions are described below, with special reference to those characteristics that affect migration. It should not be assumed that religious adherents follow all prescribed rules for behavior and uphold an identical worldview. Indeed, as noted by Hefner, we must assume heterogeneity and plurality in interpretation of all religions and cultures.[10]

Confucianism is pervasive among the populations of Hong Kong, Singapore, Korea, Taiwan, China, and Japan. Chan points out that even in countries where other religions are more popular (such as Malaysia), the Chinese (Confucian) community dominates commerce and industry, exhibiting the success emanating from adherence to values that are embedded in their religion.[11] Confucianism values frugality, hard work, family loyalty, respect for authority, respect for education, achievement orientation, a sense of personal obligation to group welfare (at the expense of individualism), and meritocratic institutions (that select elites at an early age). What do such values have to do with economics and ultimately with migration? The emphasis on frugality stimulates household savings, ensuring a reservoir of funds to cover the costs of relocation. The willingness to work hard and the motivation to achieve are conducive to overall increases in production and productivity, as well as to migration (in order to better oneself, even at the cost of harder working conditions in the new location). The respect for education ensures a popular effort to build the human capital stock, as well as an investment in oneself that is likely to pay off in future job searches in foreign lands. The Confucian emphasis on hierarchy can both retard economic growth (insofar as it limits occupational mobility) and stimulate it (insofar as it fosters inequality, which underlies the emergence of the heroic entrepreneur, envisioned by Schumpeter to be the cornerstone of economic growth[12]). The emphasis on respect for authority tends to hamper creativity and foster conformity, a deadly trait in the effort to modernize. (The effects of this are evident in Singapore, where the government is openly concerned with the lack of creativity among its population. Creativity is necessary to compete in the information economy, yet traditional Confucianist culture suffocates it).[13] The emphasis on both hierarchy and authority exerts a pull on the potential migrant, discouraging migration (since family loyalty, respect for authority, and a sense of obligation to the group all favor staying together and staying in one place).

Islam dominates in parts of Africa, Asia, and the Middle East, guiding the lives of millions of people worldwide. The behavioral norms, laid out in the Koran and the Sunna, promote social responsibility and altruism (thus defining *Homo Islamicus* as preferable to the neoclassical *Homo Economicus*). In production, these norms dictate how much people can earn and how they must treat others; in consumption, they dictate what can be consumed and under which circumstances.[14] Moreover, behavioral norms dictate that Islamic men must pay *zakat*, a tax that varies with their wealth (and that forms the basis of fiscal policy because it takes from those who have and redistributes to those who have not).[15] Finally, interest payments on investment are carefully guarded by Islamic governments since the practice of *riba* (an ancient form of moneylending) has been banned by the Koran. While Christianity and Judaism also have explicit views on interest, Islam alone actually tries to enforce its religious views, especially in Pakistan and Iran.[16] In their efforts, Islamic leaders encounter resistance. Since modern economies require compensation for foregone consumption (savings and investments), interest has an ambiguous function in Islamic economies.[17]

Following these norms and rules, the strict adherence to Islam produces a focus on social issues that, according to some scholars, is counterproductive to modern economic growth (according to Timur Kuran, a focus on individual pursuit of economic needs would stimulate the economy more[18]). What is the effect of Islamic values and rules on migration? Once again, the religious practices can produce both a push and a pull. The emphasis on social responsibility and the inconsistencies associated with interest may prove too cumbersome for some individuals. Alternatively, the economic and social security provided by a system that professes not to abandon its poor, destitute, and unemployed may act as a deterrent to migration into unknown lands with unknown prospects. In addition, the role of the community is important. Islamic law and tradition do not allow for the voluntary building of a life in a non-Islamic country. Indeed, Lewis has argued that the early interpretations of the Koran only accounted for involuntary residence of a Muslim in a non-Islamic environment.[19] Later and more moderate interpretations condone the migration of Muslims and their residence in non-Islamic states provided that they adhere to the edicts of Islam and also that they attempt to convert nonbelievers into their faith.[20] Ahmed has described how Islam (as well as Hinduism) is an obstacle to migration since 'both Islam and Hindusim do not encourage the pious to go outside their own civilisational sphere.

Traditionally high-caste Hindus were not supposed to cross the sea and abandon India. Similarly, Islam divided the world into the *Dar-ul-Islam* (abode of peace where Muslims were in power) and *Dar-ul-Harb* (abode of war, where the enemies of Islam held power).'[21]

The Protestant religion, popular in the United States, Canada, and Australia, has been associated with the rise and spread of capitalism ever since the early 1900s, when Weber pointed out the economic importance of the Protestant ethic.[22] Hard work and efficiency are valued and expected from men on the farms, men in urban employment, women in the household, and women in the kitchen.[23] The religion prescribes high productivity in all endeavors. Another cornerstone of Protestantism is frugality, essential for savings and investment, and the accumulation of capital. According to Weber, it is these characteristics, coupled with the belief that it is the duty of each individual to make the most of God-given resources, that explain the economic success of Protestant groups.[24]

The Protestant values described above are all conducive to migration. Striving for efficiency and embracing hard work are fundamental in the profile of the successful migrant. An individual with a zeal for self-reliance and with an organized and systematic approach to life and work is more likely to respond to the challenge of migration.

Buddhism is associated with the principles of simplicity, conservation, and nonviolence. It values a nonconfrontational system of decision-making and conflict resolution. The stereotypic profile of a Buddhist, namely a devout, soft-spoken, and pensive individual, seems incompatible with success in the contemporary, competitive economic environment in which aggression, speed, and drive are valued. The Buddhist profile also fails to coincide with the profile of the successful migrant, who needs both aggression and drive in order to overcome the obstacles associated with the migration process.[25]

While all the above religions have elements that can be interpreted as both conducive to migration as well as impediments to it, the mere existence of religion, the differences that people attribute to each other as a result of religious affiliations, and the lengths to which believers will go in the name of their religion are often enough to induce migration. Armies have invaded countries in order to spread their religions. Leaders have induced their believers to inhabit other lands to proselytize (under the principle of *Ciu exus, regnis est*, he whose religion it is, owns the land). Believers have destroyed the religious objects of competing religions in order to induce out migrations (indeed, in the Yugoslav wars of the 1990s, people rushed to destroy others' religious buildings and artifacts in an effort to obliterate a target religion from the area, since people are more likely to migrate from a region that is intolerant to their faith).

Culture
Two other institutions, culture and family, are closely related to religion insofar as religion dictates values (that define culture) and behavior norms (that define family relations). With respect to *culture*, there is no doubt that it affects both the economy as well as migration.[26] Cultural explanations for group disparities have a long history, going back to de Tocqueville and Weber. More recently, Bauer, Sowell, Novak, Harrison and Smiley, and most recently Harrison and Huntington, all place emphasis on cultural factors to explain differences in economic performances between ethnic groups.[27] By extension, it is the norms embodied in a culture that facilitate or discourage migration. Some cultures value tradition so emphatically that a challenge (such as migration) to set patterns is strongly discouraged. In those cultures, the young are expected to follow in the footsteps of their forefathers and failure to do so may result in social ostracism. Other cultures are characterized by rigid social hierarchies that limit the mobility of their populations, both professionally and geographically. (The Indian caste system is an illustration of such immobility.[28] Since birth defines the occupation that an individual can hold throughout his or her life, the caste system therefore limits interprofessional mobility. By extension, it then also limits geographical mobility, since not all occupations are geographically transferable.) Finally, cultures that encourage risk-taking, that welcome innovation, and foster change will produce an environment conducive to migration (as, for example, the US culture).

Family
Family ties can be both an impediment and an inducement to migration. Rossi has claimed that many migration acts are directly caused by changing family conditions, while Holm, Makila and Oberg have shown the importance of considerations such as moving together, marriage, divorce, having children, growing old, and becoming an adult.[29] Nuclear and extended family ties bind an individual to others who provide a broad range of social, economic, and psychological benefits. Close family bonds and kinship ties, together with community links, are impediments to migration since they cannot be duplicated in new locations (attempts at such duplication are evident in recent migrants congregating in new locations with members of their ethnic or religious groups).[30] At the same time, a concentration of family members in a new land provides a pull for a potential migrant and an incentive to relocate.

Labor market
In addition to religion, culture, and family, one more institution determines a migrant's decision to voluntarily relocate, namely the labor

market. In addition to considerations of labor supply and demand, other characteristics of the labor market also influence the migrant. For example, vested interests such as job seniority are likely to discourage out-migration. In societies in which job security provides protection from business cycle fluctuations, workers are likely to value their accumulated years of work and the economic security associated with their seniority (in his comparison of Japanese and American firms, Thurow underscores the differing practices with respect to the lay-off of workers and turnover rates, both of which are relevant in a comparison of labor mobility[31]). Moreover, seniority-based wages, such as those popular in Japanese firms, guarantee wage increases for length of service, foster loyalty, and discourage out-migration (seniority-based wages are related to the concept of lifetime employment according to which, once hired in large firms, workers are virtually guaranteed a position for life (in Japan, this affects about 30% of the labor force)). Furthermore, an accommodating workplace that allows alternative work arrangements (such as flexible hours, flexible work location, job sharing etc.) is likely to be an impediment to relocation because of the unlikely possibility of replicability. Such accommodating environments are increasingly evident across businesses and enterprises in the United States and Canada.[32] Nontransferable pension funds place controls on geographical labor mobility since they represent a *de facto* pension blockage. (In Japan, where pensions are not movable from company to company, older workers can expect to lose about half of their benefits if they move. This causes inflexibility in labor markets and it is estimated that such barriers to changing jobs account for almost three-quarters of Japan's unemployment).[33] Finally, the possibility for labor mobility between occupations and professions is an inducement to migrate, given that migrants will be attracted to jobs where their chances for mobility are greater (since constraints exist in some cultures or countries: among the Chinese, certain jobs are closed off by regulation; in India they are closed off by the caste system; in Switzerland they are closed off by visa requirements; in Japan they are closed off by tradition). Labor mobility between occupations is most common in the United States, Canada, and Australia.

Infrastructure

Economic infrastructure is defined as the underlying amount of physical and financial capital embodied in roads, railways, waterways, airways, and other forms of transportation and communication plus water supplies, financial institutions, electricity, and public services such as health and education.[34] Infrastructure facilitates and integrates economic activities. Indeed, the quantity and quality of infrastructure is a crucial determinant of the pace and diversity of a country's economic development.[35] Improvements in infrastructure contribute to the increase in standards of living. When infrastructure is deficient and inadequate, then transportation systems prevent flows of goods, financial institutions cannot provide capital for investment, communications cannot foster exchange of ideas, and so forth. Such conditions hamper creativity and dampen the drive for self-improvement, both necessary conditions for personal and ultimately national economic growth. When infrastructure is highly developed, it facilitates the creative and entrepreneurial individual to thrive. With respect to infrastructure, the United States, Canada, Australia, Singapore, and Hong Kong are in sharp contrast to countries such as Russia, India, and Yugoslavia.

Despite the differences among these countries, their domestic ethnic populations do not have the same access to infrastructure or the opportunity to use it. This is not to imply that transport, power, and water are explicitly denied to select groups, but rather that leaders can manipulate policy to *de facto* achieve the result that *de jure* it might not be able to. For example, a central government's discretion over investment for infrastructure can lead to lower capital inflows into a region where a minority is concentrated (as, for example, the Indian government's decision on road construction in Assam; the Czech government's decision on housing projects for the Roma; and, until 1999, the Yugoslav government's decision on water access in Kosovo). Moreover, when central governments are given authority over health and education spending, they have the power to lower (or deny) access to spatially concentrated minorities (for example, the educational facilities in the Transylvania region of Romania, where large numbers of Hungarians reside, are inferior to those in other parts of the country). Given this discrepancy between ethnic groups, the nature and quality of infrastructure affects potential migrants by obstructing or catapulting them in numerous ways. These are discussed below.

Telecommunications
To the extent that the end of the twentieth century witnessed a revolution, it has been in telecommunications. With the increases in telephone usage per capita, the ease with which international media has permeated the lives of distant communities, the astonishing growth of the computer and Internet as a personal and business tool, telecommunications have modernized production and enhanced international competitiveness.

As a result of such enhanced communication, potential migrants have the capacity to more readily gain information about their desired host country as well as to more realistically assess their possibilities in those locations. The Internet has played an especially important role in providing valuable information to migrants by linking them with the diaspora across the world (indeed, the Indian websites provide not only practical information for new arrivals but also instill values and reaffirm norms of Hinduism[36]). Thus, telecommunications have succeeded in spreading information about distant locations faster and more thoroughly than any tool previously used by migrants.[37]

Housing

Few potential migrants have no concerns about housing in their future location. Rumors of families living on streets, in cardboard boxes, and under bridges reach far beyond the city limits of Calcutta, Rio de Janeiro, and Hong Kong. The existence of shantytowns, ghettos, and barrios attests to the inability of host governments to address the housing needs of newcomers. As a result, unresolved housing questions act as a deterrent to migration for all but the most desperate (indeed, in the former Soviet Union and the Czech Republic, while workers were free to move within state borders, they were restricted by the housing shortage[38]).

Another impediment to migration, limited to some traditional cultures, has to do with the huge importance of the family abode. In relatively immobile societies, such as Yugoslavia, Russia, Estonia, and the Czech Republic, the family home is often passed on from generation to generation and its walls contain family tradition and myths as much as anything else. The house represents the family identity and its members are formed by their relationship to their home. In such societies, potential migrants are deterred from leaving. By contrast, in mobile societies such as the United States, Canada, and Australia, where geographical and occupational mobility is common, a house is rarely a home because it lacks longevity and memories. As a result, mobility induces further mobility.

Transport

Since the time of the ancient Romans, transportation systems have been recognized as a key component for economic development insofar as they enable the movement of goods, services, and resources and thereby allow commercial relations to thrive. Indeed, Roman emperors were quick to build the *Via Aurelia* linking the southern capital with the northern regions; the British built roads and ports in the Indian subcontinent; and the Chinese exploited their river systems for transportation purposes. A developed, maintained, and functioning transportation system is likely to both stimulate and restrain migration. It acts as a stimulant because it provides a conduit for moving populations; it acts as a restraint because it facilitates growth and development, thereby improving conditions at home and reducing the economic incentives to leave home.

In contrast, a deteriorating infrastructure (consisting of traffic congestion, inadequate traffic management, insufficient airport security, lapsed maintenance of roads and ports, and an outdated urban transport strategy) has negative effects on overall development. It thereby decreases the economic potential of workers and makes their daily participation in the economy more difficult and unpleasant. Both the macro effect and the micro effect of a deteriorating infrastructure motivates out-migration.

Power
According to a World Bank study, power has still to reach some 2 billion people across the world.[39] In rural South Africa, where 70 percent of black Africans reside, only 11 percent of households have access to electricity.[40] In many electrified regions of the world, unreliable power restricts production and blackouts and brownouts in power systems disrupt economic and private life. Lack of power or an inadequate power supply provides motivation to the entrepreneurial migrant to relocate since infrastructure inadequacies limit his or her economic possibilities at home.

Water
Investments in water systems are made for a variety of reasons, including to enable the economy to irrigate, move waste, and produce goods and services. Intermittent water supplies, insufficient coverage, and inadequate purifying methods are all impediments to economic development. As in the case of power, water management is a crucial component of the infrastructure of a country, and its inadequacies and limitations provide a push for the achievement-oriented migrant.

Money and Banking
The function of the banking system is to ensure a safe store of assets, to provide a market for credit, to facilitate the flow of funds into investment, and to enable the execution of monetary policy. The first two functions are relevant for this study. Usually, property rights to bank assets (such as checking accounts, savings accounts, money market shares, certificates of deposits) guarantee transferability. In other words, ownership implies the right to hold and to move assets at will. Under those conditions, a migrant can easily export his or her bank assets to his or her new place of residence. In some societies, however, bank assets are not transferable across international borders. Regulations pertaining to movements of capital as well as currency convertibility limit the ability of potential migrants to expatriate their

funds. That, in turn, limits their relocation possibilities. South Africa, Zimbabwe, and Uganda are among the many countries that limit the rights of their citizens to export capital. Originally conceived as a method for forestalling the flight of capital by departing white populations in the aftermath of independence, the practice remains in effect and applies to a wide range of ethnic groups and races.

The second function of the banking system, namely the provision of the credit market, also affects migration. To the extent that modern banking systems (with their fully disclosed interest rates and pre-planned payments schedules) replace the village moneylender (whose exorbitant fees and interest rates are decided at whim), access to credit for the relocation process becomes a realistic possibility, thereby facilitating out-migration. At the same time, a functioning credit system enables an entrepreneurial individual to invest in education, to set up a business, and to otherwise participate more easily and more fully in the economy, thereby discouraging emigration.

Public Services

The vast majority of the world's population receives its education, health care, and sanitation services from the public sector. Investment in these services increases the stock of human capital and is therefore positively related to economic development. Extensive and effective public services can act as a stimulant for migration since the potential migrant who is healthy, literate, and skilled is more likely to embark upon a relocation (and is more likely to succeed in this endeavor, as discussed below). On the other hand, the domestic availability of adequate education and health care might dampen a migrant's motivation to seek them in a new location.

Personal Characteristics

Personal characteristics of the potential migrant are quintessential in determining the capacity and incentive to migrate. Characteristics endogenous to the migrant (such as age, attitude, education, and gender) affect both the willingness to move as well as the likelihood of success after the move. Characteristics related to employment (such as income and nature of present employment) as well as characteristics exogenous to the migrant (previous movement, distance to be traversed, unemployment rates, and occupational licensure) are all determinants of the propensity to migrate.

An explanation is warranted. The personal characteristics discussed below pertain to the individual potential migrant rather than to the entire ethnic group. Since they are personal characteristics, aggregation across individuals, even if members of the same ethnic group, is neither feasible nor advisable. However, an extrapolative link from the individual to the ethnic group can easily be made. Indeed, with the exception of some personal characteristics that are ethnic-neutral (such as previous movement, distance covered, and possibly even occupational licensure), most lend themselves to an ethnic interpretation that points to differences in migration propensities among ethnic populations. For example, to the extent that age is a relevant characteristic for migrating, then those ethnic groups that have higher fertility rates and a younger population also have more potential migrants (the example of the Albanians from Kosovo is compelling: their natality rate is significantly higher than that of any other ethnic groups within Yugoslavia: 28.8%, compared with 11.4% of the Serbs[41]).

Age

While scholars have focused on the different roles that age plays in migration, all agree that the young migrate more than the old. Lansing and Meuller suggest that younger people are generally more mobile.[42] Older adults find it harder to move their families, as evidence shows that people in their thirties, forties, and fifties are more rooted in their communities and lifestyles than those in the 18–24 age bracket. Moreover, the propensity to change employers decreases with increasing age. Reynolds suggests that usually workers shop around in the beginning of their career, and then settle to collect seniority pension rights and other forms of security.[43] Finally, young people are more likely to migrate than the old because, according to Fisher, Martin, and Straubhaar, migration is investment in one's human capital. The longer one's investment horizon, the more likely one is to migrate.[44]

Attitude

Migration necessitates a risk-taking attitude, a predisposition to innovation, and an openness to the outside world. Migrants welcome contacts with outside communities, they seek out excitement, and they are drawn to new experiences. The more 'modern' an individual and the more willing to take on new challenges, the more likely he or she is to migrate in search of new opportunities. The more willing to take risks, the more likely the completion of the migration act (evidence of such risk-taking attitudes is provided by rafters from Cuba to the United States). The greater their 'radius of trust' (a term political scientists use to describe if people trust only their kin and neighbors or whether their trust is more generalized), the more comfortable migrants are with the migration process. The stronger their sense of self-reliance and their focus on the future, the more successful their migration. Therefore, just as attitude is an important factor in economic development (as described by Inkeles and Smith[45]), so too attitude is crucial for the successful migration.

Education
The quantity and quality of education is positively related to skills acquisition. Research has shown that education and skills have an effect on overall labor mobility (for example, unskilled workers change jobs more frequently than the semiskilled, who change more frequently than the skilled[46]). However, if geographical mobility is disaggregated from overall mobility, then the evidence is less clear: on the one hand, the highly skilled are more likely to migrate because of their marketability while, on the other hand, the unskilled have less to lose and so are more willing to take risks in a new location.

Gender
Are women more or less likely to relocate than men? While a glance at world migration statistics indicates that males migrate more than females, there is sufficient variation to prevent a definitive answer. In traditional societies, women are less likely to migrate on their own, in the absence of male kin. Yet, evidence of expatriate Jamaican nurses and Filipino domestic workers points to exceptions. In Western cultures, skilled, single women respond to economic incentives to migrate. At the same time, women who are not the primary bread-winners tend to follow, rather than lead, their husbands in relocation.

Income and wealth
A crucial consideration in the migration decision is current income and the prospects for future income. These are compared to the expected income in a new location. The greater the differential, the greater the incentive to relocate. Wealth is also a consideration in the migration decision, since an accumulated stock of assets enhances the capacity of migrants to undertake a risky and expensive relocation process.

Present employment
Income derived from present employment is not the only job characteristic that affects the migration decision. Work conditions, benefits, and prospects for advancements are all relevant in the migrant's cost/benefit analysis. Clearly, the better the overall employment experience, the lower the desire for change. This inverse relationship between satisfaction with present work and the push to migrate extends to all aspects of work: for example, when a benefits package is associated with length of service, the propensity to change employers decreases with increasing length of service.

Previous movement
Every time people move, they suffer the loss of the accumulated location-specific advantages.[47] Nevertheless, those who have moved in the past are more likely to move again in the future. Once they have overcome the inertia of the first move, undergone the adjustment process, and disassociated themselves from their traditional setting, they are more likely to value the opportunities of new relocations over the bonds to their geographical origins. Previous movement is even found to affect short distance commuting: Lansing and Mueller found that people who have moved in the past are much more likely to commute to a job 50 miles or more away than someone who has never moved.[48]

Distance
The propensity to migrate varies inversely with the distance a person must move.[49] Moving from rural Bihar to Calcutta entails fewer costs, lower risks, and less permanence than moving to New York. While the pay-offs of relocating further away may be greater, the obstacles associated with getting there might be insurmountable. Hence, long distances are an impediment to migration while short distances are more manageable and therefore more likely. This is supported by evidence of global migration patterns, which clearly indicate that internal migration is significantly more common than international.

Unemployment rates
Rates of unemployment both at home and in the destination affect migration. Unemployed people are more likely to migrate. To the extent that potential migrants have information, they will be less likely to migrate into a region with high employment rates. While that flies in the face of facts (namely, clear evidence of rural migrants moving to cities with high unemployment rates), it is less of a discrepancy than it seems at first sight for two reasons. First, not all potential migrants have accurate information about work opportunities, and second, not all potential migrants have realistic views of their own abilities to beat the odds.

Occupational licensure
Societies require certification of competency for a variety of tasks: driving automobiles, scuba diving, flying airplanes, administering medication etc. Some of these are transferable across countries while others require retesting to requalify in the new location. Complicated recertification procedures are an impediment to potential migrants whose occupations require acceptable licenses. Skilled workers in particular are deterred from migrating by regulations requiring occupational licenses for employment. Medicine and law are examples

of professions that restrict entry to those who are licensed within a particular state. Thus, a doctor from India weighs the ramification of US medical regulations in his/her evaluation of potential migration. Clearly, occupational licensure is not an issue for unskilled workers whose lack of skills are universal.

MACROECONOMIC COSTS AND BENEFITS OF MIGRATION

Large waves of economic migrants have enabled economic development in host regions, including the United States, the Middle East, and Germany. At the same time, losing states have suffered from the loss of human capital, as, for example, when Jews emigrated from the Soviet Union. While there is no doubt that population movements have economic, political, and demographic implications for both the host and home regions, there is disagreement as to the nature of the net effect. In the words of the World Bank, 'migration is usually beneficial to both sending and receiving countries'.[50] This optimistic view is not universal: some argue that migration is bad for home countries because it only serves the interest of international capital.[51] Alternatively, there are those who argue that the effect of migration is too complicated and unresolved to make a clear assessment.[52] What are the elements of this debate about the net effects of migration? When workers migrate, losing and receiving regions incur costs and reap benefits. The relative importance of the costs and the benefits underlies immigration and emigration policies of countries (these are discussed in chapter 7). Indeed, when the pain associated with inflows of migrants becomes too high, then countries alter their immigration policies to stop the flow (such pain was clear in Greece, where the depression of the late 1920s was directly related to the inflow of refugees from Turkey in 1922–23[53]). Alternatively, when the benefits exceed the costs, immigration policies become more receptive.

The greatest benefit of immigration to host countries is the inflow of skilled workers. The resulting brain-gain (which complements another country's brain-drain) is due to the fact that the training of the migrants took place at the expense of another government (indeed, countries such as the United States and Switzerland have been absorbers of qualified workers for decades: it is estimated that the United States saved some $4 billion in training costs of its labor force from the Second World War until the 1960s[54]). Moreover, the benefits of skilled immigrants extend beyond their earning and productive capacity to the work ethic they bring with them: for example, the Cuban community in South Florida has invigorated the area with its enthusiasm and drive.

Receiving regions reap benefits even when immigrant workers are unskilled, since they are often willing to perform undesirable and dangerous tasks, many of which are shunned by indigenous populations (witness the demand, in the US, for migrant farm workers from Mexico or the demand, in Switzerland, for street sweepers from Turkey). Furthermore, since these workers are often not adequately protected by laws, they may therefore be easily dismissed during an economic downturn.

Receiving regions also benefit from the inflow of financial assets that often accompanies the arrival of a new population. If these migrants have personal assets, they will be spent, saved, or invested in the host country. There is a benefit even if they have no assets (such as when people arrive, penniless, after forcible displacement from their home countries). It ranges from the bilateral or multilateral financial assistance that regions receive in order to cope with refugees (such as what Croatia received from the German and US governments to accept refugees from Bosnia), to direct payments for repatriation (such as was paid by Germany to the Romanian government to take back refugees that have relocated to Germany).[55] This financial assistance often motivates cash-strapped countries to absorb both involuntary and voluntary immigrants.[56]

Lest too rosy a picture is depicted for receiving regions, the incurred costs must also be mentioned. Direct costs include those associated with resettlement and integration: housing, education, policing, transportation, water, and health controls, and so on. Over time, indirect costs also become evident. These include the ramifications of the envy of the indigenous population that perceives its livelihood is threatened, its living costs are rising, and the competition for scarce resources has been unfairly sharpened (such envy produced anti-foreign bias across Germany, Britain, and France in the 1990s).

Benefits and costs are evident in the losing regions also. The principal benefit accrues when a country reduces its surplus of labor and thus relieves the demand for employment, the downward pressure on wages, and the strain on infrastructure. Countries with high population densities and insufficient opportunities for their workers, such as Bangladesh, encourage out-migration. Alternatively, countries relieve political pressures by encouraging or forcing populations to emigrate (note the Mariel boat lift orchestrated by the Cuban government).

In losing countries, the cost of emigration is high because they lose the employment and productivity that the migrant would have contributed. In addition, they lose the migrant's taxes (resulting in a decrease in government revenue), savings (which would result in a decrease in the rate of investment) and fertility (resulting in a decrease in the future human capital pool). But the most pronounced long-term cost associated with emigration is the loss of human capital. While scholars disagree as to how to measure the magnitude of such a brain-drain,[57] they do agree that the price a losing region pays in terms of economic growth potential is great. Losses are incurred when a state pays for education and training of migrants who then emigrate before they make a contribution to the economy. The more trained the migrant, the greater the loss. From ancient times, brain-drain has been a problem for losing societies: indeed, the movement of intellectuals from Athens to Alexandria and from Constantinople to Western Europe led to the awakening of one culture at the expense of the other.[58] In the mid-twentieth century, a large movement of human capital left Europe for the United States; in the late 1980s and early 1990s, significant quantities of human capital moved out of the Balkans, and so forth.[59]

LAISSEZ-FAIRE MIGRATION

It was proposed in chapter 1 that interethnic competition affects migration by ethnicity. In other words, some influences on the migration decision are shared by all members of an ethnic group and thus color an individual's decision. In its broadest manifestation, when ethnic bifurcation is present, members of a marginalized ethnic group generally have an incentive to relocate to a more accommodating and receptive environment. At the same time, empowered ethnic groups have a disincentive to move since their privileged status confers benefits unlikely to be found outside state borders. In this chapter, institutions, infrastructure, and personal characteristics have been studied and their influence on voluntary migration decisions discussed. While they do not weigh equally in a migrant's decision (religious teaching has more impact than electrification, for example), these influences underscore that ethnic groups do not share advantages and impediments, nor do they face the same capacities and incentives. This ethnic difference in migration is even more pronounced during involuntary migration (see chapter 5). It is also more pronounced when domestic policies induce a desired migration response (either to stay or to go) by harassing, restricting, and pressuring targeted ethnic groups (see chapters 6 and 7). Such restrictions to voluntary migration, both in home and host countries, support the contention that migration is, in reality, far from *laissez-faire*. In other words, pure *laissez-faire* migration, which entails unfettered movements of people in response to a variety of incentives, does not exist. Since migration is the way in which the manpower demands of economies are met, efficiency in labor markets is not achieved because labor does not flow to where demand exceeds supply. Thus, ethnic characteristics that influence the capacity and incentive to relocate have an impact on migration, as much as government restrictions that explicitly dictate who goes and who stays.

NEW TRENDS IN LABOR MIGRATION: LONG-DISTANCE COMMUTING

Immigrants today are not like the immigrants of yesterday. Many of them have neither severed their ties to their homeland, nor are permanently ensconced in their host country. They move around, they go back and forth, they make new ties and they maintain old ties. They participate in the politics and economies of everywhere they go. As a result of increased communications and cheaper transportation, location polygamy characterizes immigrant populations as never before. Evidence from the United States supports this: some 20 percent of immigrants leave within ten years of their arrival, and one third leave again over their lifetime.[60]

Such location polygamy is also observed among workers within state borders. Not only do domestic migrants tend to move around a lot, but novel ways of bridging the spatial gap between home and workplace have emerged. The United States, where suburbs, bedroom communities, and long daily commutes were first encountered, is yet again at the forefront of a new trend: long-distance commuting (also known as sleep-away commuting). Such commuting is characterized by spatial separation between home and workplace that is too long to traverse in one day. Four features define it: overnight stays, regularity, distance, and choice.[61] This still leaves a lot of ambiguity as to what sleep-away commuting is and is not. This ambiguity, coupled with the novelty of the phenomenon, explains why little data exist on long-distance commuting and therefore why it is so difficult to assess just how prevalent it is.

Indeed, there are no country-wide statistics that enable an assessment of the prevalence of long-distance commuting. The US Bureau of the Census does not collect information on it. The Departments of Labor and Transportation publish commuting information, as does the Journey to Work survey, but none include a separate category for sleep-away commuting. There are also no large-scale studies that present country-wide trends. Instead, several small-scale studies have addressed the issue. In their study of commuting during 1950–63, Lansing and Mueller surveyed a random sample of 3,991 families and found that 7 percent of all heads of families traveled back and forth to a job 50 miles or more from their place of residence.[62] These workers fall into three categories. Those who commuted daily or several times a week (2%), those who commuted weekly (2%) and those who commuted at longer intervals (3%). Moreover, 13 percent of their sample commuted and/or went away temporarily at one time or other during that time period. In 1972, Homstrom found that 75 percent of dual-career couples had, at some point, been faced with the question of whether to engage in commuting relationships in order to pursue career goals.[63] In addition, in her study of commuting couples, Driedger lamented the lack of hard data on commuting, but proposed that this is a phenomenon closely tied to dual-career couples.[64] She goes on to cite Homstrom's findings in connection with the fact that dual-career couples have only increased since then, thereby implying that sleep-away commuting is even more prevalent in the minds of a particular set of workers than ever before. Thus, independent researchers, as well as work organizations and the media, have indicated that long-distance commuting is an unmeasured phenomenon that is to be taken seriously.[65]

At its core, long-distance commuting occurs because of labor supply and demand. Simply put, there is a supply of workers willing to travel long distances and set up temporary housing in order to work at a given job. Workers who opt for this high-risk, nontraditional solution have made a personal cost/benefit analysis and have decided that the benefits of commuting outweigh the costs.[66] At the same time, there is a supply of workplaces that are willing to accommodate their workers and their personal needs in order to retain them. However, a deeper analysis reveals macrofeatures of the post-industrial economies that explain why long-distance commuting has arisen and why it is likely to become even more prevalent in the future. These are: (a) *Employment*. Most jobs in the United States are in the service sector. Professional and white-collar jobs are numerous and will in all likelihood continue to grow. These are exactly the jobs that are conducive to long-distance commuting; (b) *The Workplace*. Increasingly, workplaces are tolerating flexibility in hours and location; more businesses are becoming family friendly in order to attract and retain skilled workers. Evidence abounds of businesses so desperate for appropriately skilled workers that they are willing to let them commute or open small offices elsewhere just to accommodate their personal needs;[67] (c) *The Composition of the Labor Force by Sex*. Increasingly, women are entering the labor force. At the end of the twentieth century, 66 percent of American women were in the labor force, 59 percent of married women were employed, and some 8 million women in the labor force had children under the age of six. As these women climb the professional ladder, their commitment to their careers rises, reducing the likelihood that they will relocate in order to accommodate their spouse's careers (indeed, there was a drop in the married executives who relocated in 1999, as more of those who relocate are single and do not have spouses who are nurturing their own careers[68]). Such immobility is conducive to long-distance commuting; (d) *The Demographic Composition of the Population*. The Baby Boom generation is more likely to pay attention to the careers and the desires of both partners, especially once the children have moved away. In so doing, they are more likely to engage in long-distance commuting; (e) *Income and Wealth*. The current middle-aged cohort enjoys an unprecedented accumulation of wealth. A wealthier population is more likely to incur the expense of commuting in order to satisfy personal and career goals, thereby increasing the likelihood of commuting; (f) *Transportation*. There are currently more and cheaper ways of getting from one point to another than ever before, enabling an easy and inexpensive commute; (g) *Norms of Acceptable Behavior*. Nontraditional solutions to work–family conflicts are increasingly becoming acceptable in order to accommodate nontraditional families and nontraditional workplaces.

The emergence of long-distance commuting has implications across a wide spectrum as a result of the changes that it has produced. At the level of the economy, long-distance commuting affects the labor market, worker productivity, consumption patterns, as well as the development of various industries (including transportation, housing, hotel, and travel). In the workplace, the institutionalization of commuting as a viable option, the alteration of workplace attitudes toward commuters, and the reevaluation of benefit packages (to include commuting benefits, housing assistance, geographically flexible health plans etc.) have occurred. The family also has accommodated to the demands and strains of this novel solution to living and working by making use of technology that enables members to 'keep in touch'.

What are the implications for interethnic competition, ethnic bifurcation, and ethnic migration? A small-scale survey was conducted for this study in order to assess the professional and ethnic/racial orientation of long-distance commuters.[69] Commuters responses to a detailed questionnaire, coupled with secondary research, enabled an identification of the professional and personal profile of the successful long-distance commuter. In essence, it was found that success in long-distance commuting is most likely for the mid-career professional male or female who has a supportive partner and workplace, as well as children in their teens or beyond. Business and academia were the most common professions in the sample. among the respondents.

The evidence with respect to ethnic orientation of long-distance commuters is inconclusive. While a variety of religious, racial, and ethnic backgrounds was present among the respondents, non-Hispanic

Caucasians overwhelmingly dominated the sample (this result may be due to biases inherent in the snowball method of selection[70]). However, none of the respondents perceived that personal characteristics (theirs or of others) had any bearing on their commute, on the willingness of their workplace to accommodate their commuting needs, nor on their family's cost/benefit analysis that resulted in commuting. These perceptions of the respondents point to the irrelevance of ethnicity in upper-crust professions and support the findings presented in chapter 3. They show the success in eradicating interethnic animosities at high levels of growth and in high-income, professional jobs.

NOTES

1 Paul Hochinos, *Free To Hate* (New York: Routledge, 1993), p. 217.
2 It can be argued that these two extremes are possible albeit unlikely in reality. Even with freedom of choice, a migrant is constrained by personal, institutional and policy restraints, both in the home and the host countries; even in involuntary migration, rational choice theory tells us that at least one alternative always exists, namely death. This distinction between voluntary and involuntary migration has become especially poignant in the allocation of blame that is ongoing among Balkan ethnic groups. An example includes the acrimonious mutual accusations by Serbs and Albanians as to the voluntary vs. involuntary nature of the Serbian exodus from Kosovo during 1945–1990 (according to the Albanians, the Serbs left voluntarily in order to pursue better economic opportunities elsewhere in Serbia. According to the Serbs, their departure was by no means voluntary, as they were subject to a variety of pressures, both spontaneous and organized, by the Albanian population).
3 Ted Robert Gurr, *Minorities at Risk* (Washington, DC: United States Institute of Peace, 1993), p. 314.
4 Furthermore, the US State Department estimated that if Bosnia becomes partitioned into three ethnic states, it would result in the relocation of 600,000 more Muslims, some 300,000 Croats, and 350,000 Serbs. *International Herald Tribune*, 14 July 1993.
5 Many of these refugees are housed outside the territory of the former Yugoslavia, where there is evidence of saturation. Indeed, the refugee weariness of the 1980s is turning into refugee phobia of the 1990s, as in-migration becomes a political issue and the ills of western states become increasingly blamed on the incoming migrants (witness the platform of the Lombard League in Italy). It must be noted, however, that the reluctance is largely limited to the West, in part because it is the most desired destination: considering the receptive welcome refugees have received elsewhere in the world in the past decade, such as Malawi (which is hosting 950,000 refugees although its population is only 9.5 million people) and Pakistan (which has taken in 3.6 million Afghan refugees), the Western effort pales in comparison.
6 Albert O. Hirshman, *Exit, Voice and Loyalty: Responses to Decline in Firms, Organizations, and States* (Harvard University Press, 1970), chapter 7.
7 Ishtiaq Ahmed, 'Exit, Voice and Citizenship' in Tomas Hammar, Grete Brochmann, Dristof Ramas and Thomas Faist (eds), *International Migration, Immobility and Development* (New York: Berg, 1997).

8 J. Hicks, *The Theory of Wages* (London: Macmillan, 1932); W. A. Lewis, 'Economic Development with Unlimited Supplies of Labour', *Manchester School of Economic and Social Studies* 22 (1954); G. Ranis and J. C. H. Fei, 'A Theory of Economic Development', *American Economic Review* 51 (1961); J. R. Harris and Michael P. Todaro, 'Migration, Unemployment and Development: A Two-Sector Analysis', *American Economic Review* 60 (1970); Michael Todaro, *International Migration in Developing Countries: A Review of Theory* (Geneva: ILO, 1976).

9 Michael Todaro, *Economic Development*, 7th edn (Reading, MA: Addison Wesley, 1999), p. 749.

10 Robert W. Hefner 'Introduction: Society and Morality in the New Asian Capitalisms' in *Market Cultures* (Boulder, CO: Westview Press, 1998), p. 4.

11 Steve Chan, *East Asian Dynamism*, 2nd edn (Boulder, CO: Westview Press, 1990), p. 39.

12 See chapter on Schumpeter in Benjamin Higgins, *Economic Development: Principles, Problems and Policies* (New York: Norton, 1959).

13 *New York Times*, 19 September 1999.

14 In the production process, people are free to produce and trade for profit, however, they may not cause harm to others. People cannot earn more than their efforts justify (so they must pay 'fair' wages, charge 'reasonable' prices and be content with 'normal' profits). There can be no speculation, gambling, uncertainty, or exploitation. With respect to consumption, no resources can be devoted to activities such as adultery or alcohol or pornography. People cannot engage in ostentatious conspicuous consumption (in other words, they must consume in moderation – this serves to avoid demand-pull inflation and eliminates scarcity since there is more to go around). Finally, personal consumption takes place only after voluntary donations are made to less fortunate members of the Islamic community.

15 The Koran and the Sunna clearly prescribe who it is that must give *zakat* and in what quantities (everyone gives, but the wealthy give more). The beneficiaries of *zakat* are the poor, the handicapped, the unemployed, orphans, dependents of prisoners, travelers in difficulty and debtors from legitimate activities. In reality the *zakat* produces a tiny part of the GNP and a small fraction of government expenditure on poverty relief in most countries.

16 The Torah explicitly mentions interest, a council of bishops in France in 1312 even threatened excommunication for those who engaged in extracting interest. As late as 1571, English law banned interest-taking. See *Economist*, 31 December 1999, p. 90.

17 The Koran does not ban the institution of interest as we know it today. It bans the ancient Arabian practice of *riba*, which entailed the doubling and redoubling of debt when restitution did not occur on time. This was responsible for the effective enslavement of large numbers of people. Some Islamic economists have outright banned all interest in an effort to establish an interest-free society. Others have suggested forced savings and investments and others still have suggested profit sharing. In reality, there is a lot of interest in disguise in Islamic economies.

18 Timur Kuran, 'The Economic System in Contemporary Islamic Thought' in K. S. Jomo, *Islamic Economic Alternatives* (Kuala Lumpur: Ikraq, 1993), pp. 9–48.

19 Bernard Lewis, 'Legal and Historical Reflections on the Positions of Muslim Populations under Non-Muslim rule' in Bernard Lewis and Dominique Schnapper (eds), *Muslims in Europe* (London: Printer, 1994), p. 17.

20 John Voll, 'Islamic Issues for Muslims in the United States' in Yvonne Yazbeck Haddad (ed.), *The Muslims of America* (Oxford: Oxford University Press, 1991), p. 209, cited in Yossi Shain, *Marketing the American Creed Abroad* (Cambridge: Cambridge University Press, 1999), p. 109.

21 Ishtiaq Ahmed, 'Exit', p. 179.

22 Max Weber, *The Protestant Ethic and the Spirit of Capitalism* (New York: Scribner, 1958).

23 Especially in the Calvinist view, hard work and efficiency were deemed to be signs of the person's election or eternal salvation. That view clearly linked economic characteristics with the afterlife.

24 Weber's thesis was criticized by many, including R. H. Tawney, who argued that political and social pressures and the spirit of individuality were more important than Calvinist theology in the development of capitalism. R. H. Tawney, *Religion and the Rise of Capitalism* (New York: Harcourt Brace & Co., 1926).

25 The characteristics and principles of Buddhism that seem to discourage migration can be extrapolated from the work of the British economist E. F. Schumacher. His assessment of the role of Buddhism in economic development led to the slogan 'small is beautiful'. While not focusing directly and solely on Buddhism, Schumacher proposes a development process that is compatible with culture and spiritual values, in which people matter while scarce resources are conserved and the environment is respected. Qualitative growth is emphasized and minimum waste is lauded. (E. F. Schumacher, *Small is Beautiful: Economics as if People Mattered* (New York: Harper and Row, 1973); see chapter 4, entitled 'Buddhist Economics'.) In such a development, production is labor intensive, hence increasing employment and providing alternatives for potential migrants who would be enticed to stay at home. (Also, see discussion of Buddhist economics in Peter Hess and Clark Ross, *Economic Development* (Forth Worth, TX: Dryden Press, 1997), p. 136.)

26 For a good review of the literature on the role of culture, see Stephen Hart, 'The Cultural Dimension of Social Movements: A Theoretical Reassessment and Literature Review', *Sociology of Religion* 57, 1 (1996).

27 David Osterfeld, *Prosperity Versus Planning* (Oxford: Oxford University Press, 1992), p. 49. Lawrence E. Harrison and Samuel P. Huntington (eds), *Culture Matters* (New York: Basic Books, 2000).

28 See Louis Dumont, *Homo Hierarchius* (London: Paladin, 1972).

29 P. H. Rossi, *Why Families Move*, 2nd edn (Beverley Hills, CA: Sage, 1980); E. Holm, K. Makila, and S. Oberg, 'Tidsgeografisk handlingsteori Att bilda betingade biografier' GERUM 8, Geografiska Instiutionen, Umea Universiter (1989), cited in Gunnar Malmberg, 'Time and Space in International Migration', in Hammar *et al.*, *International Migration*, p. 41.

30 In some cultures, the concept of family is stretched to include the deceased. Indeed, it has been said that family includes buried ancestors, an idea that exerts a pull on individuals not to relocate (one of the negative externalities of forced migration of ethnic groups in the Balkans has been the need to leave behind buried relatives. In the former Yugoslavia as well as in parts of Russia, some forcibly evicted families have rushed to exhume ancestral bones for reburial in a new location). The concept of the dead providing guidelines for the living has also gone a step further, as Serbs have claimed that Serbia extends to where Serbs are buried.

31 Lester C. Thurow, 'Introduction' in Lester C. Thurow (ed.), *The Management Challenge: Japanese Views* (Cambridge, MA: MIT Press), pp. 6–7.

32 See the discussion of accommodation in the work environment in Milica Z. Bookman, *The Third Career* (Westport, CT: Praeger, 2000), chapter 7.

33 *Economist*, 23 January 1999, p. 35.

34 Infrastructure has been discussed by development economists such as Paul Rosenstein-Rodan, Ragnar Nurkse, and Albert Hirshman. They used the term *social overhead capital* when referring to infrastructure. Both concepts included activities that share technical features (such as economies of scale) and economic features (such as spillovers from users to nonusers). See World Bank, *World Bank Development Report, 1994* (Oxford: Oxford University Press, 1994), p. 2.

35 Todaro, *Economic Development*, p. 741.

36 See Shain, *Marketing Creed*.

37 It should be added that such easy communication has occurred to the dismay of some leaders who would prefer an electorate less exposed to global ideas and values. Moreover, communication has the effect of inciting ethnic sentiment, forming ethnic identities, and strengthening ethnic boundaries. Surely CNN images of captured Kurd leader Abdullah Ocalan stirred fellow Kurds, and images of the Cuban boy Elian Gonzales, taken at gunpoint from his Miami relatives, stimulated Cuban–American political sentiment. Cellular telephones and e-mail have indeed added to global communication possibilities that circumvent authoritarian controls. Because of their role in liberalizing uncontrollable communication, the Moroccan government banned cellular telephones by the Sawhati ethnic group (while this ban has been lifted by the successor to King Hassan, in an effort to develop sympathy among the Sawhatis, the fear of their association with the Polisario liberation movement is strong among the Moroccan population. *Economist*, 22 January 2000, p. 48). Even in democratic Japan, CNN typically only emits in western hotels, thereby not touching the lives of the ordinary Japanese.

38 John Ham, Jan Svejnar, and Katherine Terrell, 'Czech Republic and Slovakia' in Simon Commander and Fabrizio Coricelli (eds), *Unemployment, Restructuring and the Labor Market in Eastern Europe and Russia* (Washington, DC: The World Bank, 1995), p. 93.

39 *World Bank Development Report, 1994*, p. 1.

40 Only 7% have access to flush toilets and 5% to garbage collection. Hein Marais, *South Africa Limits to Change* (London: Zed Books, 1998), p. 107.

41 Bookman, *Demographic Struggle*, p. 91.

42 John B. Lansing and Eva Mueller, *The Geographic Mobility of Labor* (Ann Arbor: University of Michigan Press, 1967).

43 Lloyd Reynolds, 'Labor Mobility' in Clark Kerr and Paul D. Staudohar (eds), *Economics of Labor in Industrial Society* (San Francisco: Jossey-Bass Publishers, 1986).

44 Peter A. Fisher, Reiner Martin, and Thomas Straubhaar, 'Should I Stay or Should I Go?' in Hammar *et al.*, *International Migration*, p. 62.

45 Alex Inkeles and David Horton Smith, *Becoming Modern: Individual Change in Six Developing Countries* (Cambridge, MA: Harvard University Press, 1974).

46 This is true whether dealing with turnover in a single year, or lifetime mobility or interindustry shifts.

47 Because of these location specific advantages, Fisher, Martin, and Straubhaar stress the value of immobility (Fisher *et al.*, 'Should I Stay?', p. 75).

48 Lansing and Mueller, *Geographical Mobility*, p. 22. Indeed, of those who have moved three or four times in their lives, about one in three has worked at a distance (while only 1 out of 10 nonmovers have worked at a distance).

49 Gravity models of migration have incorporated the importance of geographic distance into economic migration. See I. Molho, 'Theories of Migration: A Review', *Scottish Journal of Political Economy* 33 (1986), p. 406.
50 World Bank, *World Bank Development Report, 1995* (Oxford: Oxford University Press, 1995), p. 68.
51 See, for example, S. Castles and M. Miller, *The Age of Migration: International Population Movements in the Modern World* (London: Macmillan, 1993), p. 65.
52 R. Appleyard, 'International Migration and Development – An Unresolved Relationship', *International Migration* 30, 3–4 (1992).
53 Mark Mazower, *Greece and the Inter-War Economic Crisis* (Oxford: Clarendon, 1991), pp. 129–42.
54 D. N. Chorafas, *The Knowledge Revolution* (New York: McGraw-Hill, 1968), p. 56.
55 *New York Times*, 26 September 1992.
56 This was especially true of some Balkan countries during the Yugoslav wars of the 1990s. Indeed, the UN High Commissioner of Refugees has estimated that the budget necessary to deal with displaced peoples from the Yugoslav war is in the order of $15 million per month (see Danielle Joly, *Refugees-Asylum in Europe* (Boulder, CO: Westview Press, 1992), p. 83). Much of this went into the coffers of the Balkan states. Moreover, in 1992, the International Red Cross announced that it would have to more than double its budget from 16 to 37 million Swiss Francs to deal with displaced peoples in the former Yugoslavia, and the Croatian government announced that it was spending 3 million DM per day caring for 320,000 refugees (ibid., p. 84). It is also noted that there has been much ill feeling among the Serbian authorities because, although the Serbs are housing one-quarter of all the refugees, they receive only 14 percent of the Western aid for refugees (New York Times, 28 November 1992).
57 T. W. Shultz estimated losses on the basis of educational costs, Becker, Mincver, and Bowman emphasized internal rates of return. For a discussion of these, see Robert Myers, *Education and Immigration* (New York: David McKay Co., 1972), p. 178.
58 According to Gustave Arlt, 'Without the brain drain from Constantinople [1204–1453], it is hard to imagine what the later history of Europe might have been' (Chorafas, *Knowledge Revolution*, p. 7).
59 It is estimated that 20,000 educated Albanians left Albania between July 1990 and February 1991 in search of employment opportunities (*Transition* 2, 2 (February 1991)). Bulgaria lost some 200,000 people in 1989, most of whom were young people: this is expected, according to Joly, to have a very damaging effect of the economic development of the country (Joly, *Refugees*, pp. 78–77). Official Bulgarian figures claim that in 1990 alone, 248,000 people left the country, and over 60 percent were between the ages of 15 and 39 (*Horizont*, Bulgarian Radio, 23 January 1991, cited in *FRE/RL Research Report* 2, 6, 5 February 1993, p. 58). From Serbia and Montenegro, there is evidence that 100,000 to 150,000 educated professionals left during 1992, vacating numerous positions for academics, engineers and doctors (*FRE/RL News Brief*, 28 December–8 January 1993, p. 14).
60 Peter Stalker, *Workers Without Frontiers. The Impact of Globalization on International Migration* (Boulder, CO: Lynne Reinner, 2000), p. 112.
61 First, sleep-away commuting is not the same as a lot of traveling for work. There are people whose jobs entail traveling from one plant to another, from one customer to another, from one potential site to another. Their schedule is likely to be different during the following week, and different still during the

one after. Commuters are different from them insofar as they go to one place where they stay until their return home. The fact that they travel between home and work is incidental to their job, it is despite their job. Second, sleep-away commuting does not entail living away from one's family and only periodically visiting them. There are business workers who are away on long-term assignments in another country, military personnel who are stationed away from their families, blue-collar workers working for example on rigs in the North Sea. Third, sleep-away commuting entails choice insofar as commuters make their decision to work away from their homes. They are not involuntarily separated from their homes as are service people called to duty to fight a war, or prisoners on forced labor. Fourth, sleep-away commuters are not people who occasionally sleep over in their place of work because they have worked too late, the weather did not permit their return, or they had to attend a social event. Fifth, sleep-away commuters are not migrant workers. They do not uproot their families to travel from location to location in search of work.

62 Lansing and Mueller, *Geographical Mobility*, p. 20.
63 A. Homstrom, cited in Kathleen Gerson, *Hard Choices. How Women Decide About Work, Career and Motherhood* (Berkeley: University of California Press, 1985), p. 205.
64 Claire Driedger, *Commuting Couples* (Kingston, Ontario: Queens University, Industrial Relations Centre, School of Industrial Relations Research Essay Series 15, 1987), p. 2.
65 For example, *New York Times*, 2 February 2000; *Philadelphia Inquirer*, 2 April 1995; *Wall Street Journal*, 24 September 1996, 8 March 1998, 9 September 1998.
66 The work and family lives of Americans have changed drastically over the past few decades. Moreover, the average time men and women spend working has increased by 163 hours annually (an entire month!) over the past 30 years. Under these circumstances, juggling the demands of the workplace and the home has become the primary concern for millions of Americans. In the search for a workable balance between work and family, two opposing trends have become evident. In one, work and home have *merged* as workers transform their home into a workplace. In another, work and home have *diverged* as workers work further and further away from their homes. Long-distance commuting is an example of the second trend.
67 *USA Today*, 9 December 1999.
68 *Wall Street Journal*, 15 February 2000.
69 The aim of the survey was to achieve a cross-sectional sample of commuters who regularly stayed away from home on at least two consecutive nights. Further, the aim was to understand the complexities of commuting and to formulate the personal profile of the commuter. This was a small-scale research project, entailing the participation of 20 respondents. The questionnaires they filled out were then compiled and analyzed.
70 Respondents were identified through the snowball method as well as with the aid of workers in the travel industry who had contact with commuters. This method is problematic since biases exist in the choice of respondents. While a random sample within census tracts might have been preferable, it was not possible given the lack of large-scale commuting data.

5

Involuntary Migration: Ethnic Dilution, Consolidation, and Cleansing

The transportation of chained Africans to the New World, the movement of Jewish and Slavic laborers during Nazi rule in Germany, and the forcible treks of Karen men in Myanmar for jungle clearance projects are all examples of the involuntary migration of workers. They show that such forcible movements have occurred throughout history and across continents.

These examples also show the most abhorrent intersection of involuntary migration and the labor market; namely that forced labor is a way of satisfying the manpower demands of a growing economy. Slaves, or *de facto* slave workers, were transported to where their labor was most needed (as measured by sales to the highest bidder or by enforced labor, where their marginal product was highest). Involuntary movements of workers therefore played a large role in numerous economies, often enabling development where it otherwise would have been blocked by labor shortages. Due to this very important economic function, involuntary migration continued to be a significant form of migration until quite recently. Indeed, according to Eltis, it was not until the 1840s that annual voluntary European migration to the Americas exceeded the involuntary African migration.[1] Indeed, of an estimated 9 to 15 million transatlantic migrants before 1800, fewer than 10 percent were free.[2]

In addition to their economic contribution, the experience of African slaves, Jewish and Slavic forced laborers, and Karen jungle workers also points to a shared dimension that is crucial to this research: those who are involuntarily migrating and those who are enforcing the movement are not of the same ethnic group, race, religion, or language. Why do some ethnic groups force others to migrate? What economic and political goals are achieved by removing a population from a territory, especially if that population is of a distinct ethnic orientation, different from that of the rulers?

As noted in chapter 1, both the economic and political power of an ethnic group rise when its population size, relative to other groups, increases. Therefore, it is the quest for numerical superiority in a region that leads to the forcible transfer of populations.[3] As morally repugnant as the practice may seem, inducing migrations for the sake of ethnic engineering of the population has proven to be an expedient method of consolidating power. Given that slavery, indentured servitude, and forced labor have become unacceptable in the international community in the late twentieth century, they have been substituted by a less offensive form of involuntary migration that, while repugnant and flies in the face of liberal democratic norms of behavior, is not illegal according to international law.

In this chapter, a typology of involuntary population movements is developed. Three ways of forcing people to move are identified: first, people are resettled in an area in order to dilute the pre-existing population (ethnic dilution); second, people are resettled in an area in order to strengthen the desired ethnic group (ethnic consolidation); and third, people are expelled from an area to cleanse the existing population of 'undesirables' (ethnic cleansing). These methods of population transfer are described below, following an illustrative introduction of involuntary migrations worldwide.[4]

ILLUSTRATIONS OF INVOLUNTARY MIGRATION

A discussion of involuntary labor migrations must begin with slavery, a practice that existed throughout history and lingered until it was finally officially abolished in its last outpost, Mauritania, in 1980. Slavery is primarily an economic phenomenon, most clearly associated with the labor market – during labor shortages, a compliant, abundant source of cheap labor was beneficial for economic production and distribution.[5] When whites found the New World, they needed cheap workers to exploit it and they turned to the blacks of Africa. From the mid-fifteenth century to the late nineteenth, some 12 million Africans had made the voyage to the Western hemisphere.[6] Before and after, millions more had trekked by foot to the Middle East, where Arab traders sold them on the market. Everywhere they went, slaves dug in mines, cleared land, planted, and harvested. Inside homes, they cooked, cleaned, washed, and tended children.

Another form of involuntary migration entails indentured servitude. As described by Galenson and Grubb, this was a 'temporary forfeiture of some freedom' and was viewed as a way to secure a 'loan' in order to make the trip to another country, a trip that was prohibitively expensive.[7] In the past, indentured servitude was a popular way of getting from one location to another, and while it is illegal today, it remains popular among many low-skilled, poor, and unprotected people from developing countries. Indeed, Filipino women make their way to North America and Western Europe by selling their labor, in advance, in exchange for transport. Women from Eastern Europe and the former Soviet Union are lured to the West, often only to have their passports confiscated and to end up in brothels. Indeed, the United Nations estimated that some 4 million people were trafficked into servitude or prostitution each year during the late 1990s.[8] In the United States, it is estimated that each year some 100,000 people are forced into servitude, most having been smuggled into the country.[9] They are forced to work for little or no pay, under threat of death, in factories, small businesses, farms, prostitution sites, and private homes.

Involuntary migration also occurs for reasons other than the exploitation of labor. People flee from a set of international or domestic circumstances (and thereby become classified as refugees[10] or internally displaced[11]). Among the former are wars involving armed intervention and/or political warfare, such as propaganda or a victorious new political system. War situations provoked Chinese population movements in Indo-China following the victory of North Vietnam; Jewish emigration from Germany, Poland, and Croatia during the Second World War; and residence exchanges among Greeks and Turks following the Greco-Turkish war of 1922. New political systems were responsible for the pressure on Germans to leave the Soviet Union and Eastern Europe following the Second World War and Asians to leave Uganda in the 1970s. Wars of liberation or decolonization provoked a mass exodus of Portuguese from Mozambique and whites from Malawi and Rhodesia. Another component of the international circumstances of refugee creation is the redrawing of borders in peace, when it puts national, religious, or racial groups on the wrong side of a border. Indeed, mass population movements occurred on the territories of both the Soviet Union and Yugoslavia after their respective break-ups.

With respect to domestic pressures on populations to relocate, the most important is turbulence of various forms: a violent government change, such as one associated with a revolution or a *coup d'etat*, which carries with it either policies adverse to a given people or simply violence, creates refugees. In this environment, persecution on the basis of religion, race, or ethnicity, whether by sporadic harassment or planned genocide, is apt to arise and result in refugees (for example, the Armenian exodus from Turkey, the Indian flood from Guatemala, the Muslim exodus from Myanmar). However, it is noted that minorities are not the only ones suffering from what might be a brutal, dictatorial government that harasses members of society: the political opposition may also be a target, resulting in political migration (for example, the exodus of political opponents of Pinochet from Chile or of the Ayatola Khomeini from Iran).[12] Alternatively, people may be the victims of a political experiment, such as when some 90 percent of

Tanzania's peasants were herded into *ujamaa* villages (and their homes burnt to prevent their return).[13]

In the twentieth century there has been an increase in the number of politically induced population movements, some of which have entailed forced evictions. The communist revolution in Russia produced some 1.5 million refugees, while Turkish policies induced the movement of some 250,000 Armenians and later over 1 million Greeks. During and after the Second World War, Hitler's government induced migrations of 10 million people in Eastern Europe, while the partition of India caused a displacement of over 10 million Muslims and Hindus. More recently, the creation of Bangladesh uprooted over 10 million people, Sudan accepted approximately 350,000 Eritreans, Somalia took in 800,000 people fleeing Ogaden Province, the Soviet invasion of Afghanistan sent 2 million people into Pakistan, Iraq's invasion of Kuwait sent 380,000 Palestinians out of the Persian Gulf, 80,000 Cubans fled Cuba over the course of a few weeks, 100,000 Jews fled the Soviet Union in a few years during the 1970s, and some 60,000 Ingushis refugees live in squalor in Ingushetia after being cleansed from Northern Ossetia. The war in Chechnya has produced some 800,000 Chechen refugees.[14] During 1979–89, some 8 million people were driven from their homes by 'superpower proxy wars' in places such as Afghanistan, Cambodia, and El Salvador.[15] In the first three years after the end of the Cold War (1989–92), some 4.5 million refugees were produced as people fled interethnic strife. In Africa alone, rampant interethnic wars have resulted in a situation in which only four African states have not gained or lost over 1,000 refugees.[16]

Why have forced population movements and the resulting refugees received so much attention at the turn of the new millennium, given that involuntary migrations have been present throughout history? Gordenker claims that the post-Second World War involuntary migrations have several novel characteristics.[17] First, the sheer volume of refugees has risen dramatically since 1945, as has information of their plight through the mass media. Second, most refugee situations since the war have taken place in less-developed countries, with the exception of Hungary in 1956 and the former Yugoslavia in 1992. Such movements of population to and from developing countries have influenced the development plans of both the losing and the receiving region. Third, many of the population movements have been on such a large scale and have remained unresolved for so long that they have become permanent, putting strain on the immigration system of the receiving state. Indeed, the Palestinians from Israeli territory and the Chinese from Vietnam are examples of generations living outside of their native territory. Fourth, in response to the sheer volume of displacement, there has been an unprecedented increase in international organizations who assist refugees. Although most of these have been through the United Nations systems, there are also numerous efforts at the bilateral level.

ETHNIC DILUTION

Involuntary migration sometimes occurs so that ethnic composition of the receiving region is diluted by newly resettled populations. This type of resettlement, in which an ethnic group is forcibly diluted because members of a different ethnic group are pushed onto its territory, differs in goal from the desire to increase labor supply (that preceded population movements to Siberia), or to alleviate population pressures (that preceded population movements in Malaysia), or to extend into new land (that preceded Boer population movements into the African hinterland; the Treks). Indeed, ethnic resettlements target individuals not by their skills or income levels, but rather by ethnicity (or religion or language), with the goal of diminishing the political and cultural strength that the group derives in numbers. Despite the fact that it is illegal, according to the 1949 Geneva Convention, to send colonists into occupied territory,[18] such a practice nevertheless continues across the globe. When both of the above goals are combined, the result is a particularly potent tool for decreasing the economic power and opportunities of an ethnic group.

Examples include the dilution of the Golan Heights and the Gaza Strip by the infusion of Israeli citizens into these occupied territories, the dilution of Tibet due to the forced in-migrations of the Han, the dilution of western Poland by Hitler through the importation of Germans from across Eastern Europe, and in the Balkans, the dilution of the Hungarian population by the resettlement of Romanians into Transylvania and the dilution of the Istrians by the relocation of Croat refugees from Slavonia, Krajina, and Bosnia.[19] Serbian refugees from across Croatia were resettled in eastern Slavonia (indeed, some 8,000 Serbian refugees were resettled in Baranja during 1992 alone[20]), while some refugees from Bosnia were resettled in Kosovo. After the takeover of western Slavonia by Croats, some 10,000 Serbian refugees from the area were to be resettled in Kosovo.[21]

Often these dilutions are presented in misleading terms in order to mask their true intent. For example, over the course of the 1950s and 1960s, Romanians were resettled in Transylvania (from which, it is estimated, some 100,000 Hungarians were deported and resettled in other parts of Romania[22]) largely with the goal of diluting the local Hungarian population. However, the central government claimed that the resettlement was part of a manpower planning policy to increase the supply of labor in the newly industrializing region. Moreover, in the 1990s there was a proposal to relocate Russians into Siberia: 1–2 million people annually for the next decade because the demographic trends show that the population of Siberia could decline by one-third in the next 15–20 years (life expectancy of males has declined dramatically[23]). While this has been presented as an effort to reinvigorate the Siberian population and to add new supplies of labor to the economy, it may also be considered an effort at dilution of local ethnic groups, since the proposal calls for the infusion of Russian-speaking peoples from throughout the Commonwealth of Independent States. Also, in East Timor in 1994 some 1,000 Indonesians per week were said to have arrived.[24] The government claimed that this was not part of its official transmigration policy (according to which people from densely populated regions are relocated to those that are sparsely populated), but rather the expression of pull factors due to economic development in East Timor. However, the local population was skeptical since the new arrivals, with strong pro-Indonesian sentiments, were causing an unequivocal dilution of the local population (incidentally, the Indonesian policy of population resettlement was a cornerstone in the drive for independence that the East Timorese finally achieved in 1999). Lastly, during the 1980s and 1990s, Albania was trying to encourage Albanians from the north to settle in the southern areas, where, ostensibly, the population density is lower. Conveniently, this is also where Greek speakers reside, so the population movement would also serve to dilute what is left of the minority population.[25]

These examples do not negate the fact that unintended dilution sometimes occurs and that the affected ethnic leaders must enact policies to protect themselves from further erosion of the ethnic composition status quo. The dilution consists of inflows of migrants of other ethnic groups that inevitably alter the interethnic population ratio and, more specifically, the interethnic composition of the labor force. Such perceptions of inundation translate into measures that include the placement of barbed wire along state borders. This has in fact occurred in Assam, where the inflow of the Bengalis from West Bengal and Bangladesh has tilted the population ratio in favor of the Bengalis. This process has been ongoing since the 1950s, and despite the Bengali claims that the migrants make no demands in their new land, population numbers speak louder than words, resulting in strict measures restricting Bengali rights and inflow.

Another example of unintended dilution is that of the US population in South Florida following the arrival of Cuban migrants. The Mariel boatlift brought 125,000 Cubans to America and most of them settled in Dade County. In addition, each year in the 1980s and 1990s, some 5,000 illegal rafters reached the United States.[26] Then, in

August 1994, a record 20,000 were picked up by the coastguard in the Florida Straits. Cuban President Fidel Castro has asked for 100,000 more to be allowed to immigrate.[27] While public attention in the year 2000 was turned to a single case of Cuban migration, namely that of Elian Gonzales,[28] it cannot be overlooked that these migrations have unequivocally altered the ethnic ratios in South Florida.

At times, the mere prospect of a possible up-coming dilution sends shockwaves throughout a country. Indeed, the possible return of hundreds of thousands of displaced Palestinians back to the West Bank and the Gaza Strip troubles Israel's leadership since such a move would represent a dilution of the Israeli population: according to a former Israeli ambassador to the US, 'The Palestinians have never made a secret of their intention to try to bring down the Jewish state by flooding it with hundreds of thousands of Arabs from abroad.'[29] (However, some of these would simply be returning to their homeland. The question of how many actually lived in those areas before the 1967 war is in dispute: the Arabs claim that there were 800,000, while the Israelis say 200,000 to 250,000.)

ETHNIC CONSOLIDATION

In an effort to consolidate the presence of a desired ethnic group in a territory, governments may encourage selective in-migration. This is done by the adoption of a policy of receptive, selective immigration. This open-arms policy serves the purpose of strengthening the size of one group by increasing its relative size. As such, the immigration policy does not discriminate by skill or familial ties but rather by race, ethnicity, or religion. As is discussed in chapter 7, immigration policies across the world are increasingly exhibiting this tendency to be selective: witness the current changes in the Italian immigration law pertaining to immigrants from Africa, or the German attempts to discourage Roma immigration. In the Balkans, in-migration is encouraged only when the nationality of the immigrant reflects that of the titular majority. Indeed, Greece is not receptive to the inflow of illegal Albanian immigrants; Yugoslavia has strengthened its borders to control the inflow from Albania; Romania and Bulgaria are on the look-out for Roma migrants; and so on. Balkan governments do, however, welcome selected ethnic groups, especially when they are perceived as both strengthening the majority (as would result from Bulgaria's decision to accept some 700,000 Bulgarians from the former Soviet Union) while increasing economic growth (as resulted from the influx of Croat expatriates after the Cold War). In 1994, Aleksandr Vengerovsky, vice president of the Russian Parliament, said that the settling of 200,000 Russians in the Serbian territories of Bosnia was under consideration.[30] Kashmiri Muslims that emigrated to Pakistan have been invited to resettle back in Kashmir, and thus increase the ratio of Muslims to non-Muslims.[31] Similarly, the Israeli government has encouraged Jews to settle in the occupied territories of Gaza Strip and the West Bank with the aim of consolidating the Israeli presence. Finally, following the Croatian take-over of western Slavonia in May 1995, President Tudjman announced that Croatian refugees from Serbia and the Banja Luka area were to be resettled in the area.[32] The goal was to fill the void created by the departing Serbian refugees as well as to consolidate the Croat population in the region.

Ethnic consolidation efforts are sometimes so intense that they destroy the existing population. Such intensity is exemplified by the arrival of Europeans to the Americas. The demographic shifts that were induced by the Europeans occurred for several reasons. First, there was a war against the Indians, one that the Europeans easily won with superior weaponry. Second, the Europeans' continuous arrival served to steadily increase their numbers, while those of the Indians steadily decreased (in North America, there may have been some 1 million native populations when Europeans arrived, while in South America there were even more (some 15 million in Mexico)). In the north, unlike in Mexico, there were more Europeans than Indians by the eighteenth century. Third, Europeans brought diseases to which the Indians were not immune, resulting in widespread deaths.[33]

ETHNIC CLEANSING

Involuntary migration also takes place when a targeted population is forced out of a region, thus cleansing it of 'undesirables'. This results in an immediate increase in the relative size of the desired ethnic group. The population that is forced to depart is prevented from returning, and is often prevented from concentrating elsewhere (this is the case of ethnic Hungarians who were dispersed across Romania; Vlahs and Pomak Turks, who were dispersed across Bulgaria; as well as Greeks, who were dispersed throughout Albania). Alternatively, those who have been cleansed are sent to a region where they were previously concentrated or where their conationals reside (e.g. Germans from Eastern Europe after the Second World War were sent to Germany).

Ethnic cleansing has become the preferred term for forced population movements whose purpose is to cleanse a region of an undesirable ethnic group. Bell-Fialkoff has defined ethnic cleansing as 'the expulsion of an "undesirable" population from a given territory due to religious or ethnic discrimination, political, strategic, or ideological considerations, or a combination of these'.[34] Ethnic cleansing has been in operation across the globe since time immemorial.[35] As Bell-Fialkoff points out in his study of the practice, it is 'historically speaking neither new nor remarkable'.[36] In the Americas, the arrival of whites led to attempts at extermination of the indigenous American Indian populations, and when that failed, their containment on reservations. Jews have been expelled throughout Europe and throughout history, culminating in the Holocaust of the mid-twentieth century. Turks cleansed regions of the Armenians, Eastern Europe cleansed their states of Germans (removing over 10 million people in one sweep[37]), Stalin resettled entire nationalities (Chechens, Kalmyuks, Ingush, Karachai, Balkars, and Crimean Tatars).[38] Asians were forced from Uganda, and Chinese were forced from Vietnam. Ethnic cleansing is a practice usually associated with war (although as is clear from the examples above, this is not necessarily a prerequisite). McGarry and O'Leary remind us of wartime population movements, such as Oliver Cromwell's transplantation strategies in Ireland, Tsarist and Turkish policies in the Caucuses in the nineteenth century, Stalin's movement of the Volga Germans, Cossacks and others. Pfaff called them 'horrific wartime and post-war acts of demographic surgery'.[39]

As a result of extensive media exposure, the practice of ethnic cleansing has been brought into the popular consciousness and has come to be associated with the Yugoslav wars of the 1990s. Yet, as it is not appropriate to identify ethnic cleansing as something new to the current era, it is also not appropriate to view it as limited to the Yugoslav context. As during the First and Second World Wars, Serbs, Croats, Bosnian Muslims, and Kosovo Albanians were ethnically cleansed and were themselves the perpetrators of cleansing. In this most recent bout of cleansing, namely in the 1990s, according to sheer numbers of people displaced, the Serbs were undoubtedly the most culpable. The evidence points to extensive ethnic cleansing by Serbs in Croatia and Bosnia-Herzegovina. While the total numbers are unclear and unreliable, a regional analysis indicates that, for example, around Banja Luka, fewer than 50,000 Muslims and Croats are left out of a pre-war population of 550,000.[40] In Eastern Bosnia, according to the 1991 census, there were 18,699 Muslims living around Vlasenica, of which there are none left.[41] Most recently, Serbian forces (in conjunction with NATO bombing) displaced over half a million Albanians from Kosovo.

However, while Serbian forces have expelled undesirable populations, they are not alone in their efforts to create ethnically pure regions. Ethnic cleansing took place among the Croats and the Muslims, also: for example, some 15,000 Bosnian Croats were cleansed from Vares by Bosnian Muslims.[42] Croats expelled Bosnian Muslims from Herzegovina in such large numbers that Lord Owen suggested in 1992 that Croatia too should be given sanctions for its role in ethnic cleansing.[43] Moreover, Serbs also have been victims of similar tactics and have been expelled from Herzegovina and western Slavonia. The Serbian community of Mostar was cleansed (the pre-war population of 24,000 people was entirely eradicated) as well as from Zenica, Travnik, Bosanski Brod, and so on. Finally, some 200,000 Serbs from Krajina were evicted during the summer of 1995, and others continue to be cleansed from Kosovo in the aftermath of the 1999 armed struggle.

The Yugoslav war is a dirty civil war, in which neighbor has turned against neighbor, and each group is trying to be the first to cleanse undesirables lest they be cleansed instead. As the *Economist* aptly put it, it is a war in which the options are to 'cleanse or be cleansed'.[44]

Contemporary examples of ethnic cleansing outside of Yugoslavia also abound. Sometimes ethnic cleansing is openly proposed but not yet executed, as in the Czech Republic, by the Republican Party (that is represented in Parliament), whose program includes the intention to 'solve the problem of the Roma by resettling them' (a polite term for expulsion).[45] At other times, ethnic cleansing is successfully executed, as the following examples attest. (a) In Georgia (when 200,000 Georgians from Abkhazia were forced to flee during the course of 1992–93).[46] (b) In South Africa between 1960 and 1980, some 3.5 million blacks were removed from their land by the white government and put on reserves (black homelands), the only place where they were allowed to own land (this amounted to 13% of the country).[47] (c) According to human rights activists, more than 70 villages in southeastern Turkey were emptied of Kurds in the period between March and June 1994; during 1990 to 1994, 800 villages were evacuated under government pressure; the town of Cizre was abandoned, under pressure, by more than half of its 60,000 residents between January and June 1994; some 8,000 Kurds have crossed into northern Iraq (some of which were among the 1.5 million that crossed to Turkey from Iraq after the Gulf War).[48] Some 874 villages and hamlets in the southeast of Turkey were cleansed and burned to the ground by the army.[49] Death squads have been responsible for the assassination of hundreds of Kurdish doctors, lawyers, writers, human rights activists, and political leaders as well as numerous kidnappings.[50] (d) During the reign of terror of Macias Nguena Biyogo in Equatorial Guinea, Idi Amin in Uganda and Jean-Bedel Bokassa in the Central African Republic, the targets were always a distinct ethnic group, and the violence perpetrated against them included the forced departure of large groups of people, accompanied by looting and death. (e) In El Salvador, the massacre at El Mozote in 1982 was done by the government to villagers reported to be sympathetic to guerillas. Some 750 people, mostly women and children refugees from other less safe areas, were slaughtered over the course of one weekend.[51] (f) Russians left Tajikistan at a rate of approximately 2,000 people per month during the early 1990s (at the time of independence, 600,000 Russians lived in the republic, in mid-1994 only some 80,000 were left[52]). While these are voluntary migrations, Russians have been cleansed from the key positions in politics and industry that they previously occupied. (g) Entire cities formerly occupied by Azerbaijanis have been burned and pillaged and children taken hostage by the Armenians.[53] Similar events have occurred on Armenian territories. Refugees from the Azeri war with Armenia came to Iran, where 50,000 came in a few weeks in the fall of 1993.[54] (h) Since the invasion of East Timor in 1974, there have been mass killings and evictions of Timorese civilians by the Indonesian government. It is claimed that, of a pre-invasion population of 688,000, some 100,000 to 200,000 peoples have died as a result of the conflict. (i) It was estimated in 1994 that some 90,000 blacks lived in the bondage of the Berbers in Mauritania, while 300,000 former or freed slaves continued to serve their former masters because of economic dependence or psychological factors. When taken into bondage following the sporadic sweeping through and cleansing of their villages, slaves were stripped of their ethnic and religious orientation, and were often forced to take on the religion of their owner.[55] (j) Hawaiians claim they have native rights to land, and that the white man came to their islands and cleansed them from their territory. As a result, they now demand sovereignty for the 140,000 native Hawaiians, who make up 12.7 percent of the population.[56] (k) In Georgia, in Abkhazia, one-half of the population (that was Georgian) was either killed or forced to leave.[57] (l) In Greek Macedonia, Bulgarians were expelled in the early 1920s and 1944. Together with the Turkish-Greek population exchange of the early 1920s, that action made Greek Macedonia virtually completely Greek. (m) Some 30,000 refugees from Tajikistan were forced to leave their homes during the civil war.[58] (n) In the 1991 census, Hungarians in Vojvodina numbered 430,946 or 22 percent of the population of 2.13 million. Since then, 35,000 have fled in response to real or perceived anti-Hungarian activity.[59] (o) Saddam Hussein gassed some 5,000 people in the Kurdish town of Halabja in 1988 during the Iran–Iraq war. At this time, more than 100,000 Kurds were forcibly relocated to areas on the Saudi border.[60] (p) In Bhutan, the government is repressing and torturing the Nepali-speaking minority, forcing thousands to flee to Nepal and India.[61] (q) On Cyprus, before the Turkish intervention of 1974 there were 120,000 Turkish Cypriots, comprising less than 20 percent of the total. Turkish settlers were brought in. Turks and Greeks on the island were displaced, in the order of 150,000 Greeks and 45,000 Turks. (r) In the early 1950s, Malaysia forcibly resettled over 500,000 rural Chinese into new villages (and in an attempt to neutralize their antigovernment sentiments, provided them with some basic needs).[62]

Given its global popularity as a means of altering the ethnic composition of a population (and thus, as a form of interethnic competition), a discussion of the methods by which ethnic cleansing is achieved is in order. First, ethnic groups may be subjected to coerced departures. Individuals or entire communities are simply given a time period during which they must vacate their homes; alternatively they are forced at gunpoint to collect their belongings with no lead time. Examples abound in the current Yugoslav war. In eastern and northwestern Bosnia, Serbs forced Muslims, often at gunpoint, to vacate their homes.[63] On 29 October 1991, Croatian radio gave Serbs 48 hours to leave their homes: the announcer called it a 'depopulation plan'. On 1 November 1991, there followed a mass destruction in which 58,000 Serbs were evicted from 250 villages in western Slavonia in Croatia.[64]

Second, ethnic groups may be harassed in order to induce their departure. Indeed, people will leave their homes, their land, and their jobs if conditions are made sufficiently difficult for their continued survival. Whether they perceive to be threatened by death if they fail to comply, or simply to be prevented from functioning in the workplace or in the neighborhood, their perceived harassment induces migration. It is difficult to define the parameters of voluntary and involuntary migration under duress: the resultant migration *de facto* translates into a situation similar to coerced departure, although it *de jure* differs from it.

There are numerous ways in which members of a target ethnic group may be pressured and harassed to relocate. Sometimes, rights such as police protection are denied to a certain group (there is evidence of this form of harassment in Rwanda and in the former Yugoslavia[65]). Economic pressures are sometimes exerted on a target population. These are discussed at length in chapter 6, suffice it to say here that they include the dismissal of members of an ethnic group or the negation of their property rights.[66]

In addition to economic harassment, rape has recently received much attention as a result of the Yugoslav war. Based on the investigation of the United Nations War Crimes Commission, rapes in the former Yugoslavia have been divided into five categories, and only in one of these is harassment the goal.[67] When it is a policy of harassment, women of a target ethnic group are humiliated and terrorized during the rape process and as a result are likely to migrate from the contested territory. Rape is a part of most war experiences, and according to Enloe, it is usually not random violence but rather is structured by 'class and ethnic inequalities'.[68] She describes how, amid the rapes that took place in the Gulf War, ethnicity and class strongly determined which women were more likely to be raped.[69] Interethnic rape has characterized the war in Bosnia-Herzegovina, although, despite all the publicity, the evidence pertaining to its extent is not at all clear.[70]

Another form of harassment that is evident in many less developed countries is the placing of landmines on land that one hopes to vacate or prevent people from inhabiting. While this practice amounts to indiscriminate killing since it can affect anybody regardless of ethnicity, age, or gender, in effect the ethnicity is controlled since mines are placed in regions inhabited by the targeted undesirable group. Although landmines were prohibited in 1983, their use continues unabated, and their scope has even been enlarged. According to the *Economist*, 'some 100 million mines lie scattered in more than 60 countries', thus manipulating migratory trends and preventing refugees from returning home.[71] The countries where this practice is most common are Cambodia, Afghanistan, Angola, Mozambique, and Somalia.

Third, ethnic cleansing may take the form of cultural cleansing. In this case, ethnic groups are pressured into leaving a territory if the symbols of their culture are eradicated. The practice has come to be called cultural cleansing, and includes the destruction of churches, temples, mosques, museums, historical collections, art work, and sacred books. Moreover, it includes the elimination of minority educational institutions, the suppression of minority languages, the obstruction of contacts with relatives abroad, the dissolution of ethnic communities, and even the falsification of historical and demographic data.

Cultural cleansing has been practiced by numerous ethnic groups. Bosnian Serbs have destroyed numerous Muslim cultural sites in Bosnia in an effort to eradicate 'evidence of Islam in the Serbian historical space'.[72] Croats have destroyed symbols of Orthodoxy in western Slavonia.[73] Hungarians are protesting the cultural cleansing of their peoples because Gheorghe Funar, the Romanian nationalist mayor of Cluj, wants to conduct archaeological digs at the site of a monument to the medieval Hungarian leader, King Mathias.[74]

Finally, ethnic cleansing may be achieved by a financial transaction. Indeed, it is possible to eliminate a target population from a region by paying another state to absorb its members. Germany has recently engaged in this form of ethnic cleansing by signing an agreement with the Romanian government to repatriate Romas: it is estimated that $20 million is being given to reintegrate some 50,000 Romanian Romas.[75]

In conclusion, two points need to be made. First, it is noted that involuntary population migrations, including ethnic dilution, ethnic consolidation, and ethnic cleansing, can further be subdivided into planned transfers (that have been arrived at by consensus) and unplanned transfers (that are void of a consensus). Most of the examples of interethnic population transfers described above are of the unplanned variety, characterized by coercion. In these, people are forced to leave their homes without any effort at compensation, negotiation, or plan for future residence, thereby amplifying the human suffering that is entailed in any relocation. This suffering can be decreased if population transfers are planned and negotiated. Examples of such transfers include the Punjab, where advance warning of partition made the violent migrations of Hindus and Muslims less violent than they otherwise would have been. Also, when Turkey and Greece exchanged populations in 1922–23, their negotiated settlement resulted in the transfer of some 2 million people. Finally, the overt and negotiated expulsion of the Germans at the end of the Second World War resulted in the resettlement of some 10 million Germans. If more interethnic population transfers were planned, the damage to people and property would be significantly lower.

Second, population transfers aimed at achieving political aims, while not a new phenomenon, have become more pronounced in the post-Cold War disorder. In part, this is due to the current popularity of the principle of self-determination based on ethnicity, which underscores the importance of the ethnic (or religious) composition of a population. However, the importance of numbers in determining both the political and economic power of a group relative to others is only valid in a legal system in which rights are based on groups rather than individuals (such a system is different from one based on the Renner–Bauer model, according to which 'national rights should be accorded to individual persons rather than exclusively to territorial groupings'[76]). As long as the ethnic group rather than the individual is the relevant unit within society, pressures will exist to increase the relative numbers of 'desirable' people. As long as nationalists think that they can achieve self-determination on the basis of the ethnic population of a territory, then they will strive to create an ethnically pure population in the region or regions they covet. The quickest way to achieve this goal is by forcing populations to relocate. Refugees carry with them emotional baggage that can translate into political support for nationalist policies to a degree unlikely among peoples not directly touched by this experience. Hence the popularity of the practices of ethnic dilution, consolidation, and cleansing.

POPULATION MOVEMENTS AND THE DEMOGRAPHIC STRUGGLE FOR POWER

Three seemingly unrelated events of the late twentieth century have recently been on the front pages of American newspapers: the war in Kosovo, the US census of the year 2000, and the custody battle over Elian Gonzales, the Cuban boy rescued at sea. What can these three events possibly have in common?

They are all, fundamentally, about a power struggle based on population numbers. All are related, in different ways, to the political power that is derived from the size of one ethnic (or religious or racial) group relative to the others. In Kosovo, two such groups, the Albanians and the Serbs, are struggling to claim their rights over territory. On the grounds of numerical supremacy in the present, the Albanian population demands independence from Yugoslavia. On the grounds of numerical supremacy in the past, Serbs demand control over their historical territories. To tilt the relative numbers in their favor, first the Serbs and then the Albanians engaged in evictions of undesirable populations.

With respect to the census, there is an ongoing debate about the use of statistical sampling in order to count people who could not be enumerated in the traditional way.[77] The stakes are high because the results of the census are used to reapportion seats in the House of Representatives among Democrats and Republicans and to divide billions of federal dollars. Who was undercounted in the previous census? The minorities (blacks and Hispanics) who, by the way, tend to vote Democratic. Also undercounted are recent immigrants. Close to 6 million undocumented immigrants live in the United States, and 275,000 arrive each year.[78] It is these people that the census wants to enumerate, since their exact number is important knowledge for the communities that absorb them. These communities provide them with health care and social services, housing assistance, education, and jobs training. As a result, billions of dollars of federal funding are riding on this census.

The custody battle over Elian Gonzales, a six-year-old boy from Cuba, had political ramifications that have not yet subsided at the time of writing. Al Gore's presidential campaign was affected, Miami was paralyzed with demonstrations and a work stoppage, local politicians Alex Penelas and Joe Carollo vowed to disobey federal rules; the chief of police resigned; and the city manager was fired. The question of whether Elian Gonzales should live with his father in Cuba or his great-uncle in the United States has evoked visceral responses from both sides of the cultural divide. Those who supported his staying in the US were prepared to form a human chain around his uncle's house to prevent federal agents from turning him over to the father. Some were reported to be willing to die in order to protect him. Those who believed he should be returned to Cuba were equally strong in their views, seeing reunification with the sole surviving parent as the overriding principle. Incidentally, it is Miami's Cuban Americans that support Elian's stay in the United States, while blacks, Jews, non-Cuban Hispanics, and others have united in their opposition. The city became enveloped in interethnic intolerance and animosity.

Back to the comparison of the three events: the war in Kosovo, the debate over the US census, and Elian's custody battle all share a common denominator: the interethnic competition for power. In- and out-migration affects the relative size of ethnic populations and thereby their power. In the case of Kosovo, since the Second World War, in-migrations of Albanians and out-migrations of Serbs have fundamentally altered the ethnic composition of Kosovo over the past 50 years, so that today Albanians account for over 90 percent of the population. In the case of the census, migrations alter the number of minorities residents and voters in any given district, thus impacting on the magnitude of federal dollar inflows and underscoring the importance of their relative numbers. In the custody battle for Elian, the power of the Cuban community in Miami became evident. Their ability to influence local politics underscored the dynamic nature of the ethnic composition of Miami-Dade. Immigration of Cubans to the area over the past four decades had altered the ethnic composition of the county, making them the dominant ethnic group (numerically, and therefore politically and economically). There are 800,000 Cubans among the 2.1 million residents in Miami-Dade. The power associated with this dominance was clear to non-Cubans when two mayors (Cuban) vowed not to uphold federal law while the two scapegoats, police chief O'Brien and city manager Warshaw, were not Cuban. Moreover, the Elian Gonzales affair might affect migration in yet one more way. As a result of the brazen display of Cuban power during the custody battle, non-Cubans are motivated to migrate out of Miami.[79] They will vote with their feet and many will believe their dislocation was not voluntary.

The three events described above are examples of different groups trying to increase their power by increasing the number of people of 'their kind' in a given territory. They are indications of the demographic struggle for power. Forced population movements, while not directly part of these examples, are undoubtedly one of the ways in which the demographic struggle plays out. In the process, it ties together interethnic competition and migration.

NOTES

1 D. Eltis, 'Free and Coerced Transatlantic Migrations: Some Comparisons', *American Historical Review*, quoted in Timothy J. Hatton and Jeffrey G. Williamson, *The Age of Mass Migration* (Oxford: Oxford University Press, 1998), p. 7.

2 Herman M. Schwartz, *States Versus Markets* (New York: St Martin's Press, 1994), p. 117.

3 Differential interethnic voluntary migration rates may also cause reversals in population ratios. However, these are often more likely to be caused by pursuit of land and food (for example, massive Bengali migration into Assam threatens the population ratio). As such, they are not part of a policy in the demographic struggle for power, and thus were not within the scope of this study.

4 Kuper lists euphemisms that have been used to describe the population that has been transplanted. He quotes Alexander Solzhenitsyn, who referred to 'special settlers' for the exiled nations. From the vocabulary of Nazi Germany, he describes the following phrases: resettlement of alien elements, evacuation, special treatment, cleaning up operation, securing the army's rear, and executive measure. Leo Kuper, *Genocide* (New Haven: Yale University Press, 1981), pp. 104–5.

5 It is also an economic phenomenon in a counterproductive way. According to Jay Mandle, the availability of slave labor on plantations tended to retard innovation – why innovate when workers were readily available and relatively cheap? See Jay Mandle, *The Roots of Black Poverty* (Durham: Duke University Press, 1978).

6 *Economist*, millennium special edition, 31 December 1999, p. 69.

7 D. W. Galenson, 'The Rise and Fall of Indentured Servitude in the Americas: An Economic Analysis', *Journal of Economic History* 44 (1984), and F. Grubb, 'The End of European Servitude in the United States: An Economic Analysis of Market Collapse, 1772–1853', *Journal of Economic History 54* (1994). Both are quoted in Hatton and Williamson, *Mass Migration*.

8 *Economist*, 8 May 1999, p. 52.

9 *Miami Herald, Parade magazine*, 20 February 2000, p. 4. A lower estimate, provided by a CIA study entitled 'International Trafficking in Women to the United States: A Contemporary Manifestation of Slavery', puts the annual number at 50,000, although it refers only to women and children. *New York Times*, 2 April 2000.

10 Refugees have been defined as those individuals that flee from man-made disasters: Gordenker defines refugees as 'persons who have left their customary homes under the pressure of fear for their present or future lives, because of immediate, overt threats or – more comprehensively – clear denials of basic human rights whose enjoyment is required for continued life over a short or longer period'. Leon Gordenker, *Refugees in International Politics* (New York: Columbia University Press, 1987), p. 63.

11 Cohen and Deng have distinguished between refugees and the internally displaced population by defining the latter as people coerced to migrate but who remain within national boundaries. Roberta Cohen and Francis M. Deng,

Masses in Flight (Washington, DC: Brookings Institution Press, 1998), p. 16.

12 Not all governments that cause population movements do so out of design or malice. Indeed, some are simply incompetent, and are unable to lead their populations or offer them adequate standards of living. For example, government incompetence led to hunger in Somalia and Ethiopia, while political instability in Lebanon in the 1970s led to chaos, and both created destabilizing population movements.

13 David Osterfeld, *Prosperity Versus Planning* (Oxford: Oxford University Press, 1992), p. 208.

14 *OMRI Daily Digest* 120, 21 June 1995.

15 *US News and World Report*, 30 November 1992, p. 36.

16 *La Repubblica*, 20 August 1992.

17 Gordenker, *Refugees*, pp. 52–9.

18 *New York Times*, 4 September 1994.

19 Joly points out that the Croatian refugees were relocated to Istria 'in order to dilute the Italian-speaking population there and possibly bolster support for the ruling Croatian Democratic Community party in an area where they had previously been defeated in elections'. Daniele Joly, *Refugees-Asylum in Europe* (Boulder, CO: Westview Press, 1992), p. 87.

20 Ibid., p. 86.

21 *OMRI Daily Digest*, 23 May 1995.

22 Transylvanian World Federation, *Genocide in Transylvania* (Astor, FL: Danubian Press, 1985), p. 23. While this may be a somewhat biased source, there are no others available.

23 *FRE/RL Daily Report*, 17 June 1994, p. 4.

24 *New York Times*, 30 October 1994.

25 Moreover, there is a pressure on land in the north due to privatization, so movement to the south would solve two problems. *Economist*, 30 April 1994, p. 60.

26 *Miami Herald*, 26 August 1994.

27 *New York Times*, 5 September 1994.

28 Elian Gonzales was rescued at sea in November 1999, on his way to Miami with his mother, who did not survive the crossing. His father's Miami relatives received him and fought in the courts for custody and then the right to an asylum hearing. The father flew to Washington to take over custody of the son, who was taken, at gunpoint, from the Miami relatives in April 2000.

29 Zalman Shoval quoted in *New York Times*, 7 May 1994.

30 *FRE/RL Daily Report*, 14 April 1994, p. 6.

31 Theodore Wright, 'The Ethnic Numbers Game in India: Hindu–Muslim conflicts Over Conversion, Family Planning, Migration and the Census' in William C. McCready (ed.), *Culture, Ethnicity and Identity* (New York: Academic Press, 1983), p. 419.

32 *OMRI Daily Digest* 113, 12 June 1995.

33 Indians in tropical areas were especially vulnerable to these diseases. Blacks were brought in to replace them (indeed, this is where the black slaves were very prominent: by the end of sixteenth century 40,000 African slaves had been imported to Mexico, adding yet another race to the social structure).

34 Andrew Bell-Fialkoff, 'A Brief History of Ethnic Cleansing', *Foreign Affairs* 72, 3 (1993), p. 110.

35 It is interesting to note that despite its frequency across the globe, it was only condemned by the World Court on 8 April 1993.

36 Ibid., p. 110.

37 One of the largest cases of ethnic cleansing in Europe in modern times, that of the Germans from Eastern Europe at the end of the Second World War, is often forgotten. At this time, some 10 million Germans were expelled from Eastern Europe. Recently, the Austrian Foreign Minister Alois Mock compared the expulsion of Sudeten Germans from Czechoslovakia to ethnic cleansing in Bosnia, since some 3 million Germans were expelled and all their property confiscated. *FRE/RL Daily Report*, 18 May 1994, p. 7.

38 On the order of some 1 million people, mostly women and children (Kuper, *Genocide*, p. 144). Stalin deported Balkars *en masse* in 1944. In 1994 Boris Yeltsin signed a decree to repatriate some of the Balkars, return historical names to settlements and localities, and to give special consideration to pension arrangements for those deported. FRE/RL Daily Report, 4 March 1994, p. 3.

39 John McGarry and Brendan O'Leary (eds), *The Politics of Ethnic Conflict Regulation* (London: Routledge, 1993), p. 5; William Pfaff, *The Wrath of Nations* (New York: Simon & Schuster, 1993), p. 90.

40 *New York Times*, 16 June 1994.

41 Ibid., 1 August 1994.

42 Ibid., 4 November 1993.

43 *FRE/RL Research Report* 1, 45, 13 November 1992, p. 77.

44 *Economist*, 6 February 1993, p. 53.

45 Paul Hochenos, *Free To Hate* (New York: Routledge, 1993), p. 225.

46 *New York Times*, 19 November 1993.

47 *Economist*, 28 May 1994, p. 35.

48 Ibid.,11 June 1994, p. 47.

49 The army claims that they did move people in order to protect them from the PKK, the Kurdish party (workers party of Kurdistan). Jeri Laber, 'The Hidden War in Turkey', *New York Review of Books* (23 June 1994), p. 47.

50 Ibid.

51 Mark Danner, *The Massacre at El Mozote: A Parable of the Cold War* (New York: Vintage, 1994).

52 *FRE/RL Daily Report*, 20 June 1994, p. 4.

53 *International Herald Tribune*, 16–17 July 1994.

54 Iran gives shelter to many refugees (2 million from Afghanistan), but the Azeris pose a special danger, since there are Azeris in Iran that found themselves on the wrong side of a border that was drawn in 1828 (indeed, 20 million people). *Economist*, 6 November 1994, pp. 49–50.

55 *New York Times*, 13 July 1994.

56 Ibid., 5 June 1994.

57 Ibid., 8 June 1994.

58 But many have returned to their homes in May 1994, after some of the civil war subsided. *FRE/RL Daily Report*, 24 May 1994, p. 4.

59 Moreover, the number of people that declare themselves Hungarian has declined, as a result of assimilation, high birth and low death rates, and emigration. *FRE/RL Research Report* 2, 48, 3 December 1993, p. 43.

60 Gurr, *Minorities*, p. 228.

61 *Miami Herald*, 25 May 1994.

62 Richard Stubbs, 'Malaysia: Avoiding Ethnic Strife in a Deeply Divided Society' in Joseph Montville (ed.), *Conflict and Peacemaking in Multiethnic Societies* (Lexington, MA: Lexington Books, 1990), p. 294.

63 *New York Times*, 16 June 1994.

64 William Dorich in *New York Times*, 3 September 1994.

65 For example, Serbs from Croatia do not enjoy police protection nor the same

legal rights as other citizens, and are urged to relocate to Serbia. *Sueddeutsche Zeitung*, 16 May 1994.

66 Examples of the former are the loss of employment experienced by Russians in Tajikistan; examples of the latter include the eviction of former Yugoslav army members from their homes in Croatia, known as *delozacija*. While the Croatian government declared moratorium on this practice in December 1993, by then several hundred were removed, and the practice continues. Indeed, 97% of those 'delodged' are Serbs, and they are replaced in their homes by Croat soldiers. *Evropske Novosti*, 8 February 1994. This tallied with a statement by President Tudjman, 'Why are there 6 000 apartments with Serbs inside and you, Croatian invalids, haven't got any?', *FRE/RL Daily Report*, 12 July 1994), p. 7.

67 The categories of rape include the following: 1. rape by individuals and small groups raping in conjunction with looting and intimidation, in the absence of war; 2. rape by individuals and small groups in conjunction with fighting, rape usually in public; 3. rape by individuals or small groups of people in detention; 4. sexual assaults for the purpose of terrorizing and humiliating people, as a part of ethnic cleansing; 5. rape of women detained in hotels for the sole purpose of sexually entertaining soldiers, rather than causing a reaction in women. *New York Times*, 12 June 1994.

68 Cynthia Enloe, *The Morning After: Sexual Politics at the End of the Cold War* (Berkeley: University of California Press, 1993), p. 168.

69 The least likely to be raped were the US female soldiers, yet over 20 were raped by their fellow US soldiers. In Kuwait, Asian women were more likely to be raped than Kuwaiti, and upper income were less likely to be than lower-income women. See ibid., chapters 5, 6, and 7.

70 See Jacques Merlino, *Les Verite Yugoslave Ne Sont Pas Toutes Bonnes a Dire* (Paris: Editions Albin Michel, 1993).

71 *Economist*, 27 November 1993, p. 42.

72 *FRE/RL Daily Report*, 16 December 1993, p. 5.

73 Davidov *et al.*, *War Damage Sustained By Orthodox Churches in Serbian Areas of Croatia in 1991* (Belgrade: Ministry of Information of the Republic of Serbia, 1991).

74 *FRE/RL Daily Report*, 27 June 1994, p. 9.

75 *New York Times*, 26 September 1992.

76 Renner and Bauer wrote about the situation in which 'national or ethnic groups were so interspersed geographically that any neat division between "their" territories was impossible'. Peter L. Berger, 'Preface' in Uri Ra'anan *et al.* (eds), *State and Nation in Multi-ethnic Societies* (Manchester: Manchester University Press, 1991), p. ix.

77 *New York Times*, 19 March 2000.

78 *Wall Street Journal*, 3 April 2000.

79 An immigration lawyer associated with the case said that if the Cuban exile community manages to keep Elian in Miami, many Anglos, blacks and non-Cuban Hispanics would feel sufficiently angered that 'they would find somewhere else to live'. *New York Times*, 1 April 2000.

6

Domestic Regulation of Migration: Inducements and Impediments

In the Sudan, the southern regions (inhabited by Christians) receive less per capita development funding than the northern regions (inhabited by Arabs). In Moldova, the local language has replaced Russian in the workplace, thus displacing nonnative speakers. In South Africa, employment restrictions during apartheid limited the access of blacks to highly skilled jobs. These are all examples of government policies that discriminate against target ethnic groups.[1]

Such discrimination runs counter to the professed values and ethics that predominate among western populations. From the perspective of the liberal, democratic tradition, in which individual rights are respected and ethnic origin is considered largely irrelevant in the eyes of the law, it may seem unlikely that leaders would or could sponsor or induce discrimination by ethnicity (or race or religion). Examples of legalized discrimination in the 'nondemocratic' parts of the world are considered, in the words of Safran, 'oppressive and inelegant',[2] and are viewed with concern by human rights activists. Indeed, examples such as the prohibition of Russians to own land in Latvia, the Iraqi draining of Shiite marshes, and employment restrictions against blacks in South Africa, are but some of the cases in which peoples are judged by ethnicity. Yet, even in societies in which the democratic tradition reigns, evidence of discriminatory policy lies not far back in their history.

This chapter addresses discriminatory policies that are economic in nature. Their goal is to apply economic pressures or offer economic incentives to the population in order to manipulate its behavior. By definition, these policies are targeted at specific ethnic groups (according to Horowitz: 'Systems of economic relations can crystallize around *opportunities afforded* and *disabilities imposed* by government policy on particular ethnic groups' (italics mine)[3]). In this way, government policies may enhance or decrease the present and future welfare of specific populations. Such policies include economic incentives to induce relocation, as well as legislation that discriminates by ethnic group with respect to taxes, property rights, labor conditions, and economic develpment.[4] Policy can thus influence the mobility of the labor force, directly or indirectly, by determining which ethnic group's workers have incentives and capacities to migrate. By inducing migration or restricting migration, a discriminatory policy manipulates the options and realities of a specific ethnic labor force. In this way, a target ethnic group can be induced to migrate in what Schatz called 'slow motion ethnic cleansing'.[5]

The economic aspects of ethnic policies as well as differential economic policies have rarely been studied by economists. The study of interethnic relations in general has been neglected by economists, since they are perceived to be the domain of anthropologists, political scientists, and sociologists.[6] However, research by Wyzan on the economic aspects of differential treatment of ethnic groups and that of Sowell on preferential policies around the world begins to fill the void in the literature.[7] Yet, to the extent that scholars in any field have addressed the issue of selective treatment of ethnic groups, they have neglected the link between differential policies and population shifts. Indeed, the study of preferential policies and affirmative action has been discussed in the literature insofar as it contradicts the concept of merit as the grounds for success within a system.[8] Also, these types of policies have been studied to ascertain their effectiveness in coping with ethnic conflict and the role of economic factors in persistent ethnic inequality. To the extent that preferential policies can eliminate the source of ethnic conflict, and to the extent that they can offset economic inequality, they are then judged worth the negative side effects, such as cost and bias against some groups. Such research leaves unanswered questions pertaining to the link between selective policies and induced migration.

DIRECT ECONOMIC INDUCEMENTS AND IMPEDIMENTS TO MIGRATION

Inducements and impediments that affect labor migrations can be divided into those that have a direct effect on migration and those that affect migration only indirectly. Direct and indirect inducements may be either overt or camouflaged. The former are those whose goals are clearly stated and whose intent is unmistakable (for example, the South African regulation that restricts land ownership of blacks). The latter are those inducements that may be interpreted as having other or multiple intents (for example, tax concessions for large families that, incidentally, happen to be largely of a single target ethnic group).

Ethnic leaders directly induce or prevent populations from migrating by using economic incentives. To discourage migration, governments extract a financial penalty: for example, the Chinese government has restricted population movements into the Beijing by requiring migrants to pay a fee of $11,600.[9] To induce in-migration, leaders pay (directly or indirectly) for the relocation of target populations (for example, Serbian authorities have provided Serbian families with economic incentives such as housing and employment to induce migration into Kosovo[10]). To induce the dispersal of peoples, leaders offer economic benefits to target populations. (For example, Hungarian graduates from vocational schools and universities have been offered employment or assigned to jobs outside their communities. Romanians are encouraged to replace them through offers of high incomes and housing opportunities in the Hungarian communities.[11]) To reduce the likelihood that temporary population relocations will become permanent, some leaders have instituted policies that act as economic disincentives for long term stay (in Switzerland, guest workers enjoy public benefits, such as education, only on a nine month cycle that coincides with the school year, thereby encouraging annual repatriations[12]). Sometimes, leaders pay directly for population relocations. The recent example of Germany's payment to Romania for the repatriation of Romanian Roma, and to Bulgaria for some 25,000 Bulgarians, is a clear example of the provision of financial inducement in order to remove an undesirable people from its territory.[13] Sometimes, the expulsion is accomplished by economic means, albeit in a roundabout manner. (For example, in Saudi Arabia, 1 million Yemeni workers lost their jobs, were denied extensions of their residency permits, and as a result had to repatriate.[14]) Lastly, leaders accept payment in exchange for allowing people to leave the country (as in Romania under Ceauşescu's rule, when exit visas were sold to Jews for $10,000 per person).

INDIRECT ECONOMIC INDUCEMENTS AND IMPEDIMENTS TO MIGRATION

Economic policy that makes an ethnic group feel less welcome, curtails its rights, and suppresses its economic development may indirectly achieve the same result as direct policy that induces or impedes migration.

In order for such indirect policy to result in selective migration of target ethnic groups, it must be based on discrimination. Discriminatory policy is one that advantages one group within society while disadvantaging another. Scholars have offered theories explaining how discrimination occurs in the labor market (i.e. Feiner), how it is rational (i.e. Becker), and how it is counterproductive for economic development (i.e. Williams). Empirical evidence has also shown that discrimination is pervasive across societies.[15] Indeed, it is pervasive not only informally, among ethnic groups engaging in interpersonal exchanges, but also formally, as reflected in government laws and regulations.

Discrimination is sometimes enshrined in national constitutions. Despite Napoleon Bonaparte's advice that constitutions should be short and obscure, numerous countries have adopted constitutions that are anything but short and obscure.[16] Indeed, many are quite elaborate documents, specifically delineating the nature of the desired discrimination. In such documents, the leadership publicly identifies the dominant ethnic group (or race) and often grants its language official status while designating other languages secondary. This explicit expression of an ethnic or linguistic hierarchy need not necessarily indicate the institutionalization of discrimination, although under conditions of pre-existing interethnic hostility, it tends to bode ill for the nontitular population. This was true of the constitutions of Sri Lanka, the new post-Yugoslav states, as well as the new Baltic post-Soviet states. In addition to those, the Malaysian constitution contains an amendment (no. 53) which grants the government the right to impose quotas for Malays for positions in public service, scholarships, and permits and licenses. In all of these countries, communal identities such as ethnic, religious, and moral are at variance with liberal Western ideas. Indeed, in many countries of the former Soviet Union and eastern and central Europe, as well as in Africa, constitutions exist but are by no means liberal in the western sense.[17] The creation of the Israeli state was meant for Jews while others, notably Israeli Arabs, were relegated to second class. Finally, the Japanese constitution of 1946, largely written by American officials during the military occupation, has two versions – one in English and one in Japanese. The English version states clearly that all people are equal under the law and that there can be no discrimination on the basis of race, creed etc. However, in the Japanese version, the term for people is *kokumin*, essentially meaning Japanese. The lack of precise definitions gives a great deal of latitude to those who look for ways to stretch boundaries of the law.

Not all economic discrimination is enshrined in the constitution. Programs based on discrimination may be associated with only some governments (such as the 'Sinhala Only' policy in effect until Jayewardene came to power in 1977, or the policy of 'Northernization' espoused by the First Nigerian Republic), or only some sectors (such as land restrictions in Fiji or restrictions of shares in new companies in Indonesia). In Israel, where there is no constitution, there is a discrepancy in government thinking on the question of institutionalized discrimination. According to Klimov, on the one hand, the Declaration of Independence (1948) establishes a Jewish state for Jews from the diaspora (thereby elevating Jews in the state to a special status), on the other hand, it promises equal rights regardless of race or religion. In South Africa, laws and practices that evolved over the past several centuries, including the policy of apartheid, in effect codified the superiority of whites over blacks. This was manifested in numerous spheres of economic life, including the removal of blacks from 'white' urban areas and their confinement to homelands (bantustans), which were to offer employment, housing, and simultaneously restrict movement.[18] (The post-apartheid government, however, reversed all that by enshrining in the constitution the right to freedom from discrimination on the grounds of race, religion, sex etc.)

Moreover, discrimination does not need to be encoded in order to exist. A study by Marx shows that Brazil did not have discrimination built into its legal structure and never experienced legal segregation between the races, and thus unlike South Africa and the United States, did not have a legacy of institutionalized racial animosities. Instead of laws biased against the African Brazilians and the indigenous Indian population, in Brazil 'the past was reconceived into a benign image, unlike elsewhere. Belief in racial tolerance was thereby reinforced, the legacy of inequality was camouflaged, and quiescence among Afro-Brazilians was encouraged'.[19]

Indirect policies that induce (or prevent) selected populations to participate in the labor force or to migrate include selective regulations pertaining to property ownership, discrimination in labor issues, selective tax policy, selectivity in development projects, ethnic discrimination in education, selective use of prices, and manipulation of natural resources. These and others are discussed below. Together, they are the government policies that affect a migrant's capacity and incentive to voluntarily migrate.

Selective Regulations Pertaining to Property Ownership

When the property rights of ethnic groups are curtailed, their members may be more prone to relocate. When a selected ethnic group is prevented from starting a new business or from receiving agricultural credit for land purchase, its members have an inducement to seek greater opportunities elsewhere.

Land

In most developing countries (as well as in many more developed countries), land provides the principal source of sustenance for a large portion of the population. Land is a source of employment, of income, of status, and of pride. As a result, regulations that determine rights to land ownership are by definition a sensitive matter, especially when they entail discrimination based on ethnicity.

Examples of such discrimination abound. Land restrictions have characterized numerous countries throughout their histories as well as in the present. Some past examples that greatly influenced present-day ownership patterns include that of the Ottoman Empire. According to the Decree of Omar II from the *Koran-al-Raya*, across the Ottoman Balkans, Orthodox Christians and Jews were restricted in owning property: 'the acquisition of real property and houses is reserved for Moslems'.[20] Another historical example is the United States. The Sioux Indians lived on territory in South Dakota that is rich in mineral deposits. The United States Congress never purchased the land, but rather passed legislation annexing Indian territories, and claimed that the tribes had agreed to the transfer. Since 1920, the Sioux have been suing the government for that land from which they were evicted.[21]

In most of these cases, newcomers had advantages that helped push original settlers on to marginal lands. This happened with blacks with the coming of the Afrikaners, the Indians with the coming of the white man, and even among local groups in Africa, such as the pagan peoples of northern Cameroon, that were pushed out by the pastoralist Fulani and the trader Hausa.[22] However, the loss of land rights is not limited to cases of newly arrived immigrants. Indeed, in Turkey, in the aftermath of the Greco-Turkish war, Greeks lost the rights to own land. In Malaysia, the foreign and merchant laborers, such as the Indians and the Chinese, that were imported during colonialism had no territorial rights.

In some cases, land discrimination is direct and applied with righteousness. The most blatant and large-scale case is that of South Africa: the Land Act of 1913 prevented blacks from owning land outside of a few arid, worthless parcels, thereby allotting 90 percent of the territory to whites. The Land Act resulted in the segregation and forced resettlement of blacks on ten ethnic reserves, where since 1960, 3.5 million blacks have been resettled because they constituted a 'surplus population'.[23] By 1966, the separation of blacks into tribal homelands was virtually complete (this state of affairs continued into the 1990s, giving President Mandela the unpleasant task of dismantling the land laws[24]). In addition, blacks did not have equal access to agricultural bank loans and support of local government in rural development programs.

While South African land policy is undergoing changes, discrimination continues in many locations, even at the turn of the new millennium. In some post-communist countries, land policies and practices have emerged that are to the detriment of the nontitular nationalities. In Latvia, for example, legislation prohibits Russians from owning land.[25] In Kosovo, while there is no legislation to support discrimination against Serbs in the purchase of land, there is anecdotal evidence that suggests widespread refusal to sell land to Serbs, as Albanians favor selling to other Albanians.

Such practices are not confined to the formerly communist countries. In Zimbabwe, a draft constitution was put to referendum in February 2000 which contained a clause giving authority to the government to confiscate white-owned land without compensation.[26] In Fiji, land has been reserved for Fijians, despite the fact that some one-half of the population is composed of Indians. According to Mayer, land could be leased to Indians but only at exorbitantly high rents, thus effectively preventing their long-term sustenance from the land.[27] In the Middle East, there has been an influx of Muslims into the previously Christian city of Bethlehem on the West Bank. There is evidence of Muslim resistance to selling property to Christians: a resident of the area explained that Muslims are 'committed to the religious aspect of owning land more than Christians'.[28]

Finally, there are instances in which land legislation has (unintentionally) had discriminatory effects on various ethnic groups. In Kazakhstan, the introduction of legislation supporting private ownership of land has been postponed numerous times because of its discriminatory effect: it is expected that it will be the Russian population that will be able to purchase land leading to a situation in which the seminomadic rural Kazakhs have no property rights on territory they have traditionally inhabited.[29]

Housing
While housing is closely related to land, it is not a principal source of income across the globe. It is, however, associated with the satisfaction of basic human needs for shelter, and thus regulation restricting ownership or lease of housing touches the very core of human existence. For this reason, legislation restricting housing rights of individuals by ethnicity or race has been at the core of criticism by the international community. The denial of housing rights is common across the globe. In Israel, restrictions on Arab residence had been in force for 52 years, preventing Israeli Arabs from living where they choose. It was only in early 2000 that Israel's high court ruled that Arabs could no longer be restricted in their living choices, and barred designation of any community as exclusively Jewish.[30] In South Africa, blacks were only allowed housing on their homelands, and it was illegal to acquire or rent housing in the white urban areas (in 1986, the Pass Laws were repealed, and blacks were allowed to relocate to the urban

areas). Similar to the South African concept of passes (that restricts mobility of blacks) is the system of permits that was popular in the Sudan: the Passports and Permits Ordinance was introduced in 1922 and gave the leadership the authority to close parts of the country to specific people and thus to restrict interethnic mobility. In Hungary, some 40 percent of the Roma population live in 'segregated rural ghettos' in small town and villages.[31] Since there is much popular resistance among Hungarians to integrating the Romas, urban housing is rarely available to them. They were even further segregated in the Czech Republic, where a 6-foot high brick wall was erected to separate them from their Czech neighbors (it was finally removed and the government paid for the purchase of the real estate of the Czech neighbors who refused to live adjacent to the Roma).[32] Finally, an integral part of the Yugoslav wars of the 1990s was the eviction of targeted ethnic groups from their homes. This process of eviction entailed signing over of property rights, under duress, to those executing the evictions. Under those circumstances, ethnicity determines the right to own property in a given territory.

Capital and business

Governments control the ethnic structure of the economy by regulating the ethnicity of capital owners and by instituting preferences by ethnicity in business dealings (such as in the granting of licenses). Such preferential policies put some groups at a disadvantage while bolstering others.[33] These policies are often introduced in order to achieve equality or redress past injustices. They often fail to achieve either goal and only succeed in eradicating a business class from a region.

Numerous historical examples illustrate the effect of these policies. In Turkey, for example, a capital levy was introduced in 1941, ostensibly applicable to all ethnic groups. However, its real goal was the eradication of the Jewish bourgeoisie and its replacement by Muslims. The exorbitant fees and the stringent regulations pertaining to their payment did in fact succeed in dramatically reducing the Jewish participation in the Turkish business community.[34] Similarly, in the post-independence period, the leaders of Tanzania and Uganda expropriated Indian businesses and property in an effort to make space for the black population. To ensure the long-term success of their strategy, they then expelled the Indians.

More recently, Malaysia introduced the discriminatory New Economic Policy. It represents an attempt by the authorities to increase the capital and investment capacities of a Malay population that had been traditionally underrepresented in industry, especially relative to the Chinese. According to the policy, 30 percent of equity had to be set aside for Malay interests, and Malay distributors had to be used as much as possible, with a minimum of 30 percent of the turnover. The restructuring of corporate wealth was to be overseen by several new public enterprises created for this purpose, the National Trust for Indigenous People, the Urban Development Authority and the National Corporation, for example. The last had as task, for example, to facilitate 'Malay ownership of industrial and commercial enterprises'.[35]

Furthermore, the Malays in Malaysia have preferential access to the stock market. Wyzan has described how the government-funded enterprises purchase stock, which they hold in trust for the Malays.[36] Horowitz describes a similar process in Indonesia, where a specified percent of shares in new companies must be held by the indigenous population.[37] In the Philippines, an informal program has emerged according to which Muslims are given preference in bank loans over others insofar as they are exempted from meeting formal requirements (such as credit-worthiness for loans).[38] Finally, in post-apartheid South Africa, the business world is experiencing so called 'black empowerment' deals, which involve important government licenses that are reserved for bidders with at least some black partners. This has occurred in the case of casinos, a television network, and radio stations.[39]

Selective Regulations Pertaining to Employment

Employment restrictions

Selected ethnic groups are subject to restrictions in employment that determine under what conditions they may work, where they may work, and what types of jobs they may perform. Most often such restrictions are unspoken and lack a formal legal enactment, so that the titular ethnic group relies on institutionalized discrimination to perpetuate its position in society. However, in some instances, employment restrictions are in fact legalized. In South Africa, since the First World War, the best occupations, skilled and semiskilled, have been reserved for whites. Moreover, in the 1920s the statutory color bar was established in the labor market. (It is noted that while businesses were instructed to follow strict apartheid rules, numerous (white) firms and managers objected to such regulation. Their objections had less to do with morality and more with profits. With jobs reserved for whites, that meant that wages were artificially kept high. Competition with blacks would have dropped wages and increased profits for the businesses.) Today, in the post-apartheid period, the Employment Equity Act (1999) obliges firms with more than 50 employees to submit annual progress reports of their efforts to make their work-force 'demographically representative' (in other words, about 75% black).[40]

In Israel, Arabs are restricted from employment insofar as they operate in a tightly regulated labor market, regulated through the restriction of travel. Indeed, Arabs are required to obtain a travel permit, which is only issued, following approval, by the nearest Jewish labor exchange.[41] During the peace negotiations between the State of Israel and the Palestinian Authority, the question of mobility of Palestinian workers to and from Israel, as well as between Gaza and the West Bank, was addressed, because it is crucial to all the economies. While Palestinians previously came to Israel in larger quantities (150,000 before the Oslo peace talks), the number in 1999 was a mere 90,000 due to restrictions that have been placed on Palestinians[42] (but not on other ethnic groups, notably those from central Europe and East Asia[43]).

Ethnic discrimination in hiring

While ethnic discrimination in hiring is most visible in government jobs, it is more pervasive in the private sector. With respect to government positions, ethnic discrimination is most likely to occur in the executive branch or the civil service, and most often as a result of preferential legislation. Examples include the following. Across the Middle East, Shiia citizens suffer in countries where Sunnis are in power and are openly excluded from plum jobs (especially in Bahrain and Saudi Arabia).[44] In Sri Lanka, the Donoughmore Constitution adopted in 1931 delineated a system of territorial representation, thereby largely excluding Tamils from the executive branch of government. In Israel, very few Arabs work in the civil service with the central government. Of the 1,860 senior officials in the government and major nongovernmental institutions, only 26 were Arabs (and most of these were employed in the religious courts).[45] While Arab exclusion from the Ministry of Defense might be justified, Klinov claims that it is prevalent also in the offices of the Bank of Israel, the Ministry of Industry and Trade, and the Social Security Institute.[46] In Malaysia, the New Economic Policy is a program of affirmative action, instituted after the 1969 race riots. This program strives to achieve 'ethnic restructuring', so that the structure of employment per sector would reflect the ethnic composition. This in effect meant that those sectors in which the Chinese were overrepresented would be altered to reflect their proportion of the population (35.8%).[47] In Nigeria, where southerners dominated in the civil service during the 1950s, a policy of northernization was introduced which succeeded in reversing the composition of the civil service so that northerners outnumbered southerners by 1965.[48] Lastly, in the Indian state of Andhra Pradesh, a prescribed percentage of government positions have been reserved for the minority Telanganas.

In the private sector, ethnic discrimination occurs as employers prefer to work with members of their own ethnic group. As a result, minority workers are at a disadvantage and have difficulty breaking into workplaces. Various forms of affirmative action regulation have restricted but not eradicated that practice. Weiner and Katzenstein have pointed out that people from Kerala (in India) have searched for employment outside of their state and found themselves discriminated against despite their high levels of education.[49] Cases of ethnic discrimination have also been reported in the former Yugoslavia. According to Bartlett, there has been an Albanization of employment in Kosovo.[50] Indeed, the Serbs in Kosovo were not being hired in part to encourage their out-migration from the region. Serbs were also the target of ethnic discrimination in hiring in Croatia: it is estimated that some 40,000 Serbs were fired from their jobs in Croatia just before the civil war broke out.[51]

In South Africa, the post-apartheid period has introduced changes in racial hiring laws. The contrast before and after 1994 is quite stark: it is reported that only one black was employed in South Africa's high security nuclear power plant during apartheid, and his job was to run away from guard dogs in order to train them to bite blacks. Today, the black majority government has introduced preferential treatment in hiring so that 95 percent of the population are the 'newly privileged' blacks.[52]

Legalized wage discrimination
Selected ethnic groups may receive remuneration packages that differ from those of the titular ethnic group. The principal component of this package is salary, although benefits and pensions may also be affected. While it is a common practice (as both Boswell and Bonacich attest[53]), it differs in manifestation as well as legitimacy. For example, wage discrimination may be the result of legislation, such as in South Africa, where white unions were given the right to collective bargaining while black workers' wages were established by the Wage Board.[54] Alternatively, the government may create conditions that indirectly allow the institutionalization of ethnic wage discrimination, such as in Romania, where President Ceauşescu abolished hourly wages and wage by piece work in 1983, replacing it with a merit system, that gave the right to the work overseer to determine merit. It is claimed that, as a result of this policy, Hungarians received lower income during this period.[55]

Linguistic restrictions in employment
While language has been introduced in chapter 2 as a component of the marginalization process, its importance as a tool of discrimination in the 1990s warrants further elaboration. As background to linguistic

discrimination policies, two questions must be asked: what is the economic role of the dominant language, and what role is there for minority tongues? These questions are debated across the globe in different forms, including southern Florida's discussion of bilingual education, the language charter under debate by the Council of Europe, and proposals for majority/minority language rights in Johannesburg, New Delhi, and Jakarta seats of power.[56]

Empowered groups sometimes officially espouse inequality between languages. Their government policies differ with respect to the tolerance awarded to minority languages: at one extreme is the highly permissive language policy (such as in the former Yugoslavia), at the other extreme is the restrictive policy (such as in France). In the latter, some allowance is made for indigenous languages (such as Breton) but not for foreign languages (such as Arabic of the Maghrebis). Some states tolerate bilingualism, such as Belgium and Canada; others operate with several languages, such as the former Yugoslavia, India, and Spain. Indeed, in the former Yugoslavia and India there exists a plurality of official languages, and only within the respective armies is there use of a single language. In Spain, one-quarter of the population uses a tongue other than Castilian. Thus, while the constitution claims that Castilian is the official language across Spain, the Autonomous Communities may designate their languages as 'coofficial' with Castilian (this happened with Catalan, Euskera (Basque language), Galician, Valencian, and Majorcan).[57]

On the other side of the globe, the elections of 1956 in Sri Lanka brought to power a coalition that favored making Sinhala the sole official language of government. Despite the fact that use of minority languages was not illegal, language became the issue behind the 1958 Tamil–Sinhalese riots. Then, in Sri Lanka the constitution of 1972 reaffirmed that Sinhalese was the only national language, to be used in official business in the north and east where Tamil predominates. As a result, large numbers of civil servants were retired.[58]

Although leaders of empowered groups have sometimes condoned the existence and use of minority languages, they have *discouraged* their use in favor of an official language. Examples abound. In Bosnia in the 1990s, there has been a rise in Islamic teaching in schools and the introduction of imported Turkish expressions into Serbo-Croatian: for a time, children were required to say *'merhaba'* for hello, and *'selam azejkum'* for good day.[59] Albanian authorities have shut down primary schools that teach in Greek (on the grounds that they have too few students) while Greeks claim that they have been prevented from setting up private schools.[60] In Wales, employment discrimination against those who spoke no Welsh was so intense that it led to the claim that there was 'apartheid based on language'.[61]

If linguistic regulations limit the official language in a place of employment, then those who are not proficient are either excluded from the labor force altogether, or relegated to the fringe in low-skilled employment. While the use of language as a weeding tool has been identified in the past in many settings, it has recently become the cornerstone of labor policies. As a result, Fisher called language policies 'the rhetoric of exclusion' since they clearly excluded non-titular tongues.[62]

Linguistic restrictions in employment have become especially popular in the new states that emerged from the former Soviet Bloc. In Estonia and Moldova, legislation was passed eliminating the use of Russian in the workplace and introducing the local languages, Estonian and Moldovan, over a period of several years. The result of such legislation was to remove native Russians, especially those that failed to assimilate by learning the local language, from positions coveted by the native population. A further result was to leave these populations without a means of livelihood, with little prospect of achieving a means, and thus with no option but to relocate. Moldova passed a law in 1989 replacing Russian by Romanian as the official language and Cyrillic by Latin as the official script. Non-Romanian native speakers previously employed in leadership positions were required to prove language proficiency through testing. In Estonia, Russians (as all foreigners) must pass a competency exam in Estonian in order to retain their jobs.[63] Latvia, as late as 1999, was still struggling to achieve a linguistic compromise with its 40 percent Russian minority: a bill, sent back to Parliament for revisions, called for the banishing of Russian from public life and imposing restrictions in the private sphere also. For example, private businesses would be required to provide a translation into Latvian of any internal discussion, however, the measure would not apply to foreign firms, only Russian firms (thus highlighting the anti-Russian discrimination).[64]

Needless to say, language politics is potentially explosive. Policy toward minority languages can easily become the source of interethnic conflict (as it did in 1976 in South Africa, where an outbreak of black student protests resulted from the compulsory use of Afrikaans as a medium of instruction). Similarly, Greenberg's study of the politics of the language reforms in the Yugoslav successor states indicates that they tend to be divisive and produce interethnic animosity, rather than assuage it.[65]

Ethnic differentiation in promotion

Ethnic discrimination in the labor markets may express itself in discrimination at the time of promotion. While hard evidence of this is sparse, some analyses of labor markets have identified differential promotion rates by ethnicity. For example, in the context of the Israeli labor markets, Klimov has suggested that there is slower promotion of Arabs than of Jews.[66] In South Africa, the process of what has come to be called Africanization is taking place, according to which senior policy jobs are going to blacks, regardless of qualification. While President Mandela in 1994 said the promotion of blacks would only occur if they were qualified, in practice it seems that there has been little regard for competence.[67]

Ethnic discrimination in education and training
In an effort to tilt the ethnic composition of the workplace in favor of one group, various discriminatory practices in education and training may be followed. These include discriminatory admission require-ments in schools, according to which members of an ethnic group are granted special rights. This occurred in Sri Lanka during 1972–77, where discriminatory admission requirements to universities enabled Sinhalese with lower grades to be admitted. Moreover, the policy of 'standardization of marks' gave preference to Sinhala speakers by giving them extra points on entrance examinations to university simply by taking the exam in Sinhala. In Tanzania, it is estimated that the required secondary school admission scores are 180 for the population of Kilimanjaro, whereas from other regions only 140 is required.[68] In South Africa, discrimination of non-European workers was done through the use of certificates of competency. The Boilers and Machinery Law of 1898, still in effect at the end of the twentieth century, states 'every person having charge of a winding engine used for raising and lowering persons shall be the holder of an engine driver's certificate of competency. No coloured person may hold an engine driver's certificate of competency.'[69] Finally, in the Soviet Union, a complex system of ethnic quotas in higher education were, in effect, somewhat akin to affirmative action policies in the United States. In both cases, it lead to discrimination in education by ethnic group.

Alternatively, legislation may discriminate in the financial benefits it gives to ethnic groups. One group may be selected to receive financial inducements in the form of scholarships or grants, and thereby make education relatively less costly and increase its participation in the educational system. In Malaysia, there is a quota system for scholar-ships whose goal is to increase the Malay population that pursues education. Another consequence is that it makes education more expensive for Chinese (who lose scholarship opportunities), inducing a larger number of them to study abroad. Another component of the total cost of education is the cost of books and supplies. If these become cheaper for one ethnic group, it is likely to change the ethnic composition of students. This occurred in Kosovo, where education is offered in both Albanian and Serbian, but according to Indic, Albanian textbooks are sold more cheaply than textbooks in Serbian.[70]

Legislation may simply deny education to a population of school-children in order to induce their out-migration or limit their future opportunities. This was common during the Soviet times, as when Soviet Germans were deported to central Asia after the German invasion in 1941, where they were denied access to higher education. Such practices occurred at the end of the twentieth century also. In China, a system of residential permits effectively limited the number of migrant families that were legally resident in the urban areas, and therefore limited the number of children from remote provinces who were entitled to education. The 3 million migrants in the Beijing area fall under this ordinance.[71]

Finally, the content of the material taught in schools may be insulting to minority ethnic groups and may reflect discrimination against them. In the predominantly Hindu state of Uttar Pradesh, the demonization of Muslims is illustrated by a math question on an elementary school test: 'If it takes four Savaks [Hindu religious workers] to demolish one mosque, how many does it take to demolish 20?'[72]

Forced labor of selected ethnic groups
Forced labor of selected ethnic groups has been present in countries in which ethnic differentiation has been institutionalized and the legal system does not provide protection to the targeted ethnic group. Forced labor implies that coercion is used to extract labor services from people, without remuneration. For example, it is claimed that ethnic Hungarians were used as forced laborers in Romania for the building of the Black Sea–Danube canal. According to Meyer and Stanglin, 'During the last 30 years, about a half million people were used as free slave laborers on the project, most of them Hungarians from Transylvania.'[73] Also, during both World Wars, Germans used Polish workers as forced labor, and Stalin ordered numerous ethnic groups to be transplanted to Siberia to be used as forced labor.

Given that data pertaining to forced labor is not readily available, it is difficult to infer just how much of forced labor is drawn from minority ethnic groups. Programs may be presented to the entire population, but only some ethnic groups *de facto* become affected. In Myanmar, two programs in the 1990s involving forced labor: one seems to be ethnic-specific, while the other seems not to be. The program that draws labor from all ethnic groups is the reconstruction of parts of Mandalay in preparation for the tourist season: it requires three labor days from each adult.[74] However, the recruiting program whereby young males are used as porters for the military in the forest areas in eastern Myanmar is not aimed at the entire population. The males are recruited from the eastern rural regions, exactly those regions in which the military is fighting rebels. While there is no hard evidence that all these youths are indeed of specific ethnic groups, the location of their residence prior to recruitment indicates that they are not of the titular majority.[75]

Miscellaneous Regulations Affecting Labor

Selective restrictions on movement

While restrictions on emigration are discussed below in chapter 7, illustrations of restrictions on domestic population movements are common and warrant introduction here. Governments enact controls to restrict internal migrations of their populations, as was evident in China and the Soviet Union for many decades. Sometimes such controls are different for different ethnic groups. An apt contemporary example is Israel. Under the terms of Palestinian autonomy, both Israel and Palestinian authorities have been given the right to determine the 'extent and conditions' of labor movements into their areas.[76] The Palestinians in Gaza have been restricted to traveling to the West Bank, nominally their 'state', because of the necessity to pass through Israeli territory. But more than that, the West Bank is apprehensive of the opening of the safe passage route because it will bring in workers from Gaza (who are willing to work for less money than local workers). With respect to employment in Israel, regulation exists such that only day workers are allowed to enter Israel, and even those are carefully selected from a group of married men over age 30 (assumed to be less of a terrorist threat).[77] The result of these restrictions is that only 15 percent of the Gaza labor force is employed in Israel, compared to 25 percent of the labor force of the West Bank.

Tax policies

Differential taxation is used to selectively favor or burden one ethnic group relative to others. Variations in tax rates and the selective use of tax incentives are ways in which taxation can be discriminatory. The goals embodied in differential taxation may be: (a) To induce out-migration of an undesirable group (for example, in Croatia after President Tudjman came to power, property taxes for non-Croatians were higher than for Croatian residents, providing a financial induce-ment for Serbs to relocate). Sometimes, differing property taxes are not legislated, but occur despite the best intentions stated in the taxation legislation, and have the effect of relocating a specific group (for example, there is evidence that blacks in the United States pay higher property taxes than whites on homes of similar value: a study by Beveridge shows that, in suburban areas, blacks pay 58% more than whites, and 30% more in urban areas[78]). (b) To punish a peoples for some committed acts. (c) To raise revenue, with the burden borne disproportionately by one group. (d) To selectively foster economic well-being by granting tax incentives to some peoples (for example, in Sri Lanka, in order to increase the economic development of the Sinhalese regions, tax incentives were used. A tax exemption for 7–10 years, a turnover tax of 2% instead of an income tax for 15 years, as well as exemption from export and import taxes and foreign exchange controls were introduced[79]). (e) To indicate a conciliatory mood toward some ethnic groups (for example, after the granting of Palestinian self-rule in 1994, the terms for the economic relations dictate that Israel will transfer to the Palestinians 75% of income tax paid by Palestinians working in Israel).[80]

These modern examples are but continuations of past discriminatory practices. In South Africa until 1914, a set of discriminatory laws existed for the Asian population (which consisted mostly of indentured immigrants from India). Among these laws was a special tax of three British pounds that the Asian population was required to pay.[81] In the Ottoman Empire, the *haraj* was collected from non-Muslims. It was a stiff and debilitating tax paid to the Sultan.[82] Finally, during colonial times in South America (roughly 1492 until 1825), the mulatos and the Indians were forced to pay tribute to the colonial powers while the Spanish population was exempt. This discriminatory practice persisted until the early part of the twentieth century. Moreover, during this period, there were two 'republics' operating in many areas, especially Mexico and Guatemala: one was for the Spaniards and one for the Indians. They had different laws, and could be kept separate because one was rural and the other urban. Today, while there is no system of differential taxation by ethnicity built into legislation across South America, two republics *de facto* still exist: there are two legal systems at work, but it is not clear if they are distinct because of ethnicity or level of income.[83]

Development policies

Discrimination by ethnicity is sometimes evident in economic development policies and programs. Authorities discriminate in several ways. They may neglect a region inhabited by an undesirable ethnic group with the goal of further impoverishing the target population and perhaps inducing out-migration. Alternatively, governments may inject money into a region inhabited by the target group in the hope of stimulating economic growth that will in turn stimulate assimilation. Examples of both policies abound. East Timor is a case of stimulated economic development, where living conditions have improved since the arrival of the Indonesian army. While it is not clear whether the proliferation of schools, medical facilities, and churches has offset the political repression of the invasion, it is nevertheless an indication of investment that has been made into the region.

Examples of regional neglect are found in many countries, including the Indian reservations in the United States and the Hill Tribe regions in India. In Sri Lanka, Hubbell points out, the discrimination against Tamil areas in the allocation of development funds: of the 40 government-sponsored enterprises established between independence and 1981, only six were in the Tamil regions of the north and east.[84] When projects were introduced into Tamil regions, such as large-scale irrigation projects, they were accompanied by the resettlement of Sinhalese peasants. In the Sudan, the southern regions (Bahr el Ghazal, Equatoria, and the Upper Nile) received significantly less government investment and resources than the north. Even during the period of the Condominium, development projects were concentrated in the north, around Khartoum, and in the valley of the Nile. Abdallah claims that this imbalance was reflected in the fact that the per capita product of the south was 50 percent below the national average. This lack of balance continued into the modern period: in 1983–84, gross domestic investment in the south was 33 percent below the national average, and 60 percent of the north's.[85]

Price policies

Price differentials by ethnicity are introduced to enable one ethnic group to achieve a higher rate of economic growth. (For example, price preferences to Malay construction firms bidding for government contracts. Such preferences have as their aim the long-run undercutting of the Chinese in private sector business, where traditionally they have been dominant.) Alternatively, a government may extend price incentives in order to encourage behavior that supports its particular ideology (in South Africa, in order to encourage the employment of whites, special tariff protection was awarded to industries with a high proportion of white workers, also called 'civilized' labor[86]). In addition, selective use of prices may have as a goal the relocation of some peoples (for example, the mayor of Teheran instituted a policy in the 1980s to drive up prices of necessities, including rents, in order to induce out-migration of new arrivals from the countryside[87]).

In addition to the government-sanctioned policies of price discrimination, localized discrimination of minority groups compounds the effect. Such micro-level cases of price discrimination range from the higher prices charged to blacks at the Adam Mark hotel chain across the United States,[88] to prostitutes in Tasmania charging recent immigrants higher prices for their services.[89]

Natural resource and environment policies

The control of natural resources empowers ethnic groups. Indeed, Turkey's possession of water in Anatolia, which might one day quench the thirst of both neighboring Arabs and Israelis, is a crucial variable in the regional balance of power.[90] So too, control of resources has had an impact on the domestic distribution of power. Exertion of power includes using resources to induce migration. Governments are known to alter geography in order to force undesirable people to move from desirable territory. By making it more difficult and more expensive to live in a territory, the population may view relocation as the only viable option, and thereby alter the demographic composition of the region. An example of this is Iraq, where the government has been trying to dislodge the Shiite Muslims from its southern regions since 1992 by diverting water from the Tigris and Euphrates rivers, and thus to dry up more than half of the vast wetlands. The economic effects of this are great: fish are no longer available, rice cannot be grown, water buffalo are restricted in their movement, and water has become too salty for drinking. The resulting scarcity has greatly affected the price of fresh water (it was selling for $1 per bucket in 1994).[91] The result of this draining of the marshes is that it pushes thousands of people into neighboring Iran (some 200,000 residents are said to have departed from the marshes since mid-1993).[92]

Food is another resource whose accessibility has been withheld and offered selectively by governments. While food policies are often couched in politically palatable terms, they often have different effects on different ethnic groups. For example, during the 20-year struggle for Eritrean independence, there seemed to be a conscious policy of starvation in Eritrea by the Ethiopian government (in order to control the activities of the separatists). As most of the separatists were of a single ethnic group, the starvation policy was *de facto* ethnic-specific. Similarly, in the USSR, the famine that occurred after the collectivization of agriculture can be viewed, according to Wyzan, as a policy of starvation directed against the Ukrainian peasants, since they formed the majority of the Kulak class targeted for extinction.[93] Also, the attacks on the rural peasant areas in El Salvador and Honduras ostensibly to eradicate supporters of Marxism were simultaneously focused on the indigenous population that was overrepresented in those areas. Finally, Turkish officials have used a variety of means to evict Kurds from southeastern Turkey. During 1993–94, they are said to have cut off food, fuel, and supplies. The Turkish army has also adopted scorched-earth tactics to damage the livelihood of the population that depends on agricultural activities.[94] These efforts have succeeded in altering the relative composition of the population in the region, as more than 800 Kurdish villages have been evacuated since 1990.

Consumer rights

Economic discrimination against selected ethnic groups may take the form of denial of consumption rights. In the absence of discriminatory practices, all individuals have the right to purchase goods and services. However, at times such rights are denied to a selected ethnic group. Such economic discrimination may take the form of denial of services, such as refusal to sell services in restaurants, clubs, and stores (for example, in Moravia, the Roma are currently denied access to swimming pools and restaurants;[95] in Tokyo, signs are posted on store fronts stating that foreigners are not allowed inside.[96]

A recent study in the United States revealed discrimination in the consumption of medication. The provision of pain medication was found to be different in predominantly black, Hispanic, or Asian neighborhoods from what it was in white neighborhoods (a study of pharmacies in New York City showed that only 25 percent of pharmacies in nonwhite areas carried enough medication while in white neighborhoods, that number was 72 percent[97]). This study follows others that found that blacks are less likely than whites to be referred for kidney transplants or surgery for early state cancer, and another that doctors are less likely to prescribe painkillers for blacks and Hispanics with broken bones or post-operative pain.[98]

Even in the aftermath of consumption, discrimination was found to take place: a study of citizens crossing the border into the United States has shown that blacks and Hispanics are more likely to be searched by customs officials than whites.[99]

DISCRIMINATORY POLICIES AND SELECTIVE MIGRATION

This chapter illustrates the global presence of discriminatory policies against minority ethnic groups. While such policies have been divided by category to facilitate the discussion, more often than not, a group that experiences discrimination in one area also experiences it in another (indeed, as Sowell points out, overseas Chinese across Asia and the Pacific have been legally discriminated against with laws forbidding them to own particular types of property, excluding them from some occupations and barring them from schools[100]).

Discriminatory policies persist despite their often negative economic effects. For example, the expulsion of ethnic Turks from Bulgaria (at a time of extreme shortage of labor) and the denial of development funding in the Tamil regions of Sri Lanka (despite the estimated high returns on investment) imply that some noneconomic needs are being satisfied by discriminatory policy. They imply that there is a trade-off between the goal of economic growth and some other goal.

In multiethnic societies that other goal is ethnic dominance. In their effort to ensure ethnic dominance in the course of interethnic competition, one group may try to stack the odds in their favor (as Olzak points out, 'rising competition encourages dominant groups of all kinds to attempt to pass exclusionary laws, enact immigration quotas, restrict labor force competition, in the form of quotas, union rules, seniority rules and other means commonly employed by professions, workers and ethnic groups to restrict entry to valued occupations'[101]).

Ethnic dominance in the aftermath of discriminatory policies is reinforced by the out-migration of undesirable peoples. As a result, inducing out-migration and thereby altering the ethnic composition of the population is often a higher priority than economic growth and development. For this reason, government policies that pressure people to stay or to go are an indication of demographic engineering. Indeed, by using economic policy to pressure an ethnic group to relocate, a government is effectively altering the relative size of ethnic groups, changing the ethnic composition of its country, and thereby changing the power base of ethnic groups. In this way, governments participate in the demographic struggle for power among ethnic groups.

While it is impossible to generalize about the precise reason for migration, let alone the precise discriminatory policy that might have led to out-migration, the discussion above is offered in support of the suggestion made in chapter 1, namely, 'as a result of discriminatory policies, selective migration ensues, in which ethnic groups are differentiated with respect to who goes and who stays'. To the extent that discriminatory policies make life easier or harder for some ethnic groups, they will be factored into the migrant's decision to relocate.

NOTES

1 Examples of governments that discriminate by ethnicity are not limited to remote locations in distant historical eras. The above examples are contemporary and are drawn from countries at different levels of development: According to the World Bank classification, Sudan is low income while South Africa and Moldova are among the middle income states. Moreover, these countries have different forms of governing, including a democratic government elected by popular participation in plural elections (Moldova), a parliamentary democracy lacking universal suffrage (South Africa during apartheid), and an authoritarian regime ruling by religious edict (Sudan). Clearly, discriminatory practices characterize governments in a variety of economic and political contexts.

2 William Safran, 'Nations, Ethnic Groups, States and Politics: A Preface and an Agenda', *Nationalism and Ethnic Politics* 1, 1 (1995), p. 2.

3 Donald Horowitz, *Ethnic Groups in Conflict* (Berkeley: University of California Press, 1985), p. 12.

4 Sometimes, when internal administrative boundaries coincide with ethnic boundaries, then the policies take on a different form. Preferential policies may entail above-average contribution to the national budget, insufficient benefit from the national budget, unfavorable terms of trade resulting from price manipulation, unfavorable regulation pertaining to investment and foreign inflows of resources etc. They may all elicit a sense of economic injustice, depending upon the relative economic position of a region. Relatively low-income regions might attribute their relatively inferior economic position to inadequate and insufficient preferential policies that might have led to unfair practices and exploitation of their resources. Relatively high-income regions may perceive themselves as the economic backbone of the state, while their neighbors drain their resources and restrain their growth. Thus, states with wide regional disparities in income constitute a ripe environment for perceptions of injustice at all levels of income.

5 Edward Schatz, 'Toward an Explanation of Non-Conflict in Multi-Ethnic Central Asia', paper presented to the meetings of the International Studies Association, 16 March 2000, p. 7.

6 Gary Becker published a study on the economics of discrimination which can apply to gender and ethnic groups. This highly controversial work focused attention on gender and race in the economy. Gary Becker, *The Economics of Discrimination* (Chicago: University of Chicago Press, 1957).

7 Michael Wyzan (ed.), *The Political Economy of Ethnic Discrimination and Affirmative Action* (New York: Praeger, 1990); Thomas Sowell, *The Economics and Politics of Race: An International Perspective* (New York: Morrow, 1983).

8 See Horowitz, *Ethnic Groups* and Myron Weiner and Mary Fainsod Katzenstein, *India's Preferential Policies: Migrants, The Middle Classes and Ethnic Equality* (Chicago: University of Chicago Press, 1981). Since the two largest cases of documented and overt programs occurred in Malaysia and India, most of the literature on the subject is specific to these cases.

9 This rule has been in effect since 1 November 1994. *Economist*, 17 September 1994, p. 4.

10 This takes place especially in those regions of Kosovo that, upon an eventual partition of Kosovo, might belong to Serbia. *Duga*, 16 April 1994, p. 78.

11 Transylvanian World Federation, *Genocide in Transylvania* (Astor, FL: Danubian Press, 1985), p. 38.

12 Indeed, the Swiss have laws that limit the duration of work permits, thus workers from Turkey, Spain, Italy, and Portugal are encouraged to retain strong ties with home and ethnic organizations and consulates. See Patrick R. Ireland, *The Policy Challenge of Ethnic Diversity* (Cambridge, MA: Harvard University Press, 1994).

13 *FRE/RL Research Report*, 1, 47, 27 November 1992, p. 64.

14 In this case, it was as punishment for Yemeni support of Iraq during the Gulf War.

15 Susan Feiner (ed.), *Race and Gender in the American Economy* (Englewood Cliffs, NJ: Prentice-Hall, 1994); Becker, *Discrimination*; Walter Williams, *South Africa's War Against Capitalism* (Westport, CT: Praeger, 1989).

16 *Economist*, 31 December 1999.

17 As a result, it is difficult for liberal western scholars to understand that constitutions may not be liberal: Graham Walker describes how western, especially American views on the constitution are intricately tied to the concept of individual rights (Graham Walker, 'The Idea of Nonliberal Consititutionalism' in Ian Shapiro and Will Kymlicka (eds), *Ethnicity and*

Group Rights (New York: New York University Press, 1997), p. 154.

18 The practice of providing employment in small industries did not in fact become established.

19 Anthony W. Marx, *Making Race and Nation* (Cambridge: Cambridge University Press, 1998), p. 8.

20 Other restrictions on non-Muslims include: the prohibition to make repairs on their buildings, to build their churches, to sue each other, to wear the same type of clothing as Muslims, to ride a horse with a saddle, to wear weapons or wide belts, to or to speak loudly. They must, on the other hand, build special hostels for Muslim travelers, host Muslims (with 'full hospitality') for three days, greet Muslims with 'full respect'. Moreover, Muslims are permitted to plow up and sow over all old cemeteries 'of the miscreants'. For the full text of the Decree of Omar II, see Appendix III in Vladimir Dedijer, *The Yugoslav Auschwitz and the Vatican* (Buffalo, NY: Prometheus Books, 1992), pp. 436–7.

21 They were awarded $106 million in 1980, which they have refused to accept since it is deemed too little. *Economist*, 23 July 1994, p. 28.

22 See Remi Clignet, 'Conflict and Culture in Traditional Societies', in Joseph Montville (ed.), *Conflict and Peacemaking in Multiethnic Societies* (Lexington, MA: Lexington Books, 1990), p. 71.

23 *New York Times*, 31 May 1994.

24 In the formulation of land reforms, the question of compensation of confiscated lands has to be addressed. Discussion is already underway for there establishment of a land claims court.

25 *Economist*, 25 July 1994, p. 51.

26 Ibid., 19 February 2000, p. 45.

27 Adrian C. Mayer, *Indians in Fiji* (Oxford: Oxford University Press, 1963), p. 62.

28 *Wall Street Journal*, 1 July 1994. Moreover, the city has completely changed composition in the past few decades, as Muslims have moved in search of employment, and in the process have dislocated the Christians from the fields they traditionally occupied (they were over represented in political and economic power, relative to their numbers): in 1970 there were 5 mosques, while in 1994 there were close to 70.

29 This legislation has been rejected in the past by Kazakhstan's Prime Minister Kazhegeldin until December 1994, at which time it has been endorsed for unexplained reasons see *FRE/RL Daily Report*, 13 December 1994.

30 *Wall Street Journal*, 9 March 2000.

31 Lynn Turgeon, 'Discrimination Against and Affirmative Action of Gypsies in Eastern Europe' in Wyzan, *Affirmative Action* p. 161.

32 This occurred in October 1999 in Usti Nad Labem. *New York Times*, 15 November 1999.

33 The benefits of such preferential policies are perceived to offset the costs associated with the resulting corruption as front people are used, for a fee, in order to obtain licenses and make contract bids.

34 Individuals were given two weeks to pay the capital levy, and failing that, their businesses were confiscated and in some cases they were sent to concentration camps.

35 Wyzan, *Affirmative Action*, p. 65.

36 Ibid., p. 73.

37 Horowitz, *Ethnic Groups*, pp. 655–6.

38 Ibid., p. 655.

39 *New York Times*, 22 February 1999.

40 *Economist*, 2 October 1999, p. 46.

41 Ruth Klinov, 'Arabs and Jews in the Israeli Labor Force: A Comparison of Education and Earnings' in Wyzan, *Affirmative Action*, p. 7.

42 Anthony Lewis, 'The Irrelevance of a Palestinian State', *New York Times Magazine* (20 June, 1999), pp. 58–9.

43 The Barak government is threatening to legalize the 100,000 undocumented workers from these countries, thus permanantly replacing the Palestinian work force. *New York Times*, 31 October 1999.

44 See Graham E. Fuller and Rend Rahim Francke, *The Arab Shi'a: The Forgotten Muslims* (New York: St Martins Press, 1999).

45 Daniel Byman, 'Immoral Majorities: A First Look at a Neglected Source of Communal Conflict', paper presented to the International Studies Association meetings in Los Angeles, 15–19 March 2000, p. 24.

46 Klinov, 'Arabs and Jews', p. 6.

47 Wyzan, *Affirmative Action*, p. 54. There are two goals of this program: one is to decrease the bias of Chinese employers in the private sector against hiring Malays, and the other is to offset this imbalance by denying access to some civil service positions to the Chinese.

48 Horowitz, *Ethnic Groups*, p. 655.

49 Kerala is the state with the highest literacy rate in India as a result of its comprehensive educational policies. As a result of discriminatory practices in other states, surplus labor from Kerala has been forced to migrate to search for employment in Persian Gulf states. Myron Weiner and Mary Fainsod Katzenstein, *India's Preferential Policies: Migrants, the Middle Classes and Ethnic Equality* (Chicago: University of Chicago Press, 1981), p. 134.

50 Will Bartlett, 'Labor Market Discrimination and Ethnic Tension in Yugoslavia: The Case of Kosovo' in Wyzan, *Affirmative Action*, pp. 197–216.

51 *New York Times*, 3 September 1994.

52 *Economist*, 2 October 1999, p. 45.

53 Edna Bonacich, 'A Theory of Ethnic Antagonism: The Split Labor Market', *American Sociological Review* 37 (1972); T. Boswell, 'A Split Labor Market Analysis of Discrimination Against Chinese Immigrants, 1850–1882', *American Sociological Review* 51 (1986). They both said that employers sometimes pay different wages to different race and ethnic groups so they could 'divide and conquer' workers more effectively.

54 Mats Lundahl, 'Will Economic Sanctions End Apartheid in South Africa? What Simple Analytical Models Can tell Us' in Wyzan, *Affirmative Action*, p. 84.

55 Transylvanian World Federation, *Genocide*, p. 52.

56 See the debate on the pros and cons of regional language rights in Europe in *Le Figaro*, 10 September 1999.

57 See Robert P. Clark, 'Spanish Democracy and Regional Democracy' in Joseph R. Rudolph, Jr. and Robert J. Thompson (eds), *Ethnoterritorial Politics, Policy, and the Western World* (Boulder, CO: Lynne Rienner Publishers, 1989), p. 18.

58 The Sinhalese claimed that this was necessary to redress the wrongs brought upon them by the discrimination against them and in favor of the Tamils during the rule by Britain.

59 This law was suspended in April 1994, *New York Times*, 2 April 1994.

60 *Economist*, 17 September 1994, p. 59.

61 This was claimed by the Archbishop of Wales. Donald Rothchild and Victor A. Olorunsola, 'Managing Competing State and Ethnic Claims' in Donald

Rothchild and Victor A. Olorunsola (eds), *State Versus Ethnic Claims: African Policy Dilemmas* (Boulder, CO: Westview Press, 1983), p. 91.

62 Sharon Fisher, 'Strengthening National Identity: The Politics of Language and Culture in Post-Independence Slovakia and Croatia', paper presented at the Annual Convention of the Association for the Study of Nationalities, April 1999, p. 4.

63 After years in which Russian was the primary language, the new state is reversing that legislation. After Estonian, English has become the second language, and Russian, while available in some schools, is not very popular. Increasingly, this is causing the emergence of a bipolar culture, in which the schism between the young people is vast.

64 *New York Times*, 16 July 1999.

65 Robert D. Greenberg, 'The Politics of Language Reform in the Yugoslav Successor States' in *East European Studies*, Meeting Report 159 (1998), p. 5. Also, see Robert D. Greenberg, 'Language, Nationalism and Serbian Politics', *East European Studies*, Meeting Report 182 (1999), p. 5.

66 Klimov, 'Arabs and Jews', p. 18.

67 *Economist*, 20 February 1999, p. 41.

68 Horowitz, *Ethnic Groups*, p. 662.

69 Transvaal Law No. 12, section 104. Cited in Walter Williams, *South Africa's War Against Capitalism* (Westport, CT: Praeger Press, 1989), p. 36.

70 Trivo Indic, quoted in Will Bartlett, 'Labor Market Discrimination and Ethnic Tension in Yugoslavia: The Case of Kosovo' in Wyzan, *Affirmative Action*, p. 208.

71 *New York Times*, 12 December 1999.

72 *Economist*, 19 February 2000, p. 6.

73 It is claimed that, among the 60,000 dissidents, priests, and landowners, there were numerous Hungarians that perished in the project. Michael Meyer and Douglas Stanglin, 'Romania's Danube Connection', *Newsweek* (30 January, 1984), quoted in Transylvanian World Federation, *Genocide*, p. 24.

74 In the project, all residents of Mandalay have been required to devote free labor to the tourist projects.

75 *New York Times*, 17 July 1994. Also, see *Economist*, 11 November 1995, p. 36.

76 Ruth Lapidoth, *Autonomy: Flexible Solutions to Ethnic Conflicts* (Washington, DC: United States Institute of Peace Press, 1996), p. 165.

77 *New York Times*, 31 October 1999.

78 Ibid., 17 August 1994. While it is improbable that this is the result of direct discrimination and racism, the fact remains that the price of suburban living for the black family is higher.

79 L. Kenneth Hubbell, 'Political and Economic Discrimination in Sri Lanka' in Wyzan, *Affirmative Action*, p. 129.

80 *Miami Herald*, 30 April 1994.

81 The laws also restricted population movements and residence of the Asians to Natal Province. It is noteworthy that at the time of these special laws, the Asian population outnumbered the whites.

82 Another form of tax was the collection of the tribute of blood, namely, the removal of non-Muslim boys aged 6 to 10 from their families forever, their forced conversion to Islam, and their training for membership in the sultan's janissary corp (to eventually fight their own people).

83 Douglas Cope, 'Race Relations in Latin America: Case Studies in Mexico and Guatemala', lecture given to the Brown Club of Dade and Broward Counties, 23 June 1994.

84 Hubbell, 'Discrimination in Sri Lanka, p. 125.

85 Adil Eltigani Ali Abdalla, 'Ethnic Conflict in the Sudan' in Wyzan, *Affirmative Action*, pp. 146, 149.

86 This policy was prevalent in the 1920s. Lundalh, 'Economic Sanctions', p. 84.

87 The number of migrants is estimated to be in the millions. *Economist*, 11 December 1993, p. 48.

88 Higher prices were accompanied by decreased service, according to the Justice Department accusation. *Wall Street Journal*, 17 December 1999.

89 This claim was made in a novel that is a fictional depiction of social and economic conditions of immigrant workers in Tasmania after the Second World War. While the claim is not supported by documentation, it is in all likelihood based on anecdotal evidence. Richard Flanagan, *The Sound of One Hand Clapping* (New York: Atlantic Monthly Press, 1997).

90 Numerous scholars have said that water will be the most important fluid of the twenty-first century. By impounding the Rivers Tigris and the Euphrates, Turkey controls much of the water in the Middle East.

91 *New York Times*, 3 November 1994.

92 A CIA report published in September 1994 claims that the number of Shiites leaving the marshes is more than 100,000–150,000 (*Miami Herald*, 8 September 1994). The number in the text is from the *New York Times*, 16 November 1994.

93 Wyzan, *Affirmative Action*, p. ixx.

94 *Economist*, 11 June 1994, p. 47.

95 *OMRI Daily Digest*, 20 October 1995.

96 In one store, a Brazilian broadcaster was asked to leave because the store did not serve foreigners. While such occurrences are common, what was surprising was that she sued the store owner and won the case, an unprecedented event in a country in which ethnic homogeneity often led to antiforeign sentiment. *New York Times*, 15 November 1999.

97 This study was conducted by Mount Sinai School of Medicine in New York City and entailed a survey of 347 pharmacies. *New York Times*, 9 April 2000.

98 *New York Times*, 9 April 2000.

99 *Miami Herald*, 10 April 2000.

100 Sowell, *Economics and Politics of Race* (New York: William Morrow, 1983).

101 Susan Olzak, *The Dynamics of Ethnic Competition and Conflict* (Stanford: Stanford University Press, 1992), p. 219.

7

International Regulation of Migration: Immigration and Emigration Policies

In February 2000 the right-wing Freedom Party joined the Austrian government after a national election.[1] The leader, Jörg Haider, has been a virulent spokesman of antiimmigrant sentiment, citing lost jobs, the loss of the Austrian identity, and the overall unpleasantness of foreigners. Haider is not alone in Europe: Italy's post-fascists (lineal heirs to Mussolini) are part of the government and a senior minister in the Franco regime founded the center–right alliance presently ruling Spain.[2] Others who share Haider's views on immigration are vying to join their countries' governments: In France, Jean-Marie Le Pen; in the United States, Patrick Buchanan; in Italy, Umberto Bossi; and in Australia, Pauline Hanson. These people lead the political debate as they claim to represent the pervasive popular mood of immigrant-fatigue.[3]

In many Western, industrialized countries, immigration has become a burning public policy issue. Questions of employment, ethnicity, race, fairness, cultural imperialism, wages, political rights, and public funding are all channeled into the immigration dialogue and become closely linked in the debate pertaining to the appropriate *number* of immigrants as well as their *countries of origin*. Visceral objections by vociferous interest groups often set the tone of the immigration debate. Immigration is racialized and immigrants are demonized often just because they look different than the host population, rather than because they are guest workers. In some countries, most notably in Germany, periodical antiforeigner outbursts indicate pent-up rage at uninvited visitors (even if their parents were invited). Such sentiments have managed to link together elements from the far right and the far left in numerous western countries.

With the exception of sporadic incidents of violence, there are few reliable barometers of overall popular sentiment pertaining to immigration. As a result, policy makers rely mostly on voter expression through support of political parties that take a stand on immigration. Alternatively, citizens express their concerns about immigration in polls and microlevel discussions. Policy makers in governments, as well

as reporters in the popular media and academics in research institutions, use this information to articulate the parameters of the
immigration debate.

According to this debate, the principal areas of concern for indigenous populations may be classified into three categories: economic,
political, and social. Underlying all three is a basic, almost visceral
response that is shared by a wide variety of citizens: fear about their
long-term position within their own societies. In other words, host
populations fear their own possible future displacement and marginalization if a large inflow of immigrants succeeds in changing the relative
ethnic composition of the population. They fear the long-term change
in relative population sizes and the change in economic and political
power that accompanies it.

In historical terms, such economic, political, and social concerns are
new and their articulation into a closed-door policy is even newer.
From the second half of the nineteenth century until 1914, there was
no restriction on traveling within Europe. This was a period of free
trade with little need to protect domestic markets and populations. At
the time of the First World War, passports were first requested for
traveling, and soon thereafter immigration controls were introduced.
Moreover, during the period of mass migrations to the New World
(namely 1850 to 1914), 55 million Europeans migrated unfettered by
policy, restrictions, quotas, and denials.[4] Host populations did not
express immigrant fatigue, nor did they bond against the newcomers.
As a result, neither the government, nor the media, nor the population
had a need for policy to regulate immigration. In the United States in
1911, the Immigration Commission pondered the question of whether
immigration is a good thing or a bad thing and for whom.[5] After four
years, they concluded that it was in fact bad, but that view did not elicit
sufficient popular support and indignation to warrant policy changes.
However, over the years the pressure to change grew, waxing and
waning in tandem with economic conditions. Now that Western
recipient countries have entered the new millennium, pressure for
policy change is once again growing. Hence, our attention turns to
policies that restrict or encourage immigration and emigration. As
mentioned in chapter 5, policies pertaining to international population movements (immigration and emigration), together with policies
associated with domestic population movements (both direct and
indirect, as discussed in chapter 6), are one of the four determinants
of a migrant's incentives and capacities (the others being institutions,
infrastructure, and personal characteristics). Policies related to international movements are discussed in this chapter.

WHO MIGRATES AND WHERE DO THEY GO?

According to the World Bank, each year some 2 to 3 million people emigrate from their countries of origin.[6] At the beginning of the twenty-first century, some 130 million people live outside their home country and that number has been rising by about 2 percent a year. While this seems slight (indeed, a mere 2.3% of the world population), it is significant because of who is moving and where they are going.

Most migrants move within their own countries. This is most evident in China, where some 200 million people have moved more than 1,000 miles (amounting to more than the worldwide total number of people living outside their countries, namely 130 million). The next largest share of migrants move across national boundaries within the less developed countries (hereafter LDCs). The remainder of migrants move from the LDCs to the more developed countries (hereafter MDCs). In the latter, population movements from the LDCs represent a major shift in immigrant origins: before the mid-1960s most migrants tended to be from eastern Europe and Russia, southern Europe and the Mediterranean, and northern Europe, all in different historical periods. Although proportionally small, migrants from LDCs to MDCs are large in absolute terms and are growing.

In the late 1990s the majority of the annual migrants were going to just four host countries: the United States, Germany, Canada, and Australia, in that order. Between 1990 and 1997 the US alone admitted close to a million immigrants each year. In 1990, the US census counted 19.7 million foreign-born people, representing a 34 percent increase over 1980 and 8 percent of the total population.[7] If we consider North America and western Europe, the stock of migrants grew by 2.5 percent per year between 1965 and 1990. Moreover, if Oceania is included (Australia, New Zealand, and the South Pacific Islands), then 1 in every 13 people living in these regions is foreign-born.

A closer look at the United States reveals that most of its current immigrants are from Mexico, followed by the Caribbean basin, and south and southeast Asia. From 1961 to 1993, over 4 million Mexicans arrived legally, comprising 21 percent of the total legal immigration into the country.[8]

While there is no doubt that the migration trends are from the less developed countries to the more developed countries, migrants are also attracted to countries that are not among the most developed in *absolute* terms but rather are *relatively* more developed than their countries of origin. Palestinians are drawn to Iraq and Kuwait, Zimbabweans to South Africa, and Sri Lankans to India.

It is also evident that traditionally net emigrant countries are turning into net immigrant countries. Italy and Spain, that previously sent migrants into northern Europe, are now the recipients of workers from northern Africa and eastern Europe.[9] Alternatively, countries have become simultaneous hosts as well as population losers: Guatemalans and Salvadorans cross the southern border into Mexico while Mexicans continue to cross the northern border into the United States. Poland, that used to send workers into western Europe, now hosts workers from Russia and other former Soviet states. Finally, Russia, while seeking immigrant status in the United States for some of its citizens, is hosting immigrants from the Caucasus, mostly from Armenia.

DEMOGRAPHIC EFFECTS OF IMMIGRATION

The demographic effects of immigration are great both in the losing as well as the receiving countries. The focus in this chapter is on the latter, which at the end of the twentieth century tended to be the more developed, industrialized, western countries. As shown by the data presented above, the influx of migrants from the developing countries (who are of a different ethnic, racial, religious, and/or linguistic background from the indigenous population) is changing the demographic composition of the receiving states.

This change is further reinforced by the fact that immigrant populations tend to have a higher rate of natural population increase than the host peoples (as, for example, the Algerians in France, the Albanians in Italy, the Turks in Germany, and the Armenians in Russia). As a result, the receiving populations have developed fertility phobias relative to the newcomers. Fertility phobias stem from perceptions of differential rates of population growth: namely, the perception that host groups have lower fertility rates in comparison with the newcomers. This perception, whether rooted in reality or not, leads to anxiety about the chances of long term survival of host populations. Since replacement fertility of 2.1 children per woman is considered necessary for a society to reproduce itself (while less results in net negative growth), ethnic groups experiencing lower growth have reason for anxiety. At the same time, fertility phobias develop when low-growth populations fear the high fertility rates among members of another ethnic group, especially if that group is neighboring or interspersed within the society, as immigrants are.

Examples of fertility phobias from around the world abound. Brzezinski warned that 'the approximately 50 million Soviet Muslims currently produce as many babies per year as the 145 million Russians'.[10] Russians were alarmed by this reproductive activity in the peripheral Soviet republics, especially when some of the Muslims were migrants within Russian borders. Moreover, the Muslim countries of the Middle East, as well as Libya and Sudan, have population growth rates of 3–4.9 percent per year and it is estimated that the populations in these countries will double in 14 years.[11] Migrants from these countries are attracted to Europe, flooding the immigration offices in France, Spain, and Italy. Israelis are also concerned because the Arab population within Israel is growing at a faster pace than that of Jews. Indeed, the Palestinians in Gaza have one of the highest birth rates in the world: 7 children per woman (in the West Bank, it is 5.6). In Israel, it is 2.7. These numbers translate into population growth of 4 percent among the Palestinians and 2 percent among the Israelis (including immigration). Israel's population, of 6 million (of which 5 million are Jews) is expected to reach 8.3 million by 2025, while the Palestinian population will reach 7.4.[12] Similarly, the Albanian ethnic minority in Yugoslavia has the highest birth rate in Europe: 35 babies for every 1,000 people. Their growth rate is stable at 2.4 percent, much higher than in the remainder of the former Yugoslavia (in Croatia, it is 0.4%) and curiously much higher than in neighboring Albania.[13] It is estimated that, with current population growth rates, the Albanians will be the most numerous population in Serbia in the first quarter of the twenty-first century.[14] In the coming year, less than one third of newborns in Serbia will not be to Serbian families.[15] Some Serbs claim that 'the major political weapon of ethnic Albanians towards achieving demographic domination in Kosovo and Metohija is a very high birth rate'.[16] This is similar to the view held by some Hindus in India. Hendre claims that Hindus will be overtaken by Muslims: 'The 10.7 percent of Muslims in 1961, in union with other religious groups, will numerically overtake the Hindus in AD 2051 so decisively that the Hindus will be at the mercy of the non-Hindus.'[17] Such fear is also evident in Kenya, where the results of the 1981 census caused panic and rejection because it showed that the population of the Kikuyu had grown at twice the rate of the dominant Luo in a single decade. The growth rate of the black population in South Africa surpassed that of the white population (the white population was one-fifth in 1951, and dropped to one-seventh in 1980). Racial differences in population growth rates are also evident in Fiji, where they underlie interracial tensions.[18]

In the United States, according to Miles, 'although migrants add less than 0.5 percent to the US population each year, immigrants and their offspring are expected to be responsible for almost two-thirds of the net population increase over the next 50 years'.[19] Weiner's calculations indicate this would mean that 70 million out of an increase of 106 million people would be migrants or descendents of migrants.[20] Huntington has also written extensively about the threat of immigration and the subsequent de-Westernization of America and even the de-Americanization in the democratic sense.[21] His fear is rooted in the expectation that by 2050 whites in America will no longer be the majority, as that status will be accorded to Hispanics, Asians, and blacks. For this reason, Huntington stresses that immigration is an emerging security imperative.

Thus, it is easy to see that differing birth rates can become a major source of concern in the prevailing climate of competing nationalisms, because they are perceived to translate into future political rebalancing. Wriggins and Guyot describe this fear: 'Projected population trends may be thought to foretell changes in the political fortunes of competing ethnic groups ... Accordingly, demographic changes may loom large in the minds of competing political leaders of groups fearful of losing their positions.'[22] Kennedy describes how there emerges 'a resentment against other peoples who reproduce at a much faster pace – the assumption being that, as in a Darwinian struggle, the faster-growing species will encroach upon, and eventually overwhelm, a population with static or declining numbers'.[23]

RESPONSES TO IMMIGRATION

In the 1800s settlers in the New World welcomed population inflows from Europe because of the popular view that they had to 'populate or perish'. Some 200 years later, a respected scholar, Samuel Huntington, has said that immigration is the single greatest threat to the United States.[24] He is far from alone in this view. Apprehension about the possible displacement and marginalization of host ethnic groups by immigrants is a strong sentiment that runs as an undercurrent throughout numerous societies. It reflects itself in a growing public backlash against open immigration on streets, in schools, in workplaces, in popular discourse, in academic literature, and in the media. The French attitude toward immigrants from north Africa, the Italian attitude toward Africans, the Swiss toward Tamils. and the British toward Pakistanis are all embodied in a popular expression of concern. Even tolerant Canadians are questioning past policies: a recent poll suggests that 41 percent of Canadians want less immigration.[25] Possibly the most violent antiforeign sentiment has been voiced in parts of the former East Germany, and mostly toward the Turkish guest workers. The Czech Republic, with its 47,000 guest workers (later expelled), follows close behind. Yet, hate activity is also evident in West Germany, as well as in other parts of west and east Europe, indicating that the anti-Turkish sentiment could not be brushed off as a mere manifestation of youth groups negatively affected by the social, economic, and political turbulence associated with reunification. In his book about the rise of hate groups in post-communist Eastern Europe, Hockenos pointed out that the incidence of antinewcomer violence is manifested in a variety of economic, social, and political contexts.[26] The common denominator in both eastern and western host countries seems to be uninvited immigration.

Across the world, several political parties have sprung up, galvanizing support on the platform of antiimmigration. Their views are centered on two goals – the closing of borders to prevent new entrants, and the expelling of some of the more recent arrivals. The party that has had the greatest success and the greatest electoral showings is the National Front in France, led by Jean-Marie Le Pen (which garners some 10–15% of the votes in national poles and wins in some communities). Germany has its own Republican Party, as does Austria (the Austrian Freedom Party, led by Jörg Haider). In Italy, Umberto Bossi leads the Northern League in its appeal to the antiimmigrant sentiment, a party that received 20 percent of the national vote in 1992. In Australia, the popularity of Pauline Hanson has lead to the term *the Hanson phenomenon*. While several immigrant parties have emerged in response to the above parties (and their platform is uniquely the protection and the increase of immigrant rights[27]), their mere existence has served to further fuel indigenous paranoia.

Meissinger *et al.* describe why antiimmigrant political parties have received as large a constituency as they have.

> Single-mindedly xenophobic, these parties have defined the foreigner issue for the public, while the center parties have failed to provide a coherent, alternative voice in the debate. The inability of the mainline parties to explain the changes migrations are creating and propose practical responses has made governments appear helpless and ineffective. This has eroded the authority of political leaders, contributing to the gains anti-foreigner right-wing parties have made.[28]

As a result, spontaneous voices of antiimmigrant sentiment, coupled with the success of organized political parties, have undoubtedly pressured governments into changing their immigration policies. However, it should be emphasized that, while present and vociferous, the antiimmigrant sentiment as expressed in the right-wing political parties and outbursts on the streets remains a minority sentiment. The majority of the populations in Western countries do not openly share the view, the method, the goal, and the reasoning behind the anti-immigrant movements. It is as a result of such moderate views, the ones expressed by mainstream political parties, that immigration policies have developed into their present form.

CLASSIFICATION OF IMMIGRANTS

Every population can be divided into citizens and noncitizens. The latter group is composed of migrants, who have been further subdivided by Meissner *et al.* into the following groups: legally admitted residents (immigrants) and nonresidents (nonimmigrants), contract labor migrants, illegal immigrants, asylum seekers, and refugees.[29]

Legal immigrants include people who are legally admitted and have been granted the status of residents. In the United States, this number was in the order of 9 million people in the 1980s and was formalized by the granting of the 'green card'.[30] In 1990 alone, the United States gave permanent residence to 1,540,000 immigrants.[31] That same year, Canada granted residency to 212,692 people and Australia to 121,227. Those who are not granted resident status but are nevertheless legally admitted tend to be temporary. They include foreign students, technically trained personnel, multinational corporation executives and managers, and experts in a wide variety of fields.

Contract labor migrants are temporary residents. The practice of contract labor migration is popular across the globe wherever there are neighboring countries with varying levels of development. Under this arrangement, temporary entry permits are granted to migrants so that they can satisfy the manpower requirements of the receiving region. As such, it is a mutually beneficial arrangement from a strictly economic point of view. Examples abound. France and Germany had a series of such guest-worker schemes (with their poorer, south European neighbors) in the 1950s and 1960s. Today, numerous Middle East countries with labor scarcity rely on foreign workers from nearby countries in south and east Asia (where surplus labor is redundant). Countries such as Saudi Arabia and Kuwait actively promote inmigration of contract laborers, while others, such as Pakistan and the Philippines, actively promote emigration of their workers.

Illegal immigrants are those who do not have the right to reside or work in the country where they find themselves. They may have slipped across the border or they may have entered legally and overstayed their welcome (as, for example, students, tourists, or temporary workers on expired visas). Most industrial countries have colonies of such immigrants. Given their status, many continue to live at the fringe of society, finding employment only in the most undesirable jobs.

Asylum seekers tend to be from countries where political repression or chaos force some people, with particular circumstances, to find life unbearable. While in the past asylum seekers were mostly defectors from communist countries, in the 1990s the countries of origin included Sri Lanka, Somalia, Libya, and the former Yugoslavia. This is the most nebulous, unclearly defined category of immigrants, and as a result, it is the most controversial. The more the case loads increase in countries, the longer the process seems to be. Yet, Western countries are reluctant to repatriate asylum seekers for humanitarian reasons.

Refugees, as described in chapter 1 above, are persons who are persecuted (or fear persecution) on the basis of their race, religion, national origin, political opinion, or social group. In the 1990s there are some 17.5 million refugees outside of their countries of origin, and a similar number within domestic borders.[32] Most of them are in the less developed countries (indeed, the 20 countries hosting the highest numbers have average per capita incomes of $700).[33] They are mostly victims of interethnic wars and civil strife. Only those who have family in the West are ever likely to be resettled permanently outside the Third World.

The above classification of immigrants is relevant in explaining their rights in host countries. There has been a recent plethora of academic writing on the subject, with a consensus that in liberal democracies the emerging legal norms grant rights to immigrants that are in accordance with international human rights and civil norms, whether their status in the host country is legal or illegal.[34] A discussion of rights for illegal workers elicits visceral responses from policy makers, the media, and the general population. One extreme position is that since these people have no right to be in a country, they should have none of the rights that citizens and legal migrants have. The opposing view reduces immigrants to their least common denominator, namely their humanity, and states that since they are human beings, they deserve the same rights as other human beings. Both views are unrealistic and a middle solution is warranted. However, such a middle ground contains a wide band of possibilities. While all countries prevent nondocumented migrants from participating in the political process, some countries grant them access to public services. Since those public services are funded by the tax revenue of their citizens, then the question of fairness comes up, as well as the possible decrease in services for the resident population associated with the increased demand.

In the United States, it was not until the time of President Carter that the question of rights for undocumented migrants was discussed. The Select Committee on Immigration and Refugee Policy, in its final report in 1981, presented a compromise between the two extreme positions noted above. It included an amnesty program, provisions for nondiscrimination in employment, increased resources for Border Patrol as well as sanctions on employers who hired illegal entrants. In other words, the committee hoped to provide amnesty to those who were already in the country while trying to stem the future flow of others.[35] In 1986, the Immigration Reform and Control Act was passed, in an effort to reduce undocumented immigration while at the same time providing amnesty to resident aliens.

Recently there have been two efforts to curtail the rights of illegal immigrants in the US. One is Proposition 187 passed in California in 1994, according to which undocumented migrants would lose all rights to public services with the exception of emergency medical care (but including education). Although the measure was challenged in the courts, it remains an indicator of antiimmigrant sentiment. Moreover, in 1996 the US government approved legislation to withdraw some state services and benefits from both legal and illegal immigrants.[36]

The rights of legal immigrants are also under dispute. A permanent resident has no voting rights, cannot serve on a jury, lacks access to some public assistance, and can be deported if he or she commits a crime. It is a step short of citizenship. Asylum seekers usually have fewer rights in the various countries in which they find themselves. During the time that their application is under consideration (which may entail a wait of several years), they tend to have different degrees of work privileges and access to social services.

CLASSIFICATION OF IMMIGRATION POLICIES

In the year 2000, Alan Greenspan suggested that the inflow of foreign workers might alleviate the current shortage of labor in the United States.[37] This statement may be the precursor to a liberation of immigration policies leading to an increase in the number of immigrants. Such high-level recognition of the economic benefit of immigrants to growing economies came as a surprise to many. It underscores just how dynamic immigration policy is. Indeed, policy is a response to domestic economic and social conditions and changes when conditions change. (For example, the Mexican boundary with the United States was not enforced until the 1920s. Then, when the inflow of workers became unbearable and the protectionist climate at home prevailed, border controls were introduced.)

For the purposes of this study, the ethnic component of immigration policies warrants attention. However, it must be preceded by a general definition of immigration policy. Immigration policies are formally articulated in the laws of a country, since control over population flows over its borders is viewed as a sovereign right. Those laws are then implemented by agencies charged with their execution. The objectives of immigration policy in most Western countries are either economic, social, or humanitarian. The relative importance of these three differs from country to country. It also differs over time in each country, as it changes with fluctuating domestic conditions and international norms.

According to Fix and Passel, US immigration policy contains aspects of the following goals: social (i.e. to reunify families), economic (i.e. to improve incomes and satisfy manpower demands), cultural (i.e. to increase diversity), moral (i.e. to ensure human rights), and security (i.e. to reduce illegal immigration).[38] In the formulation of specific immigration policies, governments must make choices among these goals and they must put them in the context of the particular prevailing national conditions. In addition, Meissner *et al.* claim that three basic questions must be answered in the formulation of immigration policies: who, how many, and from where.[39]

With respect to *who* is allowed to enter a country, the response depends upon the overriding objective of the immigration policy, as stated above. To the extent that people are given right of entry on social grounds, they must be nuclear or extended family members of current citizens. To the extent that immigration policy entails the humanitarian objective and that refugees are accepted through some form of political asylum or resettlement program, it is people fleeing from oppressive regimes and interethnic conflicts that seek entry. Sometimes, political concerns prevail, such as when the United States adapted its immigration policy in the immediate aftermath of the Tiananmen Square intervention, to allow 30,000 Chinese students to remain in the country.

Generous programs that seek to reunite family members, rectify human rights abuses, and satisfy humanitarian objectives are the subject of debate pertaining to their economic impact. Because immigrants who seek entry under these conditions are not explicitly economic assets, the question of their economic contribution is debated. Indeed, the debate rages as to whether family members contribute economically to the recipient country or merely take from its economy. Some studies show that family unification is often conducive to higher productivity, that family structures promote economic achievement, and that some immigrant businesses revitalize urban neighborhoods.[40] Moreover, it has also been claimed that the children born to such unified families are more likely to be adjusted future citizens. At the same time, other studies show little or no economic contribution of immigrant family members.

Such a debate does not exist for economic immigrants, namely those who are selected because they have sought-after skills. Such workers usually have high levels of education, language proficiency in the local tongue, employment prospects, and earning capacity. They are unlikely to be a burden to the host countries, rather their contribution to the economy is expected to be high.

In the United States, Canada, and Australia, immigration policies are increasingly skewed in favor of professional immigrants. Canada has a system that awards points for education and skills.[41] In 1997, of the 205,000 planned admission, 113,000 were admitted under the 'skilled category'. In Australia during 1998–99, more than half came under the 'skill stream'. The United States is trying to go the same route, albeit with less success: the number of employment-based visas actually dropped in 1993–95 from 147,000 to 85,000.

With respect to *how many*, immigration policies must take into consideration a country's absorptive capacity. Doing so entails paying attention to the labor market, population density, facilities such as housing, and services such as education. All of these will be strained by the inflow of migrants (especially since they tend to cluster in selected neighborhoods) and, therefore, domestic policy should be tied closely to immigration policy. This is the case in Canada, where legislation regulates the proposition of workers who are admitted for any particular occupation (in order to prevent occupations from becoming immigrant-saturated).[42] Moreover, a careful proportionality was introduced among the family, refugee and labor market streams of immigrants. Unlike that of Canada, US policy did not make a connection between immigrant levels and national objectives. As a result, its quota system (designed to select immigrants from one of several categories) has been set arbitrarily, more as a result of political currents rather than economic rationality.

Many national policies can be said to be ethnic policies when discussing *from where* migrants should come. Weiner found that ethnicity is 'the most plausible explanation for the willingness of states to accept or reject migrants'.[43] Until 1965, the United States and many Western countries based the geographical distribution of their immigrants on their own societies. In other words, the formula was to mirror the ethnic composition of the domestic population. With the same results, Canada had a policy of 'whites only' in effect until the late 1960s. Similarly, until 1972, Australia had a 'White Australia' policy, aimed specifically at Asians and southeast Asians.[44] All these policies are viewed as anachronistic and politically incorrect today. They have been replaced with laws based on neutrality of country of origin, making the ethnicity of newcomers irrelevant (with the exception of Quebec, which has its own immigration policy that favors French speakers[45]). However, ethnicity *de facto* remains an issue because most immigrants in the family category tend to be from the new immigrant category (indeed, many Asians are in-migrating because they are family members of recently arrived Asians). So too, those arriving as political asylum or refugee category tend to be from the less developed countries and recently from the former Yugoslavia.

The Immigration Act of 1990 in the United States contains a provision for 'diversity' visas. According to Jenks, 'the purpose of this category is to ensure the availability of visas for immigrants from countries from which immigration has been lower than 50,000 over the preceding five years'.[46] Does this imply that the diversity clause will increase the immigration from Third World countries? Not necessarily. It might in fact increase migration from northern Europe, a region currently underrepresented in the immigration flows to the United States. As a result, it is possible that an effort toward diversity in fact takes us back to where the country was some half a century ago.

There has been a fundamental change in the immigration policies of west European countries since the late 1990s. This change, not reflected in the policies of the US, Australia, and Canada, has resulted from the overwhelming flood of immigrants from Eastern Europe. For example, 70,000 people applied for asylum in Britain in 1999, up from just 5,000 before the Berlin Wall fell in 1989.[47] The response, viewed as both necessary and popular, was a tightening of immigration policy. In April 2000 the Immigration and Asylum Act went into effect, introducing a voucher system and dispersal of immigrants across the country.[48] Such legislation is similar to the one introduced in Germany, and following in principal what has already been introduced in Austria,[49] Switzerland, Italy, and The Netherlands.

Does this mean that there has been a convergence in immigration control policies? The literature on the subject is divided, as Money so clearly shows:[50] while some claim that immigration polices are converging (such as Cornelius, Hollifield, and Martin[51]), others disagree, focusing on states' differing border controls (Miller[52]) or on their differing abilities to control borders (Freeman[53]). Some members of the European Community are signatories to the Schengen Accords of 1985 and 1990, representing an effort to arrive at a common border control policy, to harmonize asylum practices, and to work toward a common immigration policy.[54] However, despite the creation of the so-called Schengenland,[55] regional varieties continue to dominate, as Italy and Germany continue to go their own ways.[56] Moreover, there is no evidence of a convergence in immigration and emigration policies within state boundaries. Mexico is a clear example of a country that is one of the biggest exporters of people and yet is unwilling to allow immigration into its country and is unwilling to integrate (socially and economically) those who do manage entry.

ECONOMIC ISSUES UNDERLYING THE IMMIGRATION DEBATE

In the industrializing north of the United States, organized labor was threatened by the rising number of immigrants and northbound African Americans as early as the 1880s.[57] Evidence of organized labor's opposition to Chinese and Asians in California during this period is provided by Mink.[58] According to, Saxton and Nee and Nee, such opposition extended to Asians in general.[59] Workers in the past and workers in the present are often threatened by immigrants. Their fear is rooted in their view of the economy. They view the economy as a pie. Each slice represents the share of each citizen. An influx of immigrants increases the number of slices that must be cut. The size of each slice must decrease in order to accommodate the new demand. In other words, the inflow of new arrivals lowers the standard of living of the population because it increases the competition for jobs, public services, wages, goods, infrastructure, and so forth. This argument is based on the premise that there is no economic growth (so the size of the pie fails to grow and offset the trend of diminishing slices).

Is this view substantiated by data? While a true assessment of the economic impact of immigration is warranted, it is hard to achieve because there is contradictory evidence that supports both the pro and con immigration positions. The principal consideration in determining whether immigrants are a threat and a burden is the nature of the human capital they contribute to the economy (namely, the quantity and quality of skills they bring). Whether displacement of workers occurs depends upon the skills of the newcomers relative to the skills of native workers. The evidence on this point is unclear. Borjas claims that the skill level of migrants in the United States is falling and that immigrants make no contribution to the human capital of the host country.[60] Simon points out that the skills of newcomers have actually been increasing during the 1970s, 1980s, and 1990s.[61] Moreover, some argue that low-skilled immigrants contribute to the deskilling of society,[62] while others claim their contribution revitalizes the economy by increasing the availability of those skills that are in short supply.

Another consideration is whether immigrants take jobs away from native workers? An influx of workers into an economy can have several effects on employment, depending on conditions in the labor market at the time. If there is unemployment, then immigration provides a reserve army of labor. If there is full employment, an increase in supply of workers will result in unemployment, either of the newcomers or of the newly displaced native workers. A study of contemporary Australian immigration found that even during recessions, there was no relationship between number of immigrants and unemployment. Moreover, during the post-war period of expansion, immigrants created as least as much employment as they took.[63] The evidence from the United States is convincing: the number of jobs created by immigrants exceeded the number of immigrants by 30 percent.[64]

Finally, does immigration lower the incomes of native workers? Increased competition for jobs results in decreased wages, if the economy does not expand. Falling wages and unemployment translate into a deterioration of living standards. Moreover, to the extent that immigrants remain unemployed, they might draw on public finances because they make use of public services such as health, education, and welfare.[65] Those public services are funded by taxes, so immigrants who cannot carry their own weight may become a burden to the working indigenous population.[66] In contradiction to the view, some claim that immigrants in fact increase wages of native workers by stimulating production and increasing national income.[67]

At least two views on the immigration reality are apparent. One focuses on the displacement of native workers, the decrease in wages, the increased competition for jobs, the decrease in living standards, the increased public burden, and the increased competition for social services.[68] Those who uphold this view argue against an open-door immigration policy. The other view focuses on the positive economic contribution of immigrants, including their overall stimulative effect, the skills they bring in, the dynamism they infuse, the increased supply of labor they provide, and so forth. Those who favor an open-door policy support this view. Who is right? Which side represents the 'true' facts? The empirical evidence of the costs and benefits of immigration is far from conclusive.[69] While there are studies that support both open-door as well as antiimmigration arguments, the majority of scholars studying the US experience (including LaLonde and Topel, and Butcher and Card) show that there is little if any relationship between immigration and rates of unemployment, wages and overall income within a region.[70]

SOCIAL ISSUES UNDERLYING THE IMMIGRATION DEBATE

In the mid-1990s an Algerian girl, born in France, insisted on wearing her Islamic headscarf to school. The proximate cause of the ensuing uproar is that French public schools are secular and forbid any expression of religion. However, the magnitude of the French reaction can only be understood if the incident is placed in the context of contemporary French sensibilities. The native population was and continues to be apprehensive about the displacement of its culture by immigrants. The French recognize that an influx of foreigners changes the ethnic composition of the population and by extension, changes the dominant culture.[71] Indeed, when immigrants enter a country, their baggage contains cultural norms, patterns of behavior, and worldviews that are different. Host populations fear that immigrant cultural norms may come to clash with domestic ones and over time will come to overpower them. This fear of the gradual erosion of French cultural dominance underlies the headscarf issue and is at the forefront of the immigration debate.

Another concern that has been cited in immigration debates is the dissipation of Western values such as democracy, equal moral worth, and equal access for all people. Are these liberal values affected by the inflow of immigrants? According to Whelan, immigrants with entirely different values might succeed in destroying the Western liberal tradition.[72] Michael Walzer goes a step further, claiming that citizens of democracies must take proactive steps to protect their values from immigrants. The influx of immigrants with different views of democracy and human rights might dissipate the domestic values that took so long to develop and take root in the West.[73] By comparison, Shain provides evidence that such liberal values have been adopted readily by immigrants to the United States, who are eager for the opportunity and access that it grants them.[74]

In conclusion, it must be recognized that a definitive assessment of the effect of immigrant cultural baggage on host societies must take into consideration the nature of the pre-existing host culture. There is a difference between in the cultures that immigrants encounter when they move to countries such as Australia, Canada, and the United States, and when they move to Germany, Italy, or France. In the former, host culture and values are harder to define. These countries are composed of newcomers and their dominant culture is a mosaic based on diversity and plurality. They are multicultural and they are melting-pots, both simultaneously. Immigrants have, in their relatively short history in these lands, displaced the indigenous populations that lived there for centuries. By comparison, French, Italian, and English cultures have been delineated clearly over a longer period of time. They are entrenched in the souls of their populations, they permeate the school systems, and they are reflected in the workplaces. As a result, diversity, multiethnicity, and multiculturalism associated with immigration are viewed with greater distrust and skepticism than in the New World. It follows, therefore, that a discussion of the cultural displacement and the transformation of values due to immigration must be situation-specific.

POLITICAL ISSUES UNDERLYING THE IMMIGRATION DEBATE

The most important political consideration pertaining to immigration policies has to do with the citizenship rights that immigrants acquire when they become naturalized. What exactly are those rights? There is much variety from country to country. Marshall and Bottomore's definition of citizenship clearly underscores the lack of a predetermined set of rights: 'Citizenship is a status bestowed on those who are full members of a community. All who possess the status are equal with respect to the rights and duties with which the status is endowed. *There is no universal principle that determines what those rights and duties shall be* [italics mine].'[75] Most common is the right to vote and thus to be represented, although even that is not universal (since in New Zealand noncitizens can vote in national elections, while in neighboring Australia they cannot[76]).

The issue of citizenship and naturalization depends on host country policies pertaining to naturalization – namely, do they allow immigrants to become citizens or must they remain aliens forever.[77] Two criteria apply to the citizen laws of countries: according to *jus sanguinis*, citizenship is contingent on that of one's parents while *jus soli* entitles anyone born in a country to become a citizen (the former is more common in the Old World, the latter in the New World). The two are not mutually exclusive. Brubaker claims that the *jus sanguinis* concept of citizenship and national identity in Germany gave rise to an immigration system based on temporary rotation of labor and social segregation, while the *jus soli* concept of citizenship in France drove preferences for permanent settlement and assimilation.[78] It was only in 1999, under intense pressure, that Germany allowed ethnic Turkish newborns to acquire German citizenship (no similar steps have been taken by Italy and Sweden, where the *jus sanguinis* principal still prevails). Also, third-generation Koreans born in Japan still have no such benefit.

When people acquire citizenship, their sense of belonging to the state increases, as does their capacity and incentive to participate in its culture. They also want to exert their power, express their opinion, and influence policy. The electoral system, newly opened to naturalized immigrants, allows them to do this. It empowers them. The evidence from the United States is clear: the newly empowered groups using the electoral system to exert their influence include the Cubans, Haitians, Koreans, Chinese, Vietnamese, Dominicans, and Mexicans (they supercede the traditional groups, namely the Italians, Poles, Greeks, Jews, and Germans). According to Shain, these groups have been successfully empowered: 'one of the signs that an ethnic group has achieved a respectable position in American life is its acquisition of a meaningful voice in US foreign affairs'.[79]

However, not all host countries are inclined to grant citizenship rights, to condone dual citizenship, or to empower their newcomer ethnic groups. As a result, the question of who has the right to claim citizenship and who does not has caused an escalation in interethnic conflict during the 1990s. Instead of embracing people of various ethnic groups into the state population, and thus increasing the total number of people (as occurred in the United States at the turn of the century), countries are adopting stricter rules pertaining to citizenship rights in an effort to weed out undesirable groups. New eligibility restrictions underscore the fact that *relative* numbers of target ethnic groups are more important to leaders than *total* population numbers. As a result, large numbers of peoples may be displaced or rights denied them simply because the rules of citizenship have been altered. Indeed, even in Israel, where the long-standing Law of Return grants every Jew the right to immigrate to Israel and receive citizenship, the government is currently reconsidering that arrangement.[80] Moreover, Christians are restricted from becoming citizens of Middle Eastern countries except under exceptional circumstances.[81] In Eastern Europe, Czechs have introduced laws that effectively deny citizenship to some 20,000 Romas (10% of their total population).[82] However, no contemporary case of citizenship denial has been as large-scale as that of the Russian diaspora in the former Soviet Union. The experience of ethnic Russians in the former Soviet Baltic states is an apt illustration. The number of Russian post-Second World War immigrants to Lithuania was relatively small, so they were granted immediate citizenship. Bildt claims that before the Second World War, Russians constituted less than 10 percent of the Lithuanian population, while 'Soviet policies of heavy industrialization and deliberate demographic change gradually brought wave upon wave of Russian immigrants'.[83] After independence in 1991, new standards for citizenship were set, including a certain number of years of residence, declaration of loyalty to the new state, and a knowledge of the new official language. This legislation was harsh insofar as it included a quota of only 2,000 resident aliens per year to be granted citizenship. Amid furor, the law was amended to provide for naturalization of most noncitizens by the year 2000. In Estonia, residents need only two years of residency and a language test in order to attain citizenship (among the Russians that found themselves in Estonia at the time of independence, some 48,000 have opted to become Russian citizens, while some 65,000 are undecided as to whether to take Estonian papers[84]). In Latvia, ethnic Latvians are a majority only by a very slim margin. According to the 1990 census, its total population contains 1.4 million Latvians, 900,000 Russians, 120,000 Belorussians, and 100,000 Ukrainians.[85] As a result, the citizenship regulations in Latvia are highly restrictive.

These citizenship rules in the Baltic states had a positive demographic impact on Russians and Russia. With respect to the former, the restrictive citizenship rules in Latvia have caused many of the 80,000 Ukrainians in Latvia to take Russian citizenship.[86] Given the difficulty in obtaining Latvian citizenship, they opted for Russian papers (since Ukraine does not grant citizenship to nonresidents). This Ukrainian administrative ruling has greatly tilted the demographic balance in favor of Russians in Latvia.

THE ROLE OF IMMIGRATION, ASSIMILATION, AND CITIZENSHIP REGULATION

Immigration alters the pre-existing numerical balance between ethnic groups. If it tilts the composition of the population against the leading group, its leaders might be sufficiently threatened to introduce policies that defend the status quo. In his study of the ways to change the numerical ratio of ethnic groups in India, Wright focuses on the rules pertaining to selective immigration and emigration, as well as changes in the definition and procedures for obtaining citizenship or legal status. While these measures apply to controlling incoming ethnic groups, Wright also points out that other methods can be applied to already settled, undesirable groups. These include encouraging religious conversion, inducing differential fertility, manipulating the census, differentiating or aggregating language, altering political boundaries, expelling people or exchanging populations with other countries, and genocide.[87] Wright is not the only scholar to have studied such methods of population manipulation. Baaklini also discusses them in the context of Lebanon, focusing on converting others, eliminating others, holding key positions in nonelected jobs, or 'structuring the political game and electoral process in such a way that their preeminence might last irrespective of their size'.[88] In *The Democratic Struggle for Power* (1998), I chose six methods most relevant in the 1990s (population measurement, pronatalist policies, boundary changes, economic pressures, population transfers, and assimilation). Two of these policies, population transfers and assimilation, are especially relevant in this study of immigration.

With respect to the former, ethnic leaders may encourage mass population transfers or discourage movements in order to alter the relative balance among ethnic groups. They do this through their immigration or emigration policies. Some immigration policies are an international version of the ethnic consolidation studied in chapter 5 above. In other words, to the extent that reinforcement of the pre-existing ethnic mix is a goal, then immigration policies can achieve it. Similarly, some emigration policies represent an attempt to prevent the desired ethnic group from leaving the country (such as in Romania, where Romas easily obtained exit permits while ethnic Romanians did not).

With respect to the assimilation, it is noted that it represents a speedy way of increasing the relative size of an ethnic group when other, slower policies require patience that many leaders lack. Assimilation implies the elimination of differences between groups, as the smaller (or weaker) groups are expected to conform to the larger, dominant, or titular group (indeed, Czechoslovak communist policies of assimilation tried to extinguish the Roma identity by suppressing the Romany language and traditions, turning younger generations into what Hoeckenos called 'lumpen Czechs'[89]). To induce immigrants to assimilate into the dominant culture, leaders often offer economic incentives.[90] The most effective economic incentive is participation in the dominant economy. Indeed, assimilation with respect to language, religion, and citizenship enables individuals to become economically and socially more mobile and thus entails the expectation of higher economic benefits in the form of salary, promotion, and so forth (for example, in Bulgaria, Turks had greater access to employment if they agreed to the Bulgarization of their surnames).[91]

Up until recently, it was believed that the granting of citizenship was the ultimate recognition of assimilation. According to this view, if immigrants have citizenship rights, by definition they share an interest with the native population and participate in the political process to express that interest.[92] While citizenship remained important at the turn of the new millennium, assimilation is no longer a pre-requisite for it. It is no longer even expected. Indeed, the current credo of multiculturalism has made assimilation a dirty word. With changes in expectations of migrants and host populations alike, integration has become the preferable option. Integration implies mutual acceptance of different cultures and the coexistence with those differences (the Greek community in Germany is a good example: it has achieved economic success, political voice and social acceptance without assimilation[93]). Where multiculturalism prevails, integration of ethnic groups will not be a method that leaders use for demographic engineering.

EMIGRATION POLICIES

For decades, the Berlin Wall was a potent symbol of the containment of people. While the emigration policy of East Germany was so clearly embodied in stone, other states with restive populations and pent up demand for out-migration had policies that were equally effective (albeit less newsworthy). Indeed, the Soviet Union, the East European countries of the Soviet Bloc, and China all had precisely enunciated rules and regulations that dictated who could leave the country and under what conditions. The purpose of emigration policies is to control the exit of populations. Such interference is deemed necessary because without it the demand for exit visas would overwhelm the labor market, triggering a shortage of workers and an upward pressure on wages. Moreover, when educated people emigrate, the harm to the economy is even greater due to the loss of human capital. When fertile young people emigrate, there is a potential demographic cost as the country is robbed of their offspring (in other words, future workers). When workers emigrate, the government suffers the loss of their tax revenues; when healthy individuals emigrate, the investments of the health system have been lost, and so forth.

As a result of these economic considerations, some countries control emigration through a complex system of exit permits. The difficulty of obtaining these is inversely related to the outflow of migrants. Governments sometimes shroud the emigration process in secrecy, they establish elaborate bureaucratic requirements, and they deliberately increase the complexity and the time requirements of the process, all in order to discourage the potential migrant. Exit permits are sometimes so difficult to obtain that success comes only after pressure is exerted from the international community (the Jackson–Vanik amendment, passed during the Nixon administration, linked the USSR's most-favored-nation status to the opening up of its emigration policies[94]). Sometimes, emigration is effectively discouraged by the prohibitively high cost of exit permits. This has a dual effect: containing the population and raising government revenue. It has also been found that some countries have selective emigration policies, depending on the ethnicity of the migrant (such a policy reflects the goal of cleansing a society of undesirable populations, as occurred in Romania with the sale of exit permits to Jews).

The evidence with respect to trends in emigration policies is somewhat mixed. On the one hand, countries with previously tightly controlled borders have witnessed a significant liberalization. The most poignant example pertains to the former Soviet Bloc: indeed, when the Berlin Wall was dismantled on 9 November 1989, it was actually the controlled exit policies that came crumbling down, precipitating enormous migration flows.[95] On the other hand, some countries continue to closely monitor their borders. In 2000, Cuba still restricts the free outflow of people, albeit inconsistently. While numerous citizens are desperate enough to attempt the crossing of the Florida Straits, large-scale exoduses such as the Mariel boatlift underscore the fickleness of Cuban emigration policy.[96]

Contrary to countries that restrict the outflow of their populations, there are countries that encourage it (including Bangladesh, Pakistan, the Philippines, Mexico, and Sri Lanka).[97] They actively pursue policies of labor emigration for several reasons. First, they want to relieve the domestic employment pressures by decreasing demand for labor. Second, they want their workers to gain work experience in order to bring the acquired skills back home and aid in the development of their countries. Third, they want the migrant workers to send home remittances, preferably in foreign currencies. These positive effects are viewed as offsetting the negative effects of the brain-drain and loss in labor.

ETHNIC BIFURCATION AND SELECTIVE MIGRATION

The demand for entry into coveted host countries continues to exceed the supply of openings. The motivation to migrate has not abated over time, because potential migrants are cognizant that geographical mobility brings income gains to those who move. Home countries are cognizant that migration brings higher remittances to those who stay. Host countries are cognizant that immigrants enable increased production of goods and services. Thus, migration happens and will continue to happen. However, to deny that it has been selective and that the benefits have not accrued to all the ethnic groups equally, nor have the costs been borne equally, would be misleading and would mask the ethnic character of migration in the twentieth century.

Therefore, the ethnic dimension of immigration should not be underestimated. It is clear from the foregoing chapters that marginal ethnic groups do not migrate under the same conditions as dominant groups. This is evident both with respect to location (i.e. at home and in host countries), as well as with respect to the degree of coercion (i.e. voluntary vs. involuntary migration). With respect to the former, it is clear that even within their own countries, migrants of different ethnic groups do not share the same privileges, respond to the same stimuli, experience the same pressures nor enjoy the same protection. Economic incentives are not the same for all potential migrants across ethnic groups, nor is their capacity to respond to them equal. Ethnicity is also a relevant consideration in host countries. Immigration policies of numerous host countries have turned into ethnic policies, as countries consider, positively or negatively, the ethnicity of the migrant. Indeed, in Britain, 'race relations' has been used synonymously with 'immigration policy', because since the Second World War the majority of immigrants to Britain were people 'of color'.[98] In Germany, there was a clear racialization of policies that attained prominence in the electoral politics of Helmut Kohl in 1982, since he viewed hostility to foreigners as a healthy manifestation of national pride.[99] A similar introduction of ethnicity and race into political discourse was made by the leaders of the Northern Leagues in Italy. They not only tried to create a North Italian identity (for which there is no basis other than residency), but did so principally by exclusion, namely by constructing a picture of the enemy that was emboided in the nonwhite immigrant.[100]

With respect to the voluntary/involuntary dimension of migration, again marginalized and empowered ethnic groups have different experiences. In voluntary migration, ethnicity influences the capacity and incentive to migrate (as discussed in chapter 4). In involuntary migration, ethnicity is often the focal point of government policy (as discussed in chapter 6). Thus, whether they self-select or whether they are selected by others, marginalized and empowered ethnic groups face entirely different pushes and pulls. The illustrations from across the globe (provided in chapters 4 and 5) point to this ethnic component of migration.

Therefore, migration is *de facto* selective and it is selective on the grounds of ethnicity. It is selective both at the origin (namely, in the losing country) as well as at the destination (namely, the host country).[101] It is selective both in voluntary as well as in involuntary migration. The ethnic dimension clearly emerges as crucial in the global weeding process that determines who goes, where they go, and who stays.

NOTES

1 Jörg Haider's Freedom Party also won over 22% of the votes in the October 1994 general election, after a campaign in which antiimmigration played a large role.

2 *Economist*, 5 February 2000, p. 16.

3 It should be noted that the antiimmigrant debate is not limited to the industrialized countries of the West. Examples such as the eviction of Muslim Assamese immigrants from Myanmar and Indians from Uganda dot the landscape in the Third World.

4 For a discussion of unfettered migration, see Timothy J. Hatton and Jeffrey G. Williamson, *The Age of Mass Migration* (Oxford: Oxford University Press, 1998).

5 Ibid., p. 27.

6 World Bank, *Entering the 21st Century: World Development Report 1999/2000* (Oxford: Oxford University Press, 2000), pp. 37–8.

7 John Isbister, *The Immigration Debate* (West Hartford, CT: Kumarian Press, 1996), p. 60.

8 Ibid., p 70.

9 Doris Meissner, Robert D. Hormats, Antonio Garrigues Walker, and Shijuro Ogata, *International Migration Challenges in a New Era* (New York: Trilateral Commission, 1993), p. 2.

10 Brzezinski, *Foreign Affairs* (winter 1989/90), p. 13.

11 *New York Times* (September 4, 1994).

12 Ibid., 24 February 2000. Both Israeli and Palestinian leaders have called for their populations to procreate, sometimes specifically in order to outnumber their enemies on the land.

13 Federal Statistical Office of Yugoslavia, 'The 1991 Census in Yugoslavia: Statistics and Policy' (Statistical Commission and Economic Commission for Europe, Geneva: Economic and Social Council of the United Nations, 1 May 1992), p. 9.

14 *Politika*, 4 July 1994.

15 Interview with Aleksandar Despic, ibid., 4 August 1994.

16 *Politika*, 4 July 1994.

17 S. L. Hendre, quoted in Theodore P. Wright, 'The Ethnic Numbers Game in India: Hindu–Muslim Conflicts Over Conversion, Family Planning,

Migration and the Census' in William C. McCready (ed.), *Culture, Ethnicity and Identity* (New York: Academic Press, 1983), p. 415.

18 When race and religion are not the source of fertility fears, the question of language may be. For example, in Canada, where the birth rate differences between French-speaking Quebecois and the Anglo population raises questions pertaining to the future of Quebec as the bastion of French culture in North America.

19 Jack Miles, 'Blacks vs. Browns' in Nicolaus Mills (ed.), *Arguing Immigration: The Debate Over the Changing Face of America* (New York: Simon and Schuster, 1994), p. 101, quoted in Yossi Shain, *Marketing the American Creed Abroad* (Cambridge: Cambridge University Press, 1999), p. 4.

20 Myron Weiner, *The Global Migration Crisis*, p. 12, cited in Shain, *Creed Abroad*, p. 4.

21 Samuel Huntington, 'If Not Civilization, What?: Paradigms of the Post-Cold War World', Foreign Affairs 72, 5 (1993), p. 180.

22 W. Howard Wriggins and James F. Guyot, 'Demographic Change and Politics' in W. Howard Wriggins and James F. Guyot (eds), *Population, Politics and the Future of Southern Asia* (New York: Columbia University Press, 1973), p. 6.

23 Paul Kennedy, *Preparing for the Twenty-First Century* (New York: Random House, 1993), p. 40.

24 Huntington, 'Civilization'.

25 *Economist*, 24 July 1999, Canadian Survey, p. 14.

26 Paul Hockenos, *Free To Hate* (New York: Routledge, 1993).

27 In 1999 regional elections across Italy showed the tendency of immigrants to vote for other immigrants for representation, especially with respect to immigration issues. See *Corriere Della Sera*, 11 October 1999.

28 Meissner *et al.*, *International Migration*, p. 53.

29 Ibid., pp. 3–5.

30 According to Meissner, this is more than migrated during 1901–1910, the highest previous immigration decade. Ibid., p. 3.

31 Rosemary E. Jenks, 'Immigration and Nationality Policies of Leading Migration Nations', *Population and Environment* 14, 6 (July 1993), p. 569.

32 Meissner, *International Migration*, p. 5

33 Ibid., p. 5

34 See, for example, James Hollifield, *Immigrants, Markets and States* (Cambridge, MA: Harvard University Press, 1992); David Jacobson, *Rights Across Borders: Immigration and the Decline of Citizenship* (Baltimore: Johns Hopkins University Press, 1996); Yasemin Nuhoglu Soysal, *Limits of Citizenship* (Chicago: University of Chicago Press, 1994) among others.

35 Isbister, *Immigration Debate*, p. 65.

36 See Jeannette Money, *Fences and Neighbors. The Political Geography of Immigration Control* (Ithaca: Cornell University Press, 1999), p. 1.

37 *New York Times*, 18 February 2000.

38 Michael Fix and Jeffrey S. Passel, *Immigration and Immigrants: Setting the Record Straight* (Washington, DC: Urban Institute Press, 1994), p. 13, quoted in Isbister, *Immigration Debate*, pp. 68–9.

39 Meissner, *International Migration*, p. 13.

40 Ibid., p. 14.

41 Peter Stalker, *Workers Without Frontiers. The Impact of Globalization on International Migration* (Boulder, CO: Lynne Rienner, 2000), p. 108.

42 Meissner, *International Migration*, p. 15.

43 Myron Weiner, 'Security, Stability and International Migration' in Myron

Weiner (ed.), *International Migration and Security* (Boulder, CO: Westview Press, 1993), p. 10.

44 The 'White Australia' policy had been eroding slowly during the 1950s and 1960s as more and more exceptions were made for target ethnic groups.

45 Quebec has exercised this right since 1978. Further, an agreement was signed with Canada in 1991 allowing it to preserve its own demographic and cultural identity. See Demetrios Papademetriou, 'International Migration in North America: Issues, Policies, Implication', paper prepared for the joint UN Economic Commission for Europe/UNFPA meetings in Geneva, July 1991, p. 37 cited in Meissner, *International Migration*, pp. 107–8.

46 Jenks, 'Nationality Policies', p. 580.

47 *New York Times*, 3 April 2000.

48 Under this law, asylum seekers will be given vouchers redeemable for goods worth about $58 per person (instead of cash welfare benefits, as before). Moreover, instead of being able to settle wherever they want, asylum seekers will be sent to one of 13 designated areas around the country, often far from refugee support networks.

49 Incidentally, this policy was introduced long before the notorious, antiimmigrant Freedom Party came to power.

50 Money, *Fences and Neighbors*, chapter 2.

51 Wayne A. Cornelius, Philip L. Martin, and James F. Hollifield (eds), *Controlling Immigration: A Global Perspective* (Stanford: Stanford University Press, 1994).

52 Mark Miller, 'Preface to Strategies for Immigration Control: An International Comparison'. *Annals of the American Academy of Political and Social Sciences* 534 (1994).

53 Gary P. Freeman, *Immigrant Labor and Racial Conflict in Industrial Societies. The French and British Experience 1945–75* (Princeton: Princeton University Press, 1979).

54 Signatories include Belgium, France, Germany, Luxembourg, the Netherlands, Portugal, and Spain.

55 This is the informal term that refers to the seven European Union states that have abolished internal border controls under the terms of the Maastricht Treaty. See David Cesarani and Mary Fulbrook, 'Introduction' in David Cesarani and Mary Fulbrook (eds), *Citizenship, Nationality and Migration in Europe* (London: Routledge, 1996), p. 3.

56 Italy's Martelli Law of 1990 is the first comprehensive effort to stem the flow of immigration. Italy, along with Spain, has legislation that ties immigration to employment. Germany, faced with integration of East German populations, has a unique set of problems that places it at odds with the rest of the European Community.

57 Terrance Vincent Powderly, 'Record of the Proceedings of the Eighth Regular Session of the General Assembly' on the *Terrence Vincent Powderly Papers Proceedings: General Assembly 1878–1902* (Catherwood Library Collection, School of Industrial Relations, Cornell University, Ithaca, NY, 1884), and Samuel Gompers, *Seventy Years of Life and Labor* (Ithaca, NY: Industrial Labor Relations Press, 1925; edited by Nick Salvatore in 1984), cited in Susan Ozlak, *The Dynamics of Ethnic Competition and Conflict* (Stanford: Stanford University Press, 1992), p. 31.

58 G. Mink, *Old Labor and New Immigrants in American Political Development* (Ithaca: Cornell University Press, 1986).

59 A. Saxton, *The Indispensible Enemy: Labor and the Anti-Chinese Movement in*

California (Berkeley: University of California Press, 1971); V. Nee and B. de Bary Nee, *Longtime Californ': A Documentary Study of an American Chinatown*, 2nd edn (Stanford: Stanford University Press, 1986).

60 A study by George Borjas shows that immigrants increasingly do not fit the job requirements of the growing and changing US economy. George J. Borjas, *Friends or Strangers, The Impact of Immigration on the US Economy* (New York: Basic Books, 1990).

61 Ibid.; Julian Simon, 'Public Expenditures on Immigrants to the United States, Past and Present', *Populations and Development Review* 22, 1 (1996), pp. 99–110.

62 D. M. Gordon, R. Edwards, and M. Reich, *Segmented Work, Divided Workers* (Cambridge: Cambridge University Press, 1982).

63 Stalker, *Workers Without Frontiers*, p. 88.

64 Julian Simon, 'What About Immigration', *The Freeman* (January 1986), pp. 11–12, cited in David Osterfeld, *Prosperity Versus Planning* (Oxford: Oxford University Press, 1992), p. 196.

65 Roger Martinez, 'Dispelling the Job Competition Myth: An Analysis of Undocumented Immigrants' Impact on US workers', CLPP Policy Profile 1, 1 (Berkeley, CA: Chicano/Latino Policy Project), cited in Christopher Rudolph, 'Migration and the Evolving Security Agenda', paper presented to the International Studies Association, Los Angeles, 2000, p. 6.

66 This is the simplistic model, from which other micro and macro considerations follow, such as the increase in hiring due to lower wages, the increase in production due to more workers being hired, the increase in profits for businesses who are hiring more, the increase in national income from the increased production etc. All of these may or may not occur within an open-door economy.

67 Julian Simon, *The Economic Consequences of Immigration* (Oxford: Basil Blackwell, 1989); Michael Fix and Jeffrey S. Passel, *Immigration and Immigrants, Setting the Record Straight* (Washington, DC: Urban Institute Press, 1994).

68 Among the many scholars who argue against immigration are the following. Leon F. Bouvier, *Peaceful Invasions, Immigration and Changing America* (Lanham, MD: University Press of America, 1992); Palmer Stacey and Wayne Lutton, *The Immigration Time Bomb* (Monterey, VA: American Immigration Control Foundation, 1988); Richard D. Lamm and Gary Imhoff, *The Immigration Time Bomb: The Fragmenting of America* (New York: New American Library, 1985).

69 All these economic components of the immigration debate may be summed up in the concept of theft (namely, immigrants, especially illegal immigrants, steal off the host country). This is discussed by John Isbister as a philosophical dilemma. He questions whether a host country, in this case America, is the private property of Americans (in the way in which a person owns a house) or if it is public property, to be used by the first one who arrives (in the way in which a public beach is used by the first comer). He concludes that Americans are in a weak position to claim exclusive ownership, since they themselves are recent arrivals. That argument is true of all 'new' countries, including Canada, Australia, New Zealand, and so forth. Isbister, *Immigration Debate*, pp. 218–19.

70 Robert J. LaLonde, and Robert H. Topel, 'Labor Market Adjustments to Increased Immigration' in John M. Abowd and Richard Freeman (eds), *Immigration, Trade and the Labor Market* (Chicago: University of Chicago Press,

1991); Kristin Butcher and David Card, 'Immigration and Wages: Evidence from the 1980s', *American Economic Review* 81 (1991), pp. 292–6. Donald Huddle, Arthur Corwin, and Gordon MacDonald have provided empirical evidence that illegal immigration does in fact displace native workers: see *Illegal Immigration: Job Displacement and Social Costs* (Alexandria, VA: American Immigration Control Foundation, 1985). They also show immigrants to be a public burden.

71 See the following varied literature for a discussion of culture and immigration. Michael Walzer, *What It Means To Be An American* (New York: Marsilio Publishers, 1992); Stephen Steinberg, *The Ethnic Myth, Race, Ethnicity and Class in America*, 2nd edn (Boston: Beacon Press, 1989); Nathan Glazer and Daniel Patrick Moynihan, *Beyond the Melting Pot* (Cambridge, MA: MIT Press, 1963); Peter Brimelow, *Alien Nation, Common Sense about America's Immigration Disaster* (New York: Random House, 1995); and Arthur M. Schlesinger Jr., *The Disuniting of America, Reflections on a Multi-Cultural Society* (Knoxville, TN: Whittle Direct Books, 1991).

72 Whelan and Waltzer are both quoted in Isbister, *Immigration Debate*, pp. 220–1.

73 According to other proponents of this view, Western countries should take on a heroic role in the world with the express goal of saving and educating and instilling liberal values (during colonial times, it was the 'white man's burden' to spread Western culture; in modern times, democracy and Western standards of human rights are being spread across the globe).

74 Shain, *American Creed*.

75 T. H. Marshall and Tom Bottomore, *Citizenship and Social Class* (London: Pluto Press, 1992), p. 18.

76 Voting rights in New Zealand are bestowed upon noncitizens after one year of residency. Other Western states, such as Sweden, Denmark, and in selected *lander* of Germany and cantons in Switzerland, foreign residents have voting rights in local and regional elections.

77 Rules governing naturalization vary from country to country. Requirements include specific length of residence, language proficiency, demonstration of good character, evidence of integration into the community, and the absence of criminal conviction.

78 Roger Brubaker, *Citizenship and Nationhood in France and Germany* (Cambridge, MA: Harvard University Press, 1992).

79 Shain, *American Creed*, p. x. While Glazer and Moynihan have stated that ethnic influences have become very important determinants of policy in the United States (Nathan Glazer and Daniel Patrick Moynihan (eds), *Ethnicity: Theory and Experience* (Cambrdge, MA: Harvard University Press, 1975), pp. 23–4), this view is countered by DeConde, who argues that immigrant groups have little real power, despite the fact that it looks like they do (Alexander DeConde, *Ethnicity, Race and American Foreign Policy: A History* (Boston: Northeastern University Press, 1992), p. 200).

80 The pressure is coming up because of numerous Asians that are claiming to be members of the lost tribe, causing strain on the economic and social aspect of such a receptive policy. *New York Times*, 6 October 1994.

81 Ted Robert Gurr, *Minorities at Risk* (Washington: United States Institute of Peace, 1993), p. 250.

82 *New York Times*, 27 December 1995 and 7 January 1996.

83 Carl Bildt 'The Baltic Litmus Test', *Foreign Affairs* 73, 5 (1994), p. 78.

84 *New York Times*, 1 July 1994.

85 Ibid., 24 July 1994.

86 *FRE/RL Daily Report*, 30 June 1994, p. 11.
87 Wright, 'Ethnic Numbers Game'.
88 Abdo Baaklani, 'Ethnicity and Politics in Contemporary Lebanon' in William McCready (ed.), *Culture, Ethnicity and Identity* (New York: Academic Press, 1983), p. 19.
89 Hochenos, *Free To Hate*, p. 217.
90 How does one know when assimilation has occurred? When it is not possible to distinguish between peoples visually, as one can when physical features distinguish groups, then some other form of distinguishing people must be devised. The obligatory carrying of identity cards and the right of law enforcement personnel to check on those, is one way of monitoring who has assimilated (it may also foster a system of legalized discrimination). Examples abound: in Burundi, under the rule of Juvenal Habyarimana, discrimination against the Tutsis was enabled by the required identity cards that enabled quick distinction between the Tutsis and Hutus. Similarly, Soviet citizens were required to carry identification cards which described their nationality and religion.
91 Another economic inducement, popular throughout history, had to do with land: the conversion into the principal religion may be accompanied by rights to land ownership (indeed, during the Ottoman Empire, the conversion of Slavs into Islam in Bosnia carried with it rights to land and territory not enjoyed by the raja, or the remainder of the population).
92 Extending voting rights to ethnic populations can produce a negative externality. To the extent that immigrants side (i.e. affiliate politically) with their resident ethnic group, they contribute to strengthening the power of that group in the political arena. As such, they contribute directly to interethnic competition.
93 Uwe Hunger, 'Immigration in Germany', paper presented at the meetings of the International Studies Association, Los Angeles, March 2000.
94 This underscores the power to the Jewish diaspora in the United States that spearheaded this effort in order to increase the number of Soviet Jews who could emigrate to Israel.
95 Myron Weiner, *The Global Migration Crisis* (New York: HarperCollins, 1995).
96 In 1999–2000 public attention has once again turned to Cuba's emigration policies with the custody and citizenship debate pertaining to a 6-year-old rafter, Elian Gonzales. The fact that he was found after two days at sea, drifting on a tire while 10 other rafters had perished, drew attention to the squalid conditions and high death rates of those who illegally exit their country.
97 In Mexico, immigrants were granted the right to a form of dual citizenship so that they can maintain ties to their homeland, retain their property rights, and possibly return, even if they have accepted foreign citizenship. The effect was that more Mexicans were willing to leave and take multiple citizenship. (Christopher Rudolph, 'Migration and the Evolving Security Agenda of Advanced Industrial Democracies: Toward an IR Theory of Migration Policy', paper presented to the International Studies Association meetings in Los Angeles, March 2000, p. 3).
98 See the extensive literature on British race relations and immigration policy, including Zig Layton-Henry, *The Politics of Immigration* (Oxford: Blackwell, 1992); Anthony M. Messina, *Race and Party Competition in Britain* (Oxford: Clarendon, 1989); Ira Katznelson, *Black Men, White Cities. Race, Politics and Migration in the United States 1900–30 and Britain 1948–68* (Oxford: Oxford University Press, 1973); Gary P. Freeman, *Immigrant Labor and Racial Conflict*

in Industrial Societies. The French and British Experience, 1945–1975 (Princeton: Princeton University Press, 1979).

 99 See Karen Schonwalder, 'Migration, Refugees and Ethnic Plurality as Issues of Public and Political Debates in West Germany' in Cesarani and Fulbrook, *Citizenship, Nationality*.

100 Carlo Ruzza and Oliver Schmidtke, 'The Northern League: Changing Friends and Foes and its Political Opportunity Structure' in Cesarani and Fulbrook, *Citizenship, Nationality*.

101 Such selective policy is not always successful. Sometimes, despite the best intentions of governments to weed out undesirable groups, their efforts fail and the leadership must have a contingency plan. The example of Estonia is a case in point. By 1994, only 100,000 Russians left the country, then the out-flow stopped. The rest, now reduced to 34.8% of the population, are unlikely to leave. So, did Estonia adjust to this reality? Miljan describes the set of official solutions to keeping Estonia Estonian despite the large Russian presence, such as establishing Estonian as the sole official language (others may be used for private purposes), that naturalization requires competency in the language, and that all services be available to the public in Estonian. How to achieve such lofty goals? The state program 'Integration in Estonian Society 2000–2007' adopted by Parliament in January 2000 includes, among others, the objective of transforming all Russian-language schools to Estonian after 2007. See Toivo Miljan, 'Language as National Identity, the Case of Estonia', paper presented to the annual meetings of the Association for the Study of Nationalities, 13 April 2000, p. 16.

8

Interethnic Conflict:
an Inevitable Consequence?

The past century has witnessed far-reaching social, economic, and political changes across the globe. Electronic mail has replaced the handwritten note; meal consumption on-the-go has displaced long family meals; television broadcasts into homes across the globe; cellular telephones reach from Kuala Lumpur to Cape Town, Vancouver to Buenos Aires. There has been a surprising resurgence in religious sentiment, and, vexing to many, a clear Americanization of culture across the globe. Pervasive economic growth has produced both an overall increase in the standards of living as well as a widening gap between the rich and the poor. Capitalism has become borderless, communism has largely become meaningless, and socialist ideology survives in modified form. A unipolar world has emerged, with the United States at the helm, in which the free market and democracy are the prevailing mantra. An alliance of high-income democracies, namely NATO, wins a war from the air, in sharp contrast to the Great War that opened the twentieth century, that lasted four years, and which resulted in some 37 million casualties.[1] Liberal democracies proselytize the universal applicability of their political values while authoritarian governments struggle to reject what they perceive to be yet one more form of imperialist intrusion. The debate pertaining to the usefulness of state borders for modern economies and nations has delved into once sacrosanct topics such as sovereignty and self-determination, ending the century with dilemmas similar to the ones that faced the Western world in the early 1900s.

Despite these far reaching and comprehensive changes, some things have remained constant. Alas, the saying *plus ça change, plus c'est la même chose* can be readily applied to interethnic group dynamics and relationships. At the turn of the 1900s, empires were breaking up and newly independent ethnic groups were redefining their relationship to their territory, their resources, and their neighbors. The new countries that formed from the rubble of the Ottoman and Austro-Hungarian Empires struggled to find a place for themselves and their economies in a new era. Some 100 years later, in 1999, the departure of the Portuguese from Macao marks the end, albeit a symbolic end, of European intervention in Asia. The Soviet empire faltered as fifteen new countries formed and substate regions such as Chechnya struggle to redefine the nature of their relationship with the central power. The 1990s have witnessed the creation of more sovereign states than at any other time in history, with the exception of the establishment of newly independent countries in the aftermath of the Second World War. At the same time, ethnic groups divided by international borders have united: East and West Germany and North and South Yemen paralleled the unification efforts that resulted in countries such as Czechoslovakia and Yugoslavia during an earlier era. Therefore, the beginning and the end of the twentieth century have both been a time of building new and redefining old relationships between ethnic groups.[2]

Despite signs of such redefinition, some ethnic groups continue to engage in violent interactions with each other. They are still battling over the same issues that their forefathers battled over a decade or a century ago, namely, the interethnic competition for resources. The resources may have changed and the rules of the competition may have been adjusted to accommodate for new conditions, but the essential goals as well as the manifestations of the struggle have not changed significantly over this century.

Are there no exceptions? Must interethnic conflict of necessity follow interethnic interaction? Have countries learned nothing from past mistakes and have they progressed so little during the past century with respect to interethnic relations? There are indeed exceptions to perpetual interethnic conflict. There is also cause for optimism that the conditions under which those exceptions occur can develop elsewhere, in other words, they are replicable. By describing such conditions, this study contributes to the dialogue on conflict resolution among ethnic groups. Moreover, by identifying guidelines for resolving ongoing conflicts and preempting the outburst of new ones, the processes of interethnic competition, economic change, and selective migration are tied together.

THE RELEVANCE OF POLITICAL SYSTEMS AND LEVELS OF DEVELOPMENT

Much of the current literature on interethnic issues compares liberal democracies and nonliberal authoritarian states (as illustrated by the debate pertaining to Asian values vs. Western values). Alternatively, studies focus on the differences between ardent nationalist states (those for whom legitimacy is derived from their ethnic statehood) and those willing to give up sovereignty (such as members of the European

Union). Yet, a study of countries in which interethnic strife erupts points to the relevance of two interdependent variables: the nature of the political system and the level of economic development. Political systems and levels of development tend to go hand in hand. In other words, a liberal political system tends to coexist with a market economy; a restrictive political system tends to be associated with a command economy. This relationship has been identified by numerous scholars. According to Friedman, the democratic political system is conducive to economic growth because if fosters and protects personal economic freedoms such as free markets and property rights;[3] Lipset states that there is a positive relationship between prosperity and the propensity to be democratic.[4] Finally, Barro finds that when the level of political rights is low, an expansion of those rights increases economic growth.[5]

Interethnic conflict is longer, deeper, and more violent in countries that are not liberal democracies and that are at lower levels of development. This does not imply that interethnic conflict does not occur in highly developed democracies. Indeed, evidence from Belgium, Germany, and the United States points to the contrary. However, conflict in those countries is less violent, as minorities have more recourse to protective institutions.

Political Systems, Political Values, and Political Culture

Political values and political culture influence political institutions. The content of constitutions and legislation reflects values pertaining to freedom, representation, rights, and so on. One of these is particularly relevant for this study, namely, the concept of civil and human rights.

Since the Second World War great strides have been made in the enforcement of human and minority rights. As Gottlieb points out, until recently the voting majority in the UN was made up of authoritarian states that resisted efforts to seriously monitor and enforce minority rights as part of human rights.[6] Yet, while the 1948 Universal Declaration on Human Rights has no reference to minorities, in 1992 the UN General Assembly adopted the 'Declaration on the Rights of Persons Belonging to National or Ethnic, Religious and Linguistic Minorities'.[7] This document provides a broad mandate that requires that states protect their minorities and give them rights to participate in decision making, promote education in their tongue, and enjoy their culture. In addition, the International Labor Organization defines and monitors the observance of rights of migrant workers, demanding for them entitlements from their host countries and thus protecting them.[8]

Alas, these regulations are not taken seriously by all leaders in all countries. Often, domestic policies fail to reflect the international norms pertaining to human and civic rights and acceptable social behavior. Liberal, Western democracies have been at the forefront of the movement to acknowledge, respect, and protect people in general and minorities in particular. Their political, economic, and social institutions are rooted in the concept of civil and human rights, often pitting them against countries with different traditions.

In what way are political systems and the extent to which they are based on human and civil rights relevant for an assessment of inter-ethnic conflict? There are several ways. First, as discussed in chapter 3 above, liberal democracies have ethnostabilizers that become acti-vated when interethnic conflict threatens the rights of minorities. In those countries, the constitution does not distinguish between peoples, nor does it condone discrimination among peoples.[9] In the absence of ethnostabilizers, interethnic conflict more easily spirals out of control.

Second, under conditions of universal suffrage, participation in the electoral system grants power to minorities to pursue their interests in the political arena. When marginalized groups can vote and mobilize to express their demands as a cohesive electoral block, the benefits of direct democracy are clearly visible to them. Their political power is underscored by their participation in mainstream politics, since they often get courted by competing politicians. In Israel, for example, after the Israeli–Arab community began to shift its vote from the Rakah (the pro-Arab communist party) to the mainstream parties, then all parties, including Labor and Likud, began competing for their votes.[10] Similarly, in the United States, the courting of minorities was evident in the presidential campaign of 2000, as commentators proclaimed 'Whoever wins the votes of the new immigrants will win political power in America'.[11] Such empowerment of minorities in societies with universal suffrage is not possible in countries that lack regular elections and voter representation.

Third, in a liberal democracy, minorities are more able and likely to internationalize their concerns. They have recourse to international organizations that can monitor the satisfaction of their demands. There is no doubt that international organizations, such as the United Nations bodies, nongovernmental agencies, and representations of Western governments have played an important role in minority protection worldwide. The internationalization of minority concerns also takes place via connections with diaspora communities that are condoned in liberal democracies. Such connections allow newly natur-alized and newly empowered ethnic groups to retain strong ties to their home countries that, in turn, ensure that their nationals are treated well.[12]

Fourth, numerous liberal democracies are willing to give up some of their sovereignty in exchange for benefits that accrue with supra-state unions. Such unions indicate that state boundaries are no longer deemed as important as they once were. Indeed, monetary unions, common employment policies, and shared political goals undermine independence in domestic monetary and fiscal policies. Such integration and union is accomplished more easily among liberal democracies because they share a political culture. This culture includes values concerning human and minority rights. All Western democracies have accepted the prescribed international norms of human rights. Countries that do not conform to these norms are denied membership (witness the European Union's refusal to consider Croatia's bid for membership because of its policy towards minorities).[13] Therefore, membership in suprastate unions is another way in which domestic policies towards minorities are kept in check and interethnic conflict is contained.

Thus, for all four reasons mentioned above, countries in which political values and political culture are liberal and where there is respect for human and minority rights are more likely to treat their minorities better than countries where such liberal values are absent.

Level of Development

Governments provide numerous goods and services to their populations, including their minorities and immigrants. Given that the funds for such expenditures are raised by governments principally through taxation, it follows that differences in levels of development are reflected in differences in revenue-generating capacity. Consumers, producers, savers, and investors are taxed and their income is transferred into government coffers. The higher the level of development, the higher the taxable income, and therefore the higher the tax revenue of the government. With such revenue, more developed countries can fund a wide range of programs for minorities. It is in these countries, with their generous social policies, that rights and services are extended to minorities, immigrants, noncitizens, even illegal aliens. No less-developed country shares social policies on the scale encountered in the more developed countries.

'I'd Rather Migrate to Canada Than to Turkey!'

It was stated in chapter 1 that the best conditions for a minority migrant exist in a highly developed liberal democracy. While this may sound obvious (along the lines of 'it's better to be rich, smart, and beautiful than poor, stupid, and ugly!'), it is worth emphasizing why conditions for the migrant would in fact be better. As the discussion above has shown, human and minority rights are more respected in liberal democracies. A more developed country has the resources for greater public services and welfare programs, and they have a political culture that both condones and tolerates the redistributive powers of the state to keep welfare coffers full. Therefore, a liberal industrial democracy has both the capacity (that comes from its high level of development) as well as incentive (that comes from its political values and culture) to create an environment conducive to the minimization of interethnic conflict.

Hence, it is easy to understand why potential minority immigrants are more attracted to Canada than to Turkey. It is easy to understand why Eastern Europe's biggest and most mistreated minority, the Roma, have been emigrating in large numbers, not to neighboring countries (such as Greece, Turkey, or Poland) but rather to Canada and the United States.[14]. It is easy to understand why Indonesians, Chinese, and Malaysians would like to enter Singapore, where the government prides itself on its ability to provide its citizens with the five Cs (car, condo, credit cards, cash, and career with a multinational).[15] The United States also, despite its three Gs (guns, ghettoes, and gated communities[16]) continues to attract migrants in pursuit of the American Dream. It is therefore also easy to understand why the more liberal a state is, the more it has an immigration problem, since rational migrants vie for entry into those countries where they will be most protected.

All this points to the emergence of a two tier system of countries across the globe (this concept was introduced by Martin Heisler in March 2000). In one group, countries have highly developed economies as well as a wide variety of liberal democratic institutions. Their economies are based on education, information, and human capital with which they participate in the global economy as leaders in the knowledge industry. Their politicians have to cater to their electorate, so they are always kept in line. They uphold universal values, such as human rights, which gives them a common denominator with selected other countries. That similarity encourages and enables their willingness to compromise their sovereignty and form mutually beneficial unions. The importance of their state borders is shrinking and the importance of interdependence in the international economic arena is growing. In the words of Slater, this New World 'sees the death of geography and in particular, the death of the nation-state'.[17] According to Soysal, states have become post-national, as they are now instruments for the implementation of human rights norms more than anything else.[18] Some of their sense of ethnicity is also relinquished, as they become post-national. The mobility of capital, labor, and information is crucial to them. In the words of Kaplan, countries such as these are inhabited by 'Hegel's and Fukuyama's Last Man, healthy, well fed and pampered by technology'.[19] In places where the Last Man does not exist, the First Man prevails. Indeed, 'Hobbes's First Man, condemned to a life that is poor, nasty, brutish, and short',[20] populates the vast majority of countries in the second tier. Within this group, countries are less developed, authoritarian, and tend not to uphold western values. In contrast to the developed, liberal states, these countries value their sovereignty very much. They protect their state borders ferociously and are suspicious of the global economy. They are threatened by international interactions. They do not have sufficient self-confidence in their culture, their politicians, their institutions, and their borders that they can withstand the onslaught of global integration, be it in the form of trade or migration. The leadership fosters nationalist sentiment in order to keep the citizens loyal and introverted. Their populations tend to value the boundaries of their ethnicity and their self-image is tied first and foremost to their national identity relative to others. Far from being post-national, they are entrenched in their nationality in the ethnic, not civic sense. Their economies are dependent on land, be it for agriculture or resources such as oil. Therefore, territory is very important for them and they are willing to go to war to protect it (and even to expand it).

Thus, rather than the world divided according to civilizations, as suggested by Huntington, the world is dividing into democratic–service–liberal countries and authoritarian–nationalistic countries. This division has implications for migration, namely who goes and where they aim to go.

ETHNIC AND CIVIC DOMINANCE

As it can be argued that conditions for immigrants are preferable in a liberal, highly developed democratic state, so too it can be argued that it is better to be a citizen and member of the majority than a member of a minority without citizenship rights. This is true because both the relative size of an ethnic group as well as citizenship connote dominance.[21] Dominance, in turn, is positively associated with economic, political, and social power within a society.

In multiethnic states, dominance may be defined by ethnic or civic status. With respect to the former, dominance refers to a simple majority in numbers. Indeed, the concept of ethnic dominance was introduced in chapter 1 and was defined in terms of numerical supremacy of a population. With respect to the latter, dominance is measured by the formal recognition granted to individuals by the state, namely citizenship. In the civic sense, dominance is reflected in citizenship while the marginal group is composed of noncitizens. *De jure*, any ethnic group can be part of the civic/dominant or the civic/marginal categories. Indeed, a member of a minority ethnic group can be a citizen as much as a member of the majority ethnic group can.

Table 8.1 illustrates the possible combinations of ethnic and civic dominance. When ethnic dominance is coupled with civic dominance, then the economic and political power of a people is the strongest. Similarly, when people are ethnically marginal and have no citizenship rights, they are in the weakest position. These two ends of the spectrum are clear and predictable. It is the other two, namely the marginal ethnic groups that are citizens and the dominant ethnic groups that are not citizens, whose economic and political powers are not a priori clear and predictable. Indeed, we have evidence from across multi-ethnic states of marginal ethnic groups that are citizens and as such exert power through the voting system (for example, Cuban immi-grants in the United States). There is also evidence of dominant ethnic groups that are not citizens exerting economic influence through their skills (for example, Russian workers in the Caucuses).

Table 8.1
Ethnic and Civic Dominance Possibilities

	Civic dominant	*Civic marginal*
Ethnic dominant	most powerful	undetermined
Ethnic marginal	undetermined	least powerful

CRISIS: DANGER AND OPPORTUNITY

In Chinese calligraphy, the symbol for the term *crisis* consists of two words, danger and opportunity. It reflects centuries of experience in dealing with the complexities of crisis situations. According to the wisdom embodied in the term, while in each crisis there is a danger, there is also an opportunity. The danger lies in the possibility that the crisis might continue, spread, or escalate. The opportunity lies in replacing the crisis with a far more preferable outcome. The signs of danger are often clear and intuitive while the signs of opportunities are often nebulous and even counterintuitive. An application of this Chinese concept of crisis to interethnic competition and selective migration in multiethnic states underscores both the potential dangers as well as the potential progress that can result from an interethnic crisis situation. The key ingredient in both danger and opportunity is conflict – the danger that it will escalate and become violent, and the opportunity to transform it into harmony.

Danger: Interethnic Conflict

In the medical sciences, the *tipping point* refers to the moment when everything changes, all at once. For example, viruses move through the population at a leisurely pace until, suddenly, they become an epidemic. While Gladwell recently applied the concept of the tipping point to the spread of fads,[22] it is also useful in the analysis of interethnic conflict.[23] In other words, ethnic groups may coexist in a state of subdued hostility for a long time, and then, some internal or external event, seemingly small, can produce massive interethnic conflict. How do societies know when they are close to this tipping point? Moreover, what is the catalyst that plunges a society into violence?

The academic literature offers numerous explanations for the emergence of interethnic conflict.[24] Several bodies of theory have addressed the issue at length. While they all relate it to modernization, they differ in their focus. The human ecology theories are based on incoming migrants and the niches they find for themselves.[25] It is believed that as opportunities for minorities increase and inequalities decrease, interethnic conflict will diminish. Numerous offshoots of the niche idea have developed, including Barth's contention that ethnic and racial violence follows when niches overlap.[26] Assimilation theories focus on the role of cultural difference and conclude that conflict results from partial assimilation.[27] Other theories, based on economic inequality, suggest that conflict arises between regions and ethnic groups because one is consistently at the core and dominates those on the periphery.[28] Other economic theories focus on dual labor markets and middle man minorities, in which ethnic conflict arises because some minorities have managed to create (or exploit) a niche in the economy, much to the anger of the dominant ethnic group.[29] Horowitz's contribution to the literature states that ethnic conflict results from a modernization gap between ethnic groups who have developed at different rates.[30] Competition theories focus on the conflict that erupts from interethnic competition. Olzak claims that the factors that raise the levels of competition among race and ethnic groups increase the rates of ethnic collective action. Conflicts erupt when ethnic inequalities and racially ordered systems begin to break down, due to economic change.[31] Finally, according to Olivier, conflict also erupts when institutional segregation breaks down.[32]

While the above theories all focus on interethnic conflict and the role played by minorities, others have focused on nonconflict. For example, Fearon and Laitin,[33] as well as Schatz,[34] have explored non-onflict in an effort to understand the conditions under which ethnic groups live in harmony. Also, contrary to studies that place the onus in interethnic conflict on minorities, Byman identifies majority behavior that is conducive to conflict: 'When one communal group outnumbers its rivals, controls the state, owns most of the land and otherwise dominates society, we would expect it to be magnanimous in its treatment of minority groups. Yet, the reality is often quite different … We must recognize that the majority often initiates policies that spark rebellion or refuses to compromise in the face of reasonable minority demands for fair treatment.'[35]

This brief overview of the literature serves to illustrate the voluminous scholarly efforts expended to understand both constructive and destructive ethnic group interactions. There is indeed an overabundance of literature on interethnic conflict because there is an overabundance of interethnic conflict. It is safe to say that in multi-ethnic states the principal danger associated with a crisis situation is the eruption of interethnic conflict. Whether it is sustained over the long term (as in Northern Ireland), or whether it is explosive in the short term (as in the former Yugoslavia), the danger that the economic, social, and political fabric becomes affected is indeed great.

During the pre-conflict period, the confluence of ethnic and civic dominance constitutes a particularly potent mix for the emergence and escalation of conflict among ethnic groups. What often begins as microlevel harassment turns into street fighting and verbal abuse. Soon the conflict escalates into riots, antiminority legislation, pressures for involuntary migrations, and so on. Governments and ethnic groups engage in a retaliatory spiral of confrontational measures. Often spurred on by the international community, minority groups pursue their demands as never before.[36] Sometimes, their demands take on a secessionist and irredentist tone, and nothing short of unraveling ties with other groups (and taking territory with them) will suffice.[37] Leaders react in a knee-jerk fashion, often aggravating the volatile atmosphere and the precarious balance between groups. They introduce yet more policies, which are progressively more restrictive and discriminatory. Violence, war, and the loss of life and property ensue and represent the dangers inherent in the emergence and continuation of an interethnic crisis.

In moving from interethnic animosities to open conflict, the importance of discriminatory policy (including its interference in the *laissez-faire* migration process) must be stressed. Such policy provides a catalyst for interethnic conflict. It is embodied in the tipping point. This is due to the nature of discriminatory policies. They are not based on the ancient principle of physicians, namely *primum non nocere*, first, do no harm. To the contrary, discriminatory policies by definition entail harm. When policies such as the ones discussed in chapter 6 are adopted, minority ethnic groups respond by becoming more introverted, accentuating their differences, and strengthening their bonds.

The groundwork is laid for group mobilization and for the articulation of the boundaries of their 'differentness'. At the same time, discriminatory policies discourage intergroup contact (and, according to Lake and Rothchild, they interact less and barriers are erected to further communication and conflict resolution[38]). A legal framework that allows discrimination in the workplace, the capital market, the educational system, and so forth, affects the target population economically, socially, and politically. According to Olson and Pearson, it is just such a government policy that may spark discontent and fear and lead to violent interethnic conflict: 'policy providing systematic advantage to certain groups or that are designed to disadvantage others can be viewed as a catalyst for violence'.[39] Olson and Pearson's research shows that multiethnic states with discriminatory policies are more likely to experience violence in the form of riots or ethnically related civil war than states that do not adopt such a policy.[40] Their conclusions are supported by Gurr's research, according to which minorities that engage in violent rebellion are often discriminated against politically, economically, and culturally.[41]

Discriminatory policy leads to conflict, albeit with a lag. There is often a cycle of discrimination and intergroup hostility before the actual violence begins. Such discrimination and hostility between competing groups are not constant but rather are a varying feature in multiethnic societies. Clearly, in liberal democracies, where human and minority rights are respected, the tipping point is less likely to be reached than is the case in countries where no such legislation exists, because discriminatory policy is less overt and more subdued due to human and minority rights legislation.

Opportunity: Interethnic Harmony

The literature on conflict resolution has produced a variety of suggestions, including the accelerated assimilation of ethnic groups, the accommodation of minority groups, the integration of ethnic differences into mainstream society, the repression of ethnic demands, and so on. Yet, all these suggestions overlook the underlying source of interethnic conflict, namely interethnic competition for resources, and therefore they bypass the principal source of the solution. Indeed, since it is interethnic economic competition that results in ethnic bifurcation, then it is the economy that must provide the starting point in diffusing interethnic conflict.

The potential of the economy to diffuse conflict is most evident under conditions of economic decline. As noted in chapter 2, ethnic grievances become economic grievances when the economy is contracting. The struggle for a piece of the economic pie is accentuated by the perception, common among ethnic groups, that their own group is singled out for economic hardship. In numerous locations across the globe, it was economic decline (and its concomitant increase in scarcity) that first ignited interethnic conflict. So too, it is an economic revival that would best diffuse it since, in the words of Kaplan, ethnic animosities will be 'quelled by bourgeois prosperity'.[42] It is in this spirit that Doder proposes that the future of Yugoslavia should include economic reconstruction efforts rather than military intervention on the part of the West.[43] It was also in this spirit that the western military alliance proposed a reconstruction plan for the Balkans after the NATO bombing of Yugoslavia.[44] Finally, it was in this spirit that the Stability Pact for southeast Europe was constructed.[45]

However, an overview of the world in the year 2000 showed that economic growth is not a sufficient condition for achieving the inter-ethnic tolerance upon which to base the future cohabitation of ethnic groups within political boundaries. That it is not sufficient has been clearly shown by the proliferation of numerous secessionist efforts in places such as Scotland, Wales, Spain, and Canada, indicating that economically developed regions ruled by democratic parliamentary governments are not immune to ethnically based secessionist senti-ments. While it seemed some decades ago that politicized ethnicity in the West was a trend that would never emerge again, its reemergence necessitates novel and effective ways of addressing the centrifugal and centripetal forces exerted by a multitude of interests coexisting within a political boundary.[46] Such trends should not evoke romantic reminis-cences about how successful the Austro-Hungarian and Soviet empires were in holding together disparate economic and ethnic entities, nor should we put too much hope on a supranational ideology that would unify people. (Indeed, Marxism was to play that role insofar as their adherents should have shed all vestiges of association with a small interest group. It did not succeed and no other supranational force is in the making.)

Instead, a modified program of economic growth within a pre-scribed political framework maximizes the potential to diffuse inter-ethnic conflict. This broad-based program for the political economy of multiethnic states might even go a step further and actually promote interethnic harmony. It is based on the recognition that, despite the quintessential importance of economic factors, other conditions must also be met to ensure harmony. These considerations lead to a program that includes the following: (a) broad-based ethnic group participation in economic growth (henceforth, participatory growth); (b) skill-based immigration policy; (c) acceptance of democratic choice (with special reference to political boundaries); and (d) conditionality in Western

economic relations. While more research on each of these proposals is
warranted, an initial exploration follows.

(a) During participatory growth, economic injustices perceived by
ethnic groups cease to be a focus in interethnic interactions. Individuals continue to identify with their ethnic group while recognizing
the economic benefits to be derived from interethnic competition and
cooperation. Interethnic competition, ever present as it waxes and
wanes over business cycles, can be reharnessed and refocused so as to
emphasize its constructive characteristics (this distinction is important
since competition can be destructive for the economy (as shown by
cases of politicized economic policies such as in the former Yugoslavia)
or it can be constructive (as it is in capitalist production)). An emphasis
on the development and encouragement of *constructive competition*
would serve to draw out the positive elements of the competitive
process while suppressing the negative ones. Such competition will
emerge spontaneously when the perceived benefits of cooperation
outweigh the costs.[47] Ethnic groups will then cooperate to increase the
economic pie, rather than compete for stagnant or shrinking pie slices.
Such *conducive cooperation* leads to enhanced benefits for all ethnic
groups, as cooperation becomes the conduit to economic growth.
Contemporary illustrations of how economic opportunism transcends
interethnic hostility are evident in Israel (where Jewish and Palestinian
collaboration led to the economic revival of Ramallah[48]) and in the
Sandzak area of Serbia (where a thriving economy resulted from
cooperative production and trade among Slavic Muslims, Serbs, and
Muslim Kosovars[49]).

If constructive competition and conducive cooperation result in
economic growth and development, then does that raise the possibility
of other forms of interethnic conflict? Indeed, does it take us right back
to chapter 3, to issues of ethnic bifurcation and antiimmigrant hostility
in growing economies? It does not if it is buffeted by the conditions
discussed below.

(b) Labor is a crucial resource in the production process and
migration provides a reserve army of labor for countries that need it.
If the supply of migrants is neither threatened nor restricted, then the
potential for economic growth and development is enhanced. To
ensure an unimpeded flow of workers, immigration policies must be
altered so as to be based on skills, irrespective of ethnic origin. Such a
skill-based immigration policy would serve to siphon labor into the
sectors and geographical areas in which it can best be utilized, namely,
in which its marginal product of labor is maximized. It would relieve
host countries of surplus immigrants by restricting non-skills-based
immigration (including asylum, family reunification etc.). Increased
skills-based immigration might not alter the total number of people

relocating, but it would certainly change their composition. By enabling the movement of workers to the locations in which their skills are most valued, a skills-based immigration policy would eliminate one of the main obstacles to further growth, namely the supply of appropriately skilled labor. (As noted in chapter 7, immigration policies in western European countries, Australia, and Canada are shifting the focus away from ethnicity and in favor of human capital factors.[50] The basis of discrimination in immigration policy has moved away from ethnicity and in favor of skills in a way that is appropriate to their post-industrial economies. They are, as Pugliese said, 'at the forefront of a post-industrial migration'.[51])

A skills-based immigration policy would further reinforce the changing nature of the migrant, who is no longer only a low-wage worker and no longer automatically relegated to the bottom of the occupational hierarchy. Rather, many professional migrants today hold skills that are scarce among domestic populations. They therefore come to occupy occupational niches in which locals cannot compete. (Studies show that immigrants and local populations often do not compete for the same jobs. In Canada, for example, where the foreign-born make up 17% of the population, total immigrants were found not to compete with the total native labor force.[52]) Those niches will be appropriate for their education, training, and experience.

However, a skills-based immigration policy should not and cannot attract only highly skilled workers. It will continue to draw unskilled workers since the host countries' economies are diversified and complex and therefore demand labor at all skills levels. In other words, not only will Canada and the United States draw highly skilled engineers and programers from India and China, but they will also continue to allow unskilled workers from Mexico and Central America to immigrate. Similarly, while Switzerland is biased in favor of the highly skilled doctor, its economy also needs the unskilled street sweeper.

Workers at all skills levels will fill niches in host countries and proceed to carve out new ones. Indeed, today, Filipinos work in health care in southeast Asian countries, Jamaicans hold home health care jobs in Florida, and Mexicans are gardeners in southern California.[53] Tomorrow, those same immigrants may concentrate in other occupations. The dynamic nature of employment, immigration and niche creation suggests that ethnoprofessionalism is rarely fixed over the long run and that there are opportunities for mobility of all sorts.

In this post-industrial migration, there is a valid concern that a skills-based immigration policy in host countries may impoverish home countries. There is no doubt that the loss of human capital is likely to retard growth and increase dependency. However, less developed countries are by definition at a different stage of development. As such, their manpower requirements are different. Skills appropriate for industrial production are not necessarily appropriate for a knowledge-based service economy. A competitive specialization in the production of industrial goods may prove to be more lucrative than the noncompetitive production of high-tech services.

(c) Sometimes it is not possible to diffuse interethnic conflicts within the confines of a given political state. Sometimes antagonisms run so deep that all efforts, including economic inducements and/or political repression, can neither quell nor suppress them. Sometimes ethnic groups simply refuse to cooperate, compete, and otherwise interact in any way. Under those conditions, one or more groups may pursue self-determination and opt to leave the political union of which they were a part. While such secessionist sentiment takes a variety of forms, its goals always include the creation of new territorial demarcations in which a former minority is the new majority.[54] By implication, the old majority becomes the new minority in what comes to resemble an ethnic status swap.

An ethnic group's quest for self-determination and territorial concentration is all too often accompanied by the goal of ethnic purity. In other words, not only do ethnic groups pursue majority status, but they also desire a territory devoid of minorities. How can such a goal be supported by a wide range of individuals, including educated, westernized professionals? Maybe they believe that people have to live apart before they can live together again. Maybe there is truth in the sayings 'Good fences make good neighbors' and 'The more we are separated, the better we will understand each other'. Maybe George Brock's definition of ethnic groups (namely, a people united by the common dislike of their neighbors) helps us to understand this need for ethnic purity.[55] Maybe competition theorists are right when they claim that interethnic conflict is minimized when groups occupy nonoverlapping habitats, in other words, when they live, work, and play apart from each other. Maybe when interethnic antagonism has reached the point of no return, partition into ethnically pure regions becomes the only viable solution.

Whatever logic underlies the quest for ethnic purity, it is a fact that it has come to be the most popular choice in many countries at the end of the century. Without arguing the full merits and demerits of ethnically pure states, the popular aspect of this choice must be addressed. Given the distasteful associations of ethnic purity with the practice of ethnic cleansing, it is necessary to formulate clear guidelines as to when it is an acceptable goal and when it cannot be condoned. If the goal of ethnic purity is expressed through legal means, such as a fair electoral process in which citizens, who have universal suffrage, vote for an ethnically homogeneous future, then does that make it an acceptable democratic choice? If ethnic purity represents the goal of the majority of the population, then is it not the most democratic choice? Does a democratic basis lend legitimacy to ethnic purity?

Examples from the former Yugoslavia put these questions into context. The political parties that sprung up were, without exception, nationalistic in orientation. Democratic plurality gave rise to ethnic parties that reflected the interests of a single group. Moreover, referenda were introduced to ask citizens questions about their desires for a multiethnic future.[56] The popular quest for ethnic purity was consistently shown. Those who were uncomfortable with the nationalist atmosphere (read: the new minorities) often voluntarily migrated to areas where they were more comfortable (read: where they were the majority). Alternatively, minorities were involuntarily moved from some areas. Thus, through voluntary and involuntary population movements, the ethnic landscape of the former Yugoslav states has undergone a profound transformation. A *de facto* partition has occurred across the territory. Just how much the ethnic composition of the new states have changed is as yet unclear, but the evidence there is points to a new state of ethnic purity. The ethnic mosaic that was once Bosnia is gone. Recent estimates pertaining to the 1990s in Bosnia indicate the following change over the period 1991 to 1997.[57] In the Republika Srpska, the proportion of Muslims dropped from 28 to 3 percent, while in the Muslim and Croat Federation, it grew from 52 to 72 percent. Serbs in the Republika Srpska went from 54 to 96 percent, while in the Federation they dropped from 17 to 2 percent. Finally, Croats went from 9 to 1 percent in the Republika Srpska, while in the Federation they remained at 22 percent. Such clear evidence of ethnic homogenization can also be found in Croatia. Following the large-scale expulsion of Serbs in 1995, as well as the sporadic exodus of Serbs and other non-Croats during the nationalist leadership of Franjo Tudjman, the state achieved a high degree of ethnic purity, up from the 75 percent concentration of Croats it had in 1990.[58] Moreover, as a result of decades of population movements in and out of Kosovo, culminating in the population movements around the time of the NATO intervention (mid-1999), the population of the region today is significantly more Albanian than it was even a decade before (namely, 87%). Therefore, in all regions except for Serbia proper, Montenegro, and to a certain degree, Macedonia, the goals of ethnic purity have been pursued and achieved. Even in these places, many would pursue ethnic purity if they could.

If the drive for ethnic purity is strong among a population and shows few signs of subsiding, it is unlikely that forced cohabitation will produce long-term interethnic harmony. This does not apply to highly repressive, authoritarian countries in which there is no democratic expression of choice. In those cases, harmony is not a goal and the repression of ethnic aspirations is far too strong for them to be vented. Rather, it applies to the countries that have democratic institutions through which they vote for undemocratic measures (ethnic purity at all costs). Such a paradoxical result of political liberalization prompts some to say that too much democracy, too soon, is bad. The West, that has come to be the final arbiter in self-determination disputes, either condones or condemns quests for ethnic purity. When actively condoning or condemning such practices, the West is interfering in the democratic choices.

It is argued that long-term interethnic harmony cannot be achieved if an antidemocratic ruling is imposed on the population. One glaring example of such an undemocratic solution is the Dayton Peace Accord for Bosnia. It is undemocratic because it's cornerstone is not the choice of the majority of the population, as was stated in national elections. The majority of Serbs and Croats voted against the creation of a unified Bosnia, together accounting for over 50 percent of the population and the popular vote.[59] By supporting the Muslim view of territorial integrity and professed desire for multiethnicity, the Western powers were supporting a minority view. The result is that interethnic animosities continue and are likely to continue.[60]

This argument supports a proposition made in chapter one, namely when selective migration is due to discriminatory policies, it can have the perverse effect of diminishing interethnic conflict. Indeed, when interethnic conflict is followed by secession, partition, and ethnic purity, then the conflict ceases to exist because its fundamental basis has been eliminated. It is eliminated because if successful, discriminatory policies push undesirable ethnic groups out. The exodus of ethnic groups, either through voluntary or involuntary migration, can thus be a source of stability. In this way, migration has the odd feature of being the product of interethnic conflict and at the same time a part of its solution. The largest case of ethnic cleansing in the twentieth century supports this contention. When some 10 million ethnic Germans from Eastern Europe and the Soviet Union were expelled, their departure resulted in peace and harmony as a perceived fifth column was eliminated.[61] Other examples of stability following the creation of ethnic purity (such as Croatia without Serbs, Israel without Palestinians etc.) alerts us to the potential benefits of this goal.

However, it is not lightly that one can support the popular choice of ethnic purity and advocate its implementation. The quest for ethnic purity underscores the fact that democracy does not apply to minorities and majorities equally. Moreover, the quest for ethnic purity sometimes necessitates an unpalatable action, namely the forceful dislocation of undesirable populations. As such, the quest for ethnic purity is a double-edged sword that is usually not supported or condoned by the western world.[62]

Conditions could be imposed on the realization of ethnic purity so as to minimize the negative effects and maximize the positive ones. Negative effects include the physical, economic, and emotional hardship associated with involuntary displacement, migration, loss of rights, and so on. Positive effects include stability and the realization of popular choices expressed democratically. In the effort to minimize costs and maximize benefits, the international community should use its powers of persuasion to enforce protection of minorities who suffer the consequences of ethnic purity. Such persuasion is discussed below.

(d) According to Hochenos, 'by defining themselves in terms of the dominant nationality alone, the ethnic national state establishes a hierarchy of peoples, with some more equal than others'.[63] Indeed, in numerous post-communist states, democracy is only democratic for the titular majority.[64] In an effort to ensure that political liberalization means more than just the replacement of one disadvantaged ethnic group with another, Western leaders can play an important role. With their liberal views and democratic values, they need to spearhead the effort to reverse the newly emerging undemocratic trends. The West needs to ensure that, in the long run, human rights values and minority protection do indeed become universal. Without discussing the merits and demerits of such a policy, without delving into its imperialist properties, and without questioning its similarities with religious proselytizing, it is merely stated that attention to minority rights is well placed. The protection of minority rights will ensure that, in the pursuit of ethnic purity, ethnic groups have to treat other groups according to a set of prescribed principles. The imposition of full rights and equality of all citizens, irrespective of ethnic orientation, serves to soften the blow of ethnic purity in several ways. It limits what the new ruling ethnic group can do to minorities; it increases the options of the new minorities to stay or go. If they stay, they have more protection, if they go, they go from a position of strength. With respect to the majorities, the imposition of minority rights may in effect dampen their quest for ethnic purity (since they would have to pursue it under the watchful eye of the international community, thereby making it a more unattainable goal).

How can the Western community guide multiethnic states into adopting minority protection norms and instituting mechanisms for respecting their rights? What gentle and not-so-gentle forms of persuasion does it have at its disposal? While numerous ways may exist, the economy provides the most potent answers. Indeed, it is money that speaks the loudest and reaches the farthest. Leaders across the globe are sensitive to money issues, since they are so closely related to economic growth, political power, status in the world community, and so on. Indeed, as Kaplan points out, 'it is much more important nowadays for the leader of a developing country to get a hearing before corporate investors at the world economic forum than to speak before the UN General Assembly'.[65] Therefore, money could be used as a carrot, as countries are rewarded with financial benefits in exchange for imposing minority legislation and respecting minority rights. These benefits may include access to international sources of capital, encouragement of foreign investment, participation in international decision-making processes, and access to resources and trade. Through these avenues, the West can encourage domestic policies that are based in their own norms of human rights and views of proper interethnic behavior.[66] The introduction of such conditionality in economic relations might serve to alter minority-insensitive regimes. Such a discriminating system of support of those states that show respect for minority rights might carry the message clearly and in the long run, fundamentally alter interethnic relations.

In the effort of Western states to persuade multiethnic countries across the globe to adopt minority rights, the role played by diasporas cannot be overemphasized. Diasporas residing in the West promote the spread of Western values to their home countries because they speak both languages. This nonliteral interpretation of language encompasses all aspects of culture. Since diasporas have sensitivity to home cultures, they are better positioned to guide the penetration of western values. As Shain has shown, diasporas residing in the West, especially in the United States, have already been instrumental in bringing western ideas pertaining to democracy, human rights, and respect for minorities back to their home countries.[67] Functioning as a conduit, these former immigrants can help transform interethnic relations in their home countries and in the process promote inter-ethnic harmony.

In conclusion, multiethnic states face the danger of escalating conflict as well as the opportunity to induce interethnic harmony. Such harmony is best achieved in a particular economic and political frame-work that includes participatory growth aided by skills-based immigration, within a system of democratic choice buffeted by the enforcement of minority rights. Now, the task at hand is the explor-ation of conditions under which a society recognizes the opportunities that arise from a crisis situation as well as the dangers that it might encounter. These conditions are perhaps best described by the phrase

'The worse things are, the better they are'. The concept underlying this phrase has been used by economic historian Nathan Rosenberg in explaining the source of technological change during the Industrial Revolution;[68] it was also used by Bhalla to explain the implementation of economic reforms.[69] Just as economic crises produce incentives for technological change and economic reform, so too interethnic crises may produce incentives for the pursuit of harmony.

One characteristic of populations and their institutions that enables a response to incentives for harmony is dynamism. Societies that are dynamic are ones that change, that are accepting of that change, and that adjust painlessly to such change. It is this dynamism that enables members of ethnic groups, governments, and the international community to rise to the challenge and take the opportunity to address the interethnic issue that is once again, at the beginning of the new millennium, proving its resilience. Where is this dynamism most present? The response prompts a return to an idea stated above, embodied in the phrase 'I'd rather migrate to Canada than Turkey'. Just as the best conditions for a minority migrant exist in a highly developed liberal democracy, so too the best conditions for avoiding interethnic conflict exist in a highly developed liberal democracy. Such countries exhibit the greatest dynamism in their evolving institutions, their responsive policies, and their transforming economies.

If economic development and liberal democracy produce a formula most conducive to protecting ethnic groups (be they minorities or majorities), then it bodes well for world efforts to quell interethnic conflicts. It is in the direction of enhanced democracy that many countries are heading; it is the unrelenting quest for economic growth which drives populations and their leaders across the globe. More than at any other time in the past century, a clear goal of convergence has emerged in countries outside the inner circle of leading economies. Indeed, that Argentina should want to adopt the dollar as its currency, that Ecuador has done so already, that Fernando Cardoso, a leader among the *dependencia* theorists, should become a Brazilian politician touting globalization, that Spain's former socialist, Xavier Solana, would be upholding NATO unity, point to such convergence. While even optimists will concede that universal democratization and economic growth is at best a long-run goal, to the extent that it promotes interethnic harmony, it is worth pursuing.

NOTES

1 www.sparticus.schoolnet.co.uk/FWWdeaths.htm.
2 Incidentally, both the beginning and the end of the twentieth century were associated with great men who presided over the demise of empires and the

emerging ethnic/national entities. The Turkish ruler Kemal Ataturk was hailed (by Samuel Huntington) as a visionary because he was able to give up the Ottoman Empire. Michael Gorbachev was identified (by Donald Horowitz) as another leader who gave up an empire: 'it has been said of Mikhail Gorbachev that he has the distinction of having lost three world wars. He lost the Cold War, of course. He also lost the Second World War because he lost Eastern Europe. And he managed to lose the First World War because he presided over the end of the Russian Empire. This triple defeat produced great changes in the relationship of ethnic groups to territory.' Donald Horowitz, 'Self-Determination: Politics, Philosophy, and Law' in Ian Shapiro and Will Kymlicka (eds), *Ethnicity and Group Rights* (New York: New York University Press, 1997), p. 421.

3 Milton Friedman claimed that political and economic freedoms were inter-related. See Milton Friedman, *Capitalism and Freedom* (Chicago: University of Chicago Press, 1962).

4 Seymour Martin Lipset, 'Some Social Requisites of Democracy: Economic Development and Political Legitimacy', *American Political Science Review* 53 (1959).

5 Robert J. Barro, *The Determinants of Economic Growth* (Cambridge, MA: MIT Press, 1998), p. xi.

6 Gideon Gottlieb, *Nation Against State* (New York: Council on Foreign Relations Press, 1993), p. 31.

7 In between these two documents there were several covenants on civil, political, economic and social rights that said that violation of human rights is a matter of international concern (especially Article 27 of the International Covenant on Civil and Political Rights). Then, the 1975 Helsinki Final Act involved the Eastern Bloc in the adherence to these principles.

8 While a transnational regime for minority rights existed in the 1990s, it was relatively weak. It is really a code of good behavior, as states are merely encour-aged to comply, with no effective means of imposing sanctions on members who breach the standards (see Hugh Maill, 'Introduction' in Hugh Maill (ed.), *Minority Rights in Europe* (London: Royal Institute of International Affairs, 1994), p. 3). Moreover, while Europe professes to have respect for human and minority rights, and countries of Western Europe have even gone to war against Yugoslavia ostensibly to protect the human rights of Kosovo Albanians, there are gaping holes in their policies. A glaring example is that of the Roma; 8 million stateless people across Europe whose plight is worsened by open discrimination against them in all aspects of their lives. They suffer from violence from both ends of the spectrum – from the police as well as the skinheads. The new Europe has shown little interest in breaking the cycle of isolation and prejudice and poverty that the Roma face. The Roma experience is a pan-European problem and its overdue lack of solution makes western minority and human rights a Swiss cheese policy. Nevertheless, Europe does have a policy of protecting minority rights and it is more respectful of human rights than most places across the globe.

9 Accordingly, some of the new democracies of Eastern Europe and the former Soviet Union are not liberal democracies built on the Western model, but rather nationalistic democracies, liberal only for some but not for all.

10 Daniel Byman, 'Immoral Majorities: A First Look at a Neglected Source of Communal Conflict', paper presented at the meetings of the International Studies Association, Los Angeles, 2000, p. 25.

11 *New York Times*, 5 March 2000.

12 They very often have dual citizenship and multiple loyalties. Sometimes, they have voting rights in home and home countries (such as the US citizens from the Dominican Republic, Mexico, and soon even Israel). They are the diasporas, who, according to Fred Riggs, encompass communities whose members live informally outside a homeland while maintaining active contacts with it and some variations thereof (Fred W. Riggs, *Diasporas and Ethnic Nations*, paper presented to the International Studies Association meetings in Los Angeles, March 2000, p. 3). Yossi Shain defines them as 'a people with a common ethnic-national-religious origin who reside outside a claimed or an independent home territory' (Yossi Shain, *Marketing the American Creed Abroad* (Cambridge: Cambridge University Press, 1999), p. 8). They have one foot in their home country, one foot in the host. They have citizenship in one country but often nationhood in another. Indeed, the national identity of a community may be very different from the statehood identity.

13 Incidentally, while minority protection is crucial for membership in EU now, there was no mention of it in the Amsterdam Treaty, so there is a double standard between old and new members.

14 Given their unemployment rates of 80–100% (in Slovakia), their dismal housing, education, and health care, they are looking to emigrate. There has been a large exodus since around 1997, when it became clear that the new democracy of Eastern Europe was not meant for all citizens and that their condition *en masse* was deteriorating. During the communist period, the ideology of full employment made it illegal for adults to be unemployed unless they were disabled or engaged in otherwise productive activity. Under those conditions, the Roma were employed. During the post-communist period, discrimination against them prevented their employment since preference was given to migrants from the Ukraine and from other former Soviet states. At first, most Roma emigration was to Canada, although Britain and the US were also favored. It is estimated that since 1997 some 20% of the Roma from the Czech Republic have left, and many thousands have left from Slovakia, Romania, and Hungary. *New York Times*, 2 April 2000.

15 Ibid., 19 September 1999.

16 This term was coined by a Canadian politician. *Economist*, 24 July 1999, Canada Survey, p. 3.

17 Peter Slater, *Workers Without Frontiers. The Impact of Globalization on International Migration* (Boulder, CO: Lynne Reinner, 2000), p. 2.

18 Yasemin Soysal, *Limits of Citizenship* (Chicago: University of Chicago Press, 1994).

19 Robert Kaplan, *The Coming Anarchy* (New York: Random House, 2000), p. 24.

20 Ibid.

21 Dominance of one group over another is not set in stone, as groups may be dominant one day and marginalized the next. Indeed, just like ethnic affiliation is not primordial and immutable, so too the composition of the dominant group is not constant over time. Examples of such transformations abound throughout history: the preferred Maronite Christians in Lebanon ceased to be preferred after the French departed; the Russians in Moldavia were no longer dominant after the demise of the Soviet Union etc.

22 Malcolm Gladwell, *The Tipping Point, How Little Things Can Make a Big Difference* (Boston: Little, Brown & Co., 2000).

23 Interethnic conflict is defined as one in which at least 1,000 people have been killed.

24 See the literature survey provided by David A. Lake and Donald Rothchild (eds), *The International Spread of Ethnic Conflict: Fear, Diffusion and Escalation* (Princeton: Princeton University Press, 1998), chapter 1.

25 See, for example, Robert Park and E. W. Burgess, *Introduction to the Science of Sociology* (Chicago: Chicago University Press, 1921); Amos Hawley, *Human Ecology* (New York: Ronald Press, 1950).

26 Frederick Barth, 'Ecological Relationships of Ethnic Groups in Swat, North Pakistan', *American Anthropologist* 58 (1956).

27 Also, conflicts prevent assimilation. See H. M. Blablock Jr., *Towards a Theory of Minority Group Relations* (New York: Wiley, 1967); M. Gordon, *Assimilation in American Life* (Oxford: Oxford University Press, 1964); R. M. Williams Jr., *Strangers Next Door* (Englewood Cliffs, N J: Prentice Hall, 1964).

28 See, for example, Michael Hechter, *Internal Colonialism* (Berkeley: University of California Press, 1975).

29 Edna Bonacich, 'A Theory of Ethnic Antagonism: The Split Labor Market', *American Sociological Review* 37 (1972); Edna Bonacich, 'A Theory of Middleman Minorities', *American Sociological Review* 38 (1973).

30 Donald Horowitz, *Ethnic Groups in Conflict* (Berkeley: University of California Press, 1985).

31 Susan Olzak, *The Dynamics of Ethnic Competition and Conflict* (Stanford: Stanford University Press, 1992), pp. 2–3.

32 J. Olivier, 'Collective Violence in South Africa', unpublished Ph.D. dissertation, Cornell University, Ithaca, 1989, cited in Susan Olzak, *Ethnic Competition*, p. 34.

33 David Laitin, *Identity in Formation: The Russian-Speaking Populations in the Near Abroad* (Ithaca: Cornell University Press, 1998); James D. Fearon and David D. Laitin, 'Explaining Interethnic Cooperation', *American Political Science Review* 90 (December 1996).

34 Schatz studied nonconflict in the context of multiethnic Central Asia, when he developed an explanation of 'nonconflict' in a region where one would expect it to exist. Edward Schatz, 'Toward an Explanation of Non-Conflict in Multi-Ethnic Central Asia', paper presented to the International Studies Association meetings in Los Angeles, March 2000.

35 Byman uses the term *communal group* to include ethnic, religious, tribal, and linguistic groups. A group is a people 'bound together by a belief of common heritage and group distinctiveness, often reinforced by religion, perceived kinship ties, language, and history. Daniel Byman, 'Immoral Majorities: A First Look at a neglected Source of Communal Conflict', paper presented to the meetings of the International Studies Association, Los Angeles, March 2000, p. 1.

36 According to Stanley Hoffman, 'international law, in what amounts to a revolution, has been giving [activists of all kinds] rights against their governments. It is they who destroy states, overthrow regimes and benefit from the new information technology'. *Miami Herald*, 23 January 2000.

37 For a discussion of secession and irredentist activity, see Milica Bookman, *The Economics of Secession* (New York: St Martin's Press, 1993) and Milica Bookman, *The Demographic Struggle for Power* (London: Frank Cass, 1997).

38 David A. Lake and Donald Rothchild, 'Ethnic Fears and Global Engagement: The International Spread and Management of Ethnic Conflict', Policy Paper 26, Institute on Global Conflict and Cooperation (University of California, 1996).

39 Marie L. Olson and Frederic S. Pearson, 'Policy-Making and Discrimination: Forecasting Ethnopolitical Violence', paper presented to the International Studies Association meetings in Los Angeles, March 2000, p. 3.

40 They also claim (ibid.) that more democratic multiethnic states are less likely to adopt discriminatory policies than less democratic states. Finally, they found that discriminatory policy changes are more likely to result in violence when the disadvantaged group is large in proportion to other groups in the state.

41 Ted Robert Gurr, 'A Risk Assessment Model of Ethnopolitical Rebellion: Applied to Asian Minorities in the late 1990s', paper presented at the workshop on Crisis and Conflict Early Warning Systems, University of Maryland, 14–16 November 1996, cited ibid., p. 6.

42 Kaplan, *Anarchy*, p. 22.

43 Dusko Doder, 'Yugoslavia, New War, Old Hatreds', *Foreign Policy* 91 (summer 1993), p. 22.

44 *New York Times*, 21 April 1999.

45 This pact was signed in 1999 in Cologne with the following core members: Croatia, Bosnia Macedonia, and Albania. Peripheral members are Montenegro and opposition parties of Serbia, as well as Romania and Bulgaria. The pact offers western assistance in formulating and applying regional, economic, and human rights structures to the local environment.

46 'The dissolution of ethnicity. The transcendence of nationalism. The internationalism of culture. These have been the dreams and expectations of liberals and rationalists in practically every country.' Anthony Smith, *The Ethnic Revival* (Cambridge: Cambridge University Press, 1981), p. 1.

47 Fearon and Laitin, 'Cooperation', proposed a theory of cooperation among ethnic groups and suggested that it occurs when the perceived benefits of cooperation outweigh the perceived costs. Schatz adds to that by asking what processes alter the population perceptions of costs and benefits. Schatz, 'Non-Conflict', p. 3.

48 *Wall Street Journal*, 1 June 2000.

49 In the town of Novi Pazar, there are now some 600 factories producing counterfeit Levi's, Calvin Klein and other labels worth some $100 million annually. These producers and traders, who are busting sanctions and international copyright laws, have found a way of turning Serbia's pariah status to their advantage. In the process, they have served to create an oasis of interethnic harmony as cooperation thrives. Ibid., 18 February 2000.

50 Suyama presents the following data for Australia: the proportion of immigrants that are skilled and come into Australia under the skilled immigration category has gone from 30% in 1996 to 50% in 1999. Moreover, now emphasis is on temporary migrants rather than permanent. Nobuaki Suyama, 'An analysis of Australia's Immigration and Refugee Policies', paper presented to the meetings of the International Studies Association, Los Angeles, March 2000.

51 Enrico Pugliese, 'Italy Between Emigration and Immigration and the Problems of Citizenship', in David Cesarani and Mary Fulbrook (eds), *Citizenship, Nationality and Migration in Europe* (London: Routledge, 1996), p. 114.

52 Peter Stalker, *Workers Without Frontiers. The Impact of Globalization on International Migration* (Boulder, CO: Lynne Reinner, 2000), p. 88.

53 Richard Rosecrance, *The Rise of the Virtual State* (New York: Basic Books, 1999), p. 206.

54 According to a dictionary definition, secession is 'the act of withdrawing

formally from membership in an organization, association, or alliance'. In its application to international events, the term has come to be associated with the breaking of ties (political, economic etc.) by one group of people and their territory from the larger political unit of which it was a part. The distinction between separatist, irredentist, ethnoterritorial, and secessionist movements is often blurred, both in fact and in the usage of the terms. Indeed, the popular press in the 1990s has clearly confused the distinctions, especially that between irredentist and secessionist efforts. Horowitz distinguishes between secession and irredentism in the following fashion: 'Secession is an attempt by an ethnic group claiming a homeland to withdraw with its territory from the authority of a larger state of which it is a part. Irredentism is a movement by members of an ethnic group in one state to retrieve ethnically kindred people and their territory across borders ... Irredentism involves subtracting from one state and adding to another, new or already existing; secession involves subtracting alone.' Donald Horowitz, 'Irredentas and Secessions: Adjacent Phenomena, Neglected Connections', in Naomi Chazan (ed.), *Irredentism and International Politics* (Boulder, CO: Lynne Rienner, 1991), pp. 9–10. Irredentism is a term originating with Italian liberation movements and thus was more popular in the description of events in Mittel Europa of the past century. Nevertheless, it is useful today to distinguish between it and secession insofar as it clearly distinguishes today's 'nationalist movements' according to their aims: the desire to create a Kurdistan inhabited by Kurds residing in Iraq, Turkey and Iran is irredentist in nature, as is the desire of Hungarians residing in Romania to unite their land with Hungary. Ethnoterritorial movements differ from secessionist movements insofar as the former is broader, and encompasses both secession and irredentism. According to Thompson and Rudolph, 'The term ethnoterritorial is used ... as an overarching concept for various political movements and conflicts that are derived from a group of people, *ethnos* in the Greek sense, having some identifiable geographic base within the boundaries of an existing political system'. Robert J. Thompson and Joseph R. Rudolph, Jr, 'The Ebb and Flow of Ethnoterritorial Politics in the Western World' in Joseph R. Rudolph Jr and Robert J. Thompson (eds), *Ethnoterritorial Politics, Policy and the Western World* (Boulder, CO: Lynne Rienner, 1989), p. 2. A separatist movement differs from a secessionist movement insofar as the demands of the former consist of increased autonomy in one or many areas, whereas in the latter, full independence is part of the definition of success; Allen Buchanan, *Secession* (Boulder, CO: Westview Press, 1991), p. 9.

55 Cited in Alfred Pfabigan, 'The Political Feasibility of Austro-Marxist Proposals for the Solution of the Nationality Problem of the Danubian Monarchy', in Uri Ra'anan *et al.* (eds), *State and Nation in Multi-Ethnic Societies* (Manchester: Manchester University Press, 1991), p. 54.

56 See Bookman, *Secession*, chapter 5.

57 Comments presented by Joseph Marko in his Chairperson's Introduction at the session entitled 'European Identity Formation at the Crossroads: Ethnic Homogeneity or Multicultural Diversity? The Case of Bosnia, Kosovo, and the South Tyrol in Comparison', Association of Nationality Studies meeting, New York, 13 April 2000.

58 Various tables in Savezni Zavod za Statistiku, *Statisticki Godisnjak Jugoslavije* (1990, Belgrade).

59 For a discussion of elections in Bosnia, see Robert Hayden, *Blueprints for a House Divided* (Ann Arbor: University of Michigan Press, 1999).

60 The role of memory is crucial in this discussion. The passing of time changes peoples outlooks. Time was not present in the Yugoslav wars of secession, in which too many living people had memories of injustices that occurred in the Second World War. The role of time and memory is also important. Some 70% of the Arab population has been born since 1970. This means that the population is largely composed of people with no recollection of the colonial experience, the struggle for independence, the process of nation building and the Arab–Israeli wars. See Kaplan, *Anarchy*, p. 42.

61 In addition, this population served an important economic function in their new host country, Germany, by filling the severe labor shortage of the immediate postwar period It is these refugees that enabled the industry to expand economic output. See Philip L. Martin, 'Germany: Reluctant Land of Immigration' in Controlling Immigration: A Global perspective' in W. A. Cornelius, P. L. Martin and J. F. Hollifield (eds), *Controlling Immigration: A Global Perspective* (Stanford: Stanford University Press, 1994).

62 I say usually, since there are occasions when the western world has turned a blind eye to evidence of ethnic cleansing. Not only did this happen in the example of the German exodus after the Second World War, but more recently in Croatia during Operation Sweep (1995) when over 200,000 Serbs were cleansed from the Krajina region over the course of four days. By comparison, the ethnic cleansing of Albanians from Kosovo resulted in massive western intervention in the form of NATO bombing and subsequent UN peacekeeping in the region.

63 Paul Hochenos, *Free To Hate* (New York: Routledge, 1993), p. 304.

64 Democracy as embodied in an electoral process can bring to power extremist governments that are legitimized by the democratic process. Examples abound – Bosnia in the early 1990s; Algeria (where violence erupted after its first election in 1992); pre-Second World War Germany (where galloping inflation and pervasive unemployment served to elect an authoritarian leader); and so on. Singapore is an example of a highly developed country (with respect to income per capita, it is almost equal to Canada) in which democracy lags behind. See Kaplan, *Anarchy*, p. 77.

65 Ibid., p. 80.

66 It is difficult to make this argument devoid of value judgments. The bias reflected here, and shared by other western scholars, is that the West can contribute to overall modernization and improvements in standards of living by exporting its notions of freedom, equality, and adaptability. By opening up a country, citizens' freedom of choice and movement is increased. They become more exposed to other ways through increased access to information, and they begin to compare their own economic, social, and political limitations, their inequalities and injustices. The new scrutiny will result in reevaluation and change.

67 Shain, *American Credo*. However, in addition to playing a role in opportunities for interethnic harmony, diasporas can also be a part of the danger. One example that comes to mind is the role played by the Croatian diasporas in the United States and Germany in bringing to power the nationalist government of Dr Franjo Tudjman.

68 In his discussion of the source of technological change, Rosenberg claimed that the greater the bottlenecks in labor supply, the greater the price of labor and the greater the upheaval among workers (in other words, the worse things got), the greater the likelihood of change (in other words, growth-promoting

technological innovation). Rosenberg called these focusing devices because they forced producers to focus on selected factors. Nathan Rosenberg, *Perspective on Technology* (Cambridge: Cambridge University Press, 1976), especially chapters 6 and 8.

69 Bhalla said that political instability is good for economic reform. Stable governments get comfortable and reform less while unstable governments get uncomfortable and reform more to capture votes. Surjit S. Bhalla, 'Domestic Follies, Investment Crises: East Asian Lessons for India' in Karl D. Jackson (ed.), *Asian Contagion* (Boulder, CO: Westview Press, 1999), pp. 145–6.

Index